Artists, Writers, and Diplomats' Wives

Artists, Writers, and Diplomats' Wives

Impressions of Women Travelers in Imperial Russia

Edited by Evelyn M. Cherpak

ROWMAN & LITTLEFIELD
Lanham • Boulder • New York • London

Published by Rowman & Littlefield
An imprint of The Rowman & Littlefield Publishing Group, Inc.
4501 Forbes Boulevard, Suite 200, Lanham, Maryland 20706
www.rowman.com

86-90 Paul Street, London EC2A 4NE

British Library Cataloguing in Publication Information Available

Library of Congress Cataloging-in-Publication Data

Names: Cherpak, Evelyn M. (Evelyn May), 1941– editor.
Title: Artists, writers, and diplomats' wives : impressions of women
    travelers in Imperial Russia / edited by Evelyn M. Cherpak.
Description: Lanham, Maryland : Rowman & Littlefield Publishers, [2023] |
    Includes bibliographical references and index.
Identifiers: LCCN 2023005134 (print) | LCCN 2023005135 (ebook) | ISBN
    9781538180983 (cloth) | ISBN 9781538181003 (epub)
Subjects: LCSH: Women travelers—Russia—Correspondence. | Women
    travelers—Russia—History—Sources. | Russia—Description and
    travel—Sources.
Classification: LCC DK23 .A77 2023 (print) | LCC DK23 (ebook) | DDC
    910.820947--dc23/eng/20230321
LC record available at https://lccn.loc.gov/2023005134
LC ebook record available at https://lccn.loc.gov/2023005135

Wretched and abundant,
Oppressed and peaceful,
Weak and mighty,
Mother Russia!

—Nikolai Nekrasov

Contents

~

Introduction

European travelers, mainly men, made their way to Russia early on. The first male traveler recorded was Ohthere of Hålogaland, whose "Voyages of Ohthere to the White Sea and the Baltic in the Ninth Century" appeared in volume I of Robert Kerr's *A General History and Collection of Voyages and Travels*, published in 1811. As the centuries progressed and Russia developed and became more open, both European and North American men went to Russia as diplomats, merchants, explorers, anthropologists, newspaper reporters, agronomists, and scientists. Others went solely as travelers and wrote accounts of what they saw, giving the public their first impression of this faraway and exotic land.

By the eighteenth century, several women from England and France made their way to Russia, usually with a purpose in mind. They did not travel alone but went with a companion or relative. Travel was slow and by no means easy, as they came by coach and traveled on rough roads. These women were upper-class or titled aristocrats and had connections with the Russian aristocracy, so once they reached St. Petersburg or Moscow, they stayed in private residences and mingled with members of the Tsar's court. Both Lady Elizabeth Craven from England and Elisabeth Vigée Le Brun from France arrived in Russia with a specific goal. Lady Elizabeth was to find out all she could about Russian ports, ships, and the military in 1786 for her lover, the Margrave of Brandenburg Ansbach. She traveled from St. Petersburg to Moscow and then on to the Crimea, never revealing to the people she met what her real purpose was. Elisabeth Vigée Le Brun, an accomplished portrait painter fleeing the French

Revolution, went to Russia in 1795 to paint members of the Russian nobility. She painted the granddaughters of Empress Catherine II but not Catherine herself, who died in 1796 before her sitting. Both Elizabeth and Elisabeth wrote accounts that speak to their time in Russia; Lady Elizabeth wrote a series of letters to the Margrave as she made her way from St. Petersburg to the Crimea, and Elisabeth Vigée Le Brun, who spent six years in Russia, recounted her life there in her memoirs. Their accounts give the reader a glimpse into the country's political, cultural, and social history, as well as the court of Catherine the Great.

During the first half of the nineteenth century, the only North American woman in Russia was Catherine Adams, wife of John Quincy Adams, United States Ambassador to the Imperial Court, 1809–1814; unfortunately, she did not leave a record of her life there. However, several English and Irish women lived in Russia and wrote letters home and kept diaries. The motivation for women to travel during this period varied; some, like Martha and Catherine Wilmot, were unmarried and went as invited guests of Princess Catherine Dashkova. Martha left Ireland by ship in 1803 to live as a companion to the princess at her estate, Troitskoe, and remained there for five years. Princess Dashkova was a good friend of Martha's cousin, Lady Catherine Hamilton, hence the invitation. Martha encouraged the princess to write her memoirs, as she played a part in the accession to the throne of Catherine the Great and was a learned woman and a member of the Imperial Academy. Martha's letters to her parents and siblings told of her daily life at the estate; her travels to Poltava, Moscow, and St. Petersburg; and her admiration for the princess, as well as balls, Russian Orthodox Church services, and the peasantry. Her sister, Catherine Wilmot, arrived in 1805 and returned home in 1807, taking a copy of the princess's memoirs with her. She, too, wrote letters home and kept a diary describing everyday life at the estate and her social life. Excerpts from the letters and diaries of the Wilmot sisters were published in 1934 as *The Russian Journals of Martha and Catherine Wilmot*.

Others, like Mary Holderness, went with her husband and their four children to the Crimea in 1815, where he was involved in an agricultural experiment to farm the land. She remained there for five years, then returned to England, where she wrote in great detail about the inhabitants of the Crimea, focusing on the Tatars. In 1838, Lady Elizabeth Eastlake (née Rigby) traveled alone to Estonia to visit her sister who lived in Revel (now Tallinn). At that time, Estonia was part of the Russian Empire. She wrote a two-volume account of her visit to Estonia, *Letters from the Shores of the Baltic*, focused on the people, customs, and economy. During her stay in St. Petersburg, she had an opportunity to socialize with the court of Tsar Nicholas I, to observe the manners and daily life of the upper classes, and to tour the city. She was critical of all that she saw, comparing Russia unfavorably to England. She knew that Russia would never be a liberal state, yet she wished the country well.

The construction of railways in the second half of the nineteenth century in Russia made travel between Europe and Russia and within the empire itself much easier for the determined tourist. Mary Alsop King Waddington, who traveled by rail with her husband from Paris to Moscow for the coronation of Tsar Alexander III in 1883, wrote about her time in Russia in *Letters of a Diplomat's Wife*. Her husband, William H. Waddington, was Ambassador Extraordinary, representing France at the coronation. Once she arrived in Moscow, she attended all the ceremonies, dinners, processions, and parties before and after the coronation. She described her presentation to the Empress, an audience with the Grand Duchesses, a tour of the Kremlin, the coronation, and a polonaise with Emperor Alexander III himself. All the splendor, the wealth, and the grandeur of the Russian Court comes alive in her letters, as well as her concerns about possible terrorist attacks on the Imperial couple, which, fortunately, did not happen.

Isabel F. Hapgood, an American, was fluent in Russian, which was an asset when traveling in the country as often as she did, so she was able to make all the hotel and travel arrangements herself. In *Russian Rambles*, published in 1895, she gave an account of a three-year sojourn in Russia with her mother. In this volume, she tried to correct many of the mistaken impressions that she and other tourists had of Russia and had brought home with them. The surveillance of foreigners and the censorship of their mail were a few that she averred were untrue, and she cited personal examples. Hapgood gave readers an educated tourist's view of Russia, including the sites in the cities of Moscow, St. Petersburg, and Kiev, yet she did not neglect the lesser-visited cities of Nizhni Novgorod, Yaroslavl, and Kazan. She provided detailed descriptions of the monasteries, churches, significant buildings, markets, and people of these places. Hapgood had connections with people whom she wanted to meet and those who wanted to meet her, too—Count Leo Tolstoy being one. She visited him at Yasnaya Polyana in the countryside and at his home in Moscow, where the two had lively discussions.

The English have a reputation for being adventuresome travelers, and Kate Marsden, a nurse from London, was one that fit that category. She decided to go to Russia in 1891 on a mission of mercy to improve the health and living conditions of the sick and diseased lepers. Setting out in February 1891 with a female companion, she traveled by sledge (a type of sled on wooden runners), tarantass (a four-wheeled carriage), horseback, and boat to reach her destination in Siberia. In *On Sledge and Horseback to the Outcast Siberian Lepers*, she described the roads, the cold weather, the difficulty of finding clean post-stations (inns), the food, the horses, and the people that she met along the way who helped her. Though the Tsar's government did not initially sponsor this trip or support it monetarily, once the trip was over, she was able to enlist their aid and that of the clergy for the benefit of the lepers. Her goal was to find the herb that had medicinal properties that would cure leprosy; she found the herb, but it proved ineffective. Nevertheless, Marsden wrote a dramatic description of her two-thousand-mile journey to Siberia that was motivated by her desire to be of service.

During the first two decades of the twentieth century, Russia was visited by North American women who traveled there to report to newspapers on the Russian Revolution of 1917 and its impact on the people. But in 1900, at the turn of the century, before the cataclysmic events of the Russian Revolution, an English woman, Annette M. B. Meakin, arrived in Moscow with her mother to take the Trans-Siberian Railway to Vladivostok. She wanted to be the first woman to take the railway across the country to Japan. The railway linked the eastern and western parts of Russia and was completed in 1899; for tourists, it was a way to see the almost unknown regions of the country. Annette had made several trips to Russia before embarking on the railway excursion. She described the train as a luxurious one that traveled at a slow speed and stopped at cities along the way. Annette disembarked the train to visit various towns, and she wrote about her adventures meeting local people, finding hotels and food, visiting a prison, traveling with emigrants going to Siberia, taking an ice breaker across Lake Baikal, boarding a barge to Blagovestchensk, and then taking the train again at Khabarovsk to Vladivostok. There she heard news of the Boxer Rebellion and that Russian steamboats had been sunk on the Amur River, where she had just been. Given the news of war, Annette and her mother decided not to return to Moscow via rail, instead sailing to Japan and then to the United States. Once back in England, she wrote *A Ribbon of Iron* describing her journey.

Princess Julia Cantacuzene, granddaughter of President Ulysses S. Grant, was a firsthand witness of the events leading up to the February and October Revolutions in Russia. While on a European tour, she met Prince Michael Cantacuzene in Rome and, after a whirlwind courtship, married him in 1899. She lived in Russia for seventeen years, learned the language, resided in St. Petersburg and at the family estates in the Ukraine and the Crimea, and lived the life of an aristocrat. Julia witnessed the Russo-Japanese War, the Revolution of 1905, the events of World War I, and the Russian Revolution. She was from a liberal and democratic background that led her to favor political change in Russia. To that end, she held afternoon teas where she listened to the views and opinions of the educated men of the day. But the Bolshevik Revolution of 1917 changed her life; she lost her status, her wealth, and the culture that she had adopted. Her harrowing escape by train to Sweden with few belongings marked the end of a life of wealth and privilege. Her life in Russia was recounted in *Revolutionary Days* and *My Life Here and There*.

Bessie Beatty, a newspaper reporter, arrived in Russia in June 1917, along with other reporters to report on World War I and conditions in Russia. She stayed six months, long enough to witness the Bolshevik Revolution in October. When she first arrived, Bessie visited the southwestern front twice and interviewed the officers and enlisted personnel, some of whom supported the Bolsheviks. In Petrograd, she listened to speeches of Trotsky and Lenin, met with members of the Women's Battalion who were eager to fight the enemy, and interviewed Bolshevik women in leadership positions. Like other North Americans at that time, she was not opposed to the revolution and believed it would benefit the people, despite the fact that living conditions immediately after the revolution were dire for most. When she left Russia, she knew that she had witnessed a world-changing event.

Pauline Stewart Crosley, a Navy wife, was also a witness to the events of 1917. She lived in Petrograd for ten months. Her letters to family members, published as *Intimate Letters from Petrograd*, had news of political events but also the difficulties of daily living, finding a suitable place to live, and the lack of food and fuel. Despite dodging gunfire in the streets, she was able to attend the opera and ballet and volunteered at an American hospital serving Russian soldiers. She was especially appreciative of the cultural aspects of Russian life, and the danger in the streets did not dissuade herself from attending performances. Pauline adapted to living conditions in wartime Russia, was eager to learn the language so she could communicate with Russians, and had a positive outlook, all of which made life easier there, but that did not dissuade her from condemning the atrocities that she knew about.

Emma Goldman, an anarchist, was born in Russia in 1869, then immigrated to the United States in 1886 to join her family. After years of writing, speaking, supporting strikes and the Russian Revolution, and being jailed for her anarchist activities, she wanted to see the changes in Russia for herself. Deported by the United States Government, she arrived there in 1919 with fellow anarchist Alexander Berkman. The two stayed almost two years and were able to travel and meet and interview individuals. She kept an open mind about the Bolshevik regime until the attack on the Kronstadt sailors. As a result, Emma was profoundly disillusioned and disappointed by the economic, political, and social changes that did not benefit the people, as well as the abusive treatment of anarchists. *My Disillusionment in Russia* was written once she left the country.

Marguerite Baker Harrison, an American reporter from Baltimore, found herself in a Russian jail in Moscow for ten months in 1920 because she entered the country without a visa and was a foreign intelligence agent. In fact, she was a double agent, providing the Russians with innocuous information to survive. During her months in prison, she befriended her fellow inmates and passed the time by keeping to a daily exercise routine, sewing, singing, and playing games. Once home, she lectured and wrote *Marooned in Moscow* about her experiences. Marguerite returned to Russia in 1922 and was jailed for two months, then released. This time she entered the Far Eastern Republic without a visa, not knowing that it was recently acquired by Russia.

Artist Clare Consuelo Sheridan, an Englishwoman and cousin to Winston Churchill, befriended Lev Kamenev, a Bolshevik politician in London, and went to Russia with him in September 1920 to sculpt Lenin and Trotsky and other Bolshevik leaders. She stayed for two months and, like so many others of that time, was fascinated by Russia and looked favorably upon the changes brought by the revolution. Clare returned home only to find that the British public did not support her political views, so she sailed to the United States, hoping to find a more tolerant atmosphere. She returned to Russia briefly in 1924 without incident. As the years went by, Clare became disenchanted with the Russian Revolution when she realized its negative impact on the people. But her two months in Russia were captured in *Mayfair to Moscow: Clare Sheridan's Diary*.

The selections in this book feature the writings of sixteen prominent women who visited or lived in Russia from the end of the eighteenth century to the Russian Revolution of 1917. The accounts are arranged chronologically, beginning in 1786 and ending in 1921; geographically, they extend from St. Petersburgh, Moscow, and Kiev to the Crimea and Siberia, where most women went. All of the women who wrote books and articles about their experiences were educated and informed, although those who lived in Russia for a period of time had more exposure to the political events, economic conditions, and social culture than those who briefly passed through. Some of these women were so intrigued by Russia that they returned several times during the nineteenth and twentieth centuries. The very strangeness of Russia and the turbulent events of the revolution of 1917 and its aftermath drew them back.

Through the eyes of European and North American women travelers, the people of Russia; the country's political, social, and cultural life; and the very land itself come alive in their firsthand testimonies. Their writings shed light on life in pre-revolutionary Russia and the historic events that led to the 1917 Russian Revolution and the consolidation of power by the Bolsheviks. Their stories are a window into Russia's past, as seen from a woman's point of view and experience.

All of the writings presented here are an exact rendering of what these women wrote.

~

Editor's Note

This book has chapters devoted to the travels of women in two countries that are known as Russia and Ukraine today and to their major cities. The writings of the women themselves preserve the spelling of the time period, e.g., St. Petersbourgh or St. Petersburgh in the nineteenth century versus the current St. Petersburg, and Kiev versus the more recent Kyiv, the Ukrainian spelling. Russia is the name used by the editor when referring to the country instead of the Russian Empire that lasted until 1917.

CHAPTER ONE

~

Elizabeth, Baroness Craven

A Traveler in Russia

Elizabeth, Baroness Craven, daughter of the fourth Earl of Berkeley, was born on December 17, 1750 in London. Educated at home, she was fluent in French and Italian and learned to cook, ride, dance, and shoot. At age seventeen, she had an arranged marriage to William Craven, the Sixth Baron Craven, some ten years her senior. It was an unhappy marriage as he was rude, tight-fisted, and domineering, and he drank heavily. Furthermore, he did not share her literary or theatrical interests. Before they separated in 1780, they had seven children: William, Henry, Richard Keppel, Elizabeth, Maria Margaret, Georgiana, and Arabella. Both had numerous romantic liaisons during their marriage, though, as a woman, she bore the opprobrium for her behavior rather than he.

Once they separated, Elizabeth moved to France with her son Richard Keppel. Baron Craven was given custody of the other children, who were forbidden to communicate with her. The loss of a close relationship with her daughters caused her great anguish. In France, she continued her literary efforts; she wrote poems and an opera; translated works from Italian and French into English; and wrote, produced, and acted in plays, many of which emphasized the subordinate position of women in marriage.

Elizabeth—though not a twenty-first-century feminist—was a child of the Enlightenment. Contrary to popular and legal opinion, she believed that women were rational beings and should be equal partners in a marriage. She sympathized with women who were forced into marrying someone they were incompatible with, as was her case, and railed against the inferior legal position of women inscribed in law.

1

Lady Elizabeth Craven
Wikimedia Commons

In June 1785, Henry Vernon, who saw action in the Spanish Navy during the war with Algiers, called on Elizabeth, and the two decided to take a
short trip together to the Loire Valley to visit the Chateaux. They enjoyed
traveling together and traveling itself, so this short sojourn turned into a
very long one; they went on to the south of France, then to Italy, Austria,
Poland, St. Petersburg, Moscow, the Crimea, Turkey, Greece, Bulgaria, Wal-
lachia, Hungary, Austria, and finally to Ansbach, where Christian Charles

Alexander, the Margrave of Brandenburg-Ansbach-Bareith, lived. Elizabeth returned to Paris probably in the autumn of 1786. She was one of the first European women, if not the very first, to visit the Crimea recently conquered by the Russians from the Turks.

The Margrave had taken an interest in Elizabeth when she visited him, and she and Keppel went to Ansbach in the spring of 1787, where she was treated as one of royal rank. The Margrave had many scientific and artistic interests, and Elizabeth was there to further the arts. Eventually, the Margrave decided to marry her, and he did after his invalided wife died and Elizabeth's husband died. In the meantime, Elizabeth learned German, produced her plays in the court theater, and published her first book, entitled *A Journey Through the Crimea to Constantinople: In a Series of Letters from the Right Honourable Elizabeth Lady Craven to the Margrave of Brandenburg, Ansbach and Bareith, written in the year 1786.* The book was a series of letters to the Margrave, whom she referred to as brother. She did not reveal to anyone she met the purpose of her travels in Russia; no doubt, she was taking notes on military and naval ports and ships at the Margrave's behest. The book was a bestseller, and it established her as an author of some note. Her second book was the French translation of *Letters from a Peeress of England to Her Son* that offered her son William advice on treating his wife. In 1826, at age seventy-six, she wrote her memoirs.

Once Elizabeth's husband died in October 1791, and the Margrave's wife's died the same year, the couple were free to marry, which they did in Lisbon on October 30, 1791. The Margrave abdicated his throne, and they settled in London and at the estate of Benham Park in the countryside. Later they had a house at Southampton where Elizabeth learned to sail. Although they were snubbed by King George III of England and Queen Marie Antoinette of France because of their scandal-ridden relationships, they, nevertheless, led glamorous lives. Elizabeth was known in society because of her theatrical productions and was the only female member of the Society for the Encouragement of Arts, Manufactures, and Commerce, while the Margrave was elected to the Royal Society in 1794. Both showed charity to the poor and were generous to their staff.

Elizabeth was concerned about her position in society and wanted to be recognized by the sovereigns and be presented at court, like the rest of her family had been. The Margrave interceded for her by contacting Holy Roman Emperor Francis II. Elizabeth traveled to Vienna to pay homage to Francis II, who had granted her the title of Princess Berkeley that made her a royal and ensured that her marriage was legal. However, there is no evidence that she was ever presented at court.

Elizabeth and the Margrave were happily married for fifteen years until he died of pneumonia at age seventy in 1806. While Elizabeth had two properties in England and one in Ansbach to maintain, she did not receive the pension from Prussia that was due her, and financial problems beset her. She had to rent out Benham Park, sell her house in Ansbach, and curtail her expenses. Once Napoleon was defeated and travel was safer for Europeans, she decided to move to Posillipo, outside of Naples, Italy, as living was cheaper there and her money would go further. In addition, the climate was warm and mild, unlike England. In 1817, she built a house and a small theater and tended her garden there, quickly adapting to her new environment and becoming part of local society. However, as she aged, Elizabeth became increasingly fragile and was cared for by her son Keppel. She died on January 13, 1828, and is buried in the English Cemetery in Naples.

The following selections are from *A Journey Through the Crimea to Constantinople: In a Series of Letters from the Right Honourable Elizabeth Lady Craven to the Margrave of Brandenburg, Ansbach and Bareith.*

～

Letters from Lady Craven to the Margrave of Brandenburg-Ansbach

Petersburgh, Feb. 8, 1786

The road between Warsaw and this place is one insipid flat—except just in and about the town of Nerva, where I took a sledge and flew hither. When I wrote last, dear Sir, I think I was upon the point of going to see the Princess C———, I passed two days with her at a country house of the Princess Lubomirska's, her sister-in-law. I was most sincerely glad to see her, and we parted with regret—I received a very civil message from the King, and M. de Stackelberg sent me six bottles of bishop—which I can assure you was very serviceable to me—I did not stop at Warsaw on my return from the P—, and the messenger caught me just one post on this side of Warsaw. I can conceive nothing so *enuyant* as travelling in such a country as this—one flat plain—the view terminated by a forest, which you drive through, only to arrive at the same scene you have quitted—the frost was not hard enough to make the road good, till I came to Nerva—I am something like a country Miss, gaping at the window all day here—every creature that goes about the streets, seem as if they were in a violent hurry—they drive full gallop—with one horse ply at the corner of the streets as do our hackney-coaches and chairs—Mr S— informed me, it belonged to my dignity to have six horses to my coach, in order to pay my visits; and I beg you will imagine my surprise, when I found I had a coachmen on the box, with three postillions, one to each pair of horses—and these fitting on the right-hand, I go thus full gallop, running races with every other *attelage* that falls in my way—the streets are luckily wide—and custom makes the danger less than one should imagine—

I am interrupted and therefore wish you a good night.

Petersburgh, Feb. 18, 1786

I was to have been presented to the Empress next Sunday but she graciously sent me word to come to the Hermitage on Thursday, where she keeps her court in the evening every week, and has alternately a French play or an Italian opera. Marchesini and Madame Todi are the first singers. It is but justice to say, that nothing can be more magnificent than the appearance the Empress makes when she comes into the drawing-room; she has a lively and good-humoured look and her politeness to me was very great; but I could plainly see that someone had told her I was not an English woman—for she asked me if I was not of a Scotch family. I cannot conceive why this building which she has added to the palace is called the Hermitage; it is a long suite of rooms, full of fine pictures. You are not ignorant, dear Sir, of the many collections the Empress has purchased; among the rest Lord Orford's; all these fine works want at present a person to arrange them according to their shades and size and I doubt not but the Empress will find one—

Petersburgh is a cheerful and fine looking town; the streets are extremely wide and long, the houses stucco'd to imitate white stone; none above three stories high, which certainly adds to the lively and airy appearance of them. I think, Sir, if a young woman may permit herself to judge of things otherwise than *en detail*—that not only the town, but the manner of living is upon too large a scale; the nobles seem to vie with one another in extravagancies of every sort; particularly in foreign luxuries and fashions. The fashion of the day is most ridiculous and improper for this climate; French gauzes and flowers were not intended for Russian beauties and they are sold at a price here which must ruin the buyers.

There are buildings erected for the reception of Arts and Sciences of every kind; for artists or amateurs, though but the surplus of Italy, France, and England, would find handsome encouragement and house-room from the Empress, whose respect for talents and generosity to those who possess them, have induced some, and would many more, to fix in the present capital of this vast empire; but, alas! Sir, eight months of winter; and the horrid cold

I feel, must congeal the warmest imagination; poets and painters require verdant lawns; and the flowers of fancy must fade and die, where spring is not to be found.

The Empress and the Princess d'Afhkow are the only ladies who wear the Russian dress; it is I think a very handsome one; and I am more surprised every day that nations do not preserve their own fashions and not copy one country that is at present only the ape of every other. From Cherson, the town on the Turkish frontiers, which one thousand six hundred miles from hence, are brought many provisions; from Archangel likewise this town is provided, and from African on the Caspian Sea, near two thousand miles, all the dainties, such as grapes, pears, beans, artichokes, are brought. It is natural to suppose, that the necessaries of life are dear, from these circumstances; but some of them are extremely cheap and I believe Russia is one the cheapest countries in the world to live in; if French wines and Fashions, and English comforts can be dispensed with—to these last I never felt so much attachment as at this moment. *Dans le Ligne Anglais*, a quarter where the English merchants live, I find English grates, English coal, and English hospitality, to make me feel welcome, and the fire-side cheerful. I have never yet been fortunate enough to make any acquaintance in the world of commerce; but if all English merchants and their families are as well informed and civil as those I find here I should be glad to be admitted into the city of London as a visitor, to enjoy a little rational conversation, which at the court-end is seldom to be found. How should it be otherwise?

Peter the First thought commerce an essential pillar to his empire, and the English trader was encouraged; our little island is a proof of the consequence which trade alone can give any country; and the new acquired professions of the largest empires may only become additional trouble to their masters, unless the advantages of trade give them new life.

The French Ambassador, and the Comte Sergé de Romanzow (named to Berlin) are men of wit. Mr. Ellis is with Mr. Fitzherbert; and conversation does not languish or grow insipid in their company. We are in the last part of the carnival and balls; those given by the Ambassadors are very superb; Mr. de Segur and the Duc de Serra Capriola, the Neapolitan Minister, have each given one in a very magnificent style.

I was presented to the Grand Duchess the same night that I waited upon the Empress. She has since been brought to bed. There are some young Russian ladies very pretty and much accomplished, many of them sigh after a different climate than their own and told me he had no idea of happiness in the world like that of returning to England as a private man, and purchasing a farm. Indeed, Sir, the elegance which is produced by the cleanliness and order seen with us, is found nowhere out of England; here the houses ae decorated with the most sumptuous furniture from every country but you come into a drawing-room, where the floor is made of the finest inlaid woods, through a staircase made of the coarsest wood in the rudest manner and stinking with dirt—the postillions wear sheepskins—and at a ball, when a nobleman has proposed his hand to a fair lady he often kisses her before the whole company à *propos* to this custom.

You may have heard much of Prince Potemkin; I see him everywhere, but he is reserved and converses very little with ladies. I was invited by him to dine in an immense palace he is building in the suburb; the only room finished is too particular not to be described; it is three hundred feet in length, and on the side opposite the windows there are two rows of stone pillars, whose height and breadth are proportioned to the immense size of the room, which is an oblong square; in the centre of which on the side where the windows are, it is formed into a semi-circle or what we call a bow—which bow forms another large space independent of, though in the room; this space was laid out by his English gardener into a shrubbery with borders of flowers, hyacinths, and narcissus, myrtles, orange-trees, &e.&cc. were in plenty. We were seven or eight ladies, and as many men … immense stoves concealed by the pillars were heated in order to make such a hall in such a climate supportable … but I came home quite ill with cold. It was there I heard that extraordinary music performed by men and boys, each blowing a straight horn adapted to their size … sixty-five of these musicians produce a very harmonious melody, something like an immense organ. I sat by Prince Potemkin at dinner, but except asking me to eat and drink, I cannot say I heard the sound of his voice; so am unable to tell you what species of *esprit* has raised him to the fortunes and dignities he possesses; or what occasions Mr. S— and others to call him a sensible man.

I have seen likewise that cabinet of medals and the Museum here; the last when finished, will be a very beautiful suite of rooms—Peter the Great likewise fitting in a chair, with a coat of his amiable Catharine's embroidery. I cannot help thinking, and often hear, that notwithstanding he transferred his capital to his place, and that the Empress, Prince Potemkin, and others may build palaces of the finest orders of architecture, to contain the produce of learning and commerce, that a time will come when the heads of an empire, which extends from the South to the North, will prefer basking in the rays of the sun, which cheer the mind and the body together, to eternal frost—and these stately buildings will be turned into storehouses.

Justice obliges me to say, the Empress does all she can to invite politeness, science, and comforts from other countries, to cheer these regions of ice … but, until she can alter the climate, I believe it is a fruitless trial… I am informed the spring, or rather the time of the year we call spring, is more melancholy than winter here, so I shall hasten my departure; but a conversation I had with the Swedish Minister, a few day past, will make me give up entirely the thoughts of returning into Germany through Sweden and Denmark. I shall in my next have the honour of repeating it to you; I remain with the highest respect and regard,

Your most affectionate sister,

E.C.

M_____

I shall now prepare every thing to visit the Crimea or rather the Tauride; I have been told it is a very beautiful country; and I confess I am not sorry this *enfant perdu* gives me a good excuse towards Constantinople.

There are ladies here, whom I shall be sorry to quit; who in youth are possessed of many talents, and with whom I could form an agreeable society; Italian music, the pedal harp, and our English poets are perfectly understood by them; I think often I can trace Grecian features among the females of this country, and the subtle wit of the Greek in the men; that pliability of genius which causes them to speak so many different languages well, and adopt all the inventions and arts of other countries that are good.

I am speaking without partiality, dear Sir; but I do not see here the preju-dices of the English, and the conceit of the French, nor the stiff German pride … which national foibles make often good people of each nation ex-tremely disagreeable. I am assured the Russians are deceitful—it may be so; but as I do not desire to have intimacies. I am much better pleased to find new acquaintances pleasant and civil than morose or pert.

Mine at present is a geographical intercourse with the world; and I like to find the road I travel smooth. Wit and talents will always be objects of impor-tance to me; I have found them here, and shall be sorry to quit them. Prince Repnin and his nephew Prince Kourakin, whom I often saw in England, are both here, and I look upon them as old acquaintances, as it is thirteen years since that period. The latter is grown fat.

I forgot to tell you, Sir, that the Grand Duchess was brought to bed five days after my arrival so I have only seen her the night I was presented to her, which was the same on which I was presented to the Empress; her affability is great to strangers; for Mr. S— had not announced me to her; but seeing me move from one seat to another at the opera, by the empress's desire, and probably being informed who I was, she sent for me to come to her after the spectacle which I did.

Adieu, Sir, for the present. I remain your's, with great respect and truth.

P.S. I am not a little surprised to hear people say: I shall inherit so many hundred peasants, or such a one lost a village—it is the number of men, and not of acres, that make a fortune great here; so that a plague or any distemper that would prove mortal to the peasants, would be death to the nobles pockets likewise.

I have taken leave of the Emperors, and you may judge if I do not leave Petersburg with a good impression of her politeness; she told me before the opera, that she knew my intention; but as we defer disagreeable things as long as possible, you shall not take leave till after the spectacle; these words she said with the most gracious smile; and asked me if I was satisfied with the amusements and civilities I met with. I told her I must be both stupid and ungrateful, not to regret infinitely, that I could not stay any longer; to show how sensible I was of the hospitality and magnificence with which I was treated. The Vicechancellor, Comte d'Osterman, is obliged to have a table for sixty foreigners every Wednesday; and a widow Princess de Galitzin, a supper once a week ... at Mons. d'Osterman's too, a ball every Sunday night. The Empress is at the expence of these dinners and suppers ... and I confess, I think it is an excellent and royal idea, to be certain of having houses open for the entertainment of foreign ministers and strangers of distinction ... for you know, my dear Sir, that private houses are seldom open to strangers now in most countries, for various reasons. Here I am told there are many Princes who keep a public day, as we do in England, for the convenience of our country neighbors, and expect people whom they leave a card with, to dine with them upon such a day. But, if I was to stay here ten years, I should never be prevailed upon to go to those houses to dine without invitation nor can I believe it possible the masters of them can expect a foreigner to grace their table, without being desired even by word of mouth___I am assured I shall affront__and __ but as I meet them every where, I cannot think they should be so totally ignorant of the manners of other countries, to expect me to dine at their house without asking me... There is a custom here which I think very abominable; noblemen who are engaged to marry young ladies make no ceremony, but embrace them in the midst of a large company at a ball.

I have mentioned to a few people my intention of seeing the Crimea; and I am told that the air is unwholesome, the waters poisonous, and that I shall certainly die if I go there; but as in the great world a new acquired country, like a new beauty, finds detractors, I am not in the least alarmed; for a person, not a Russian, who has been there on speculation has given me so charming a description of it, that I should not be sorry to purchase a Tartarian estate.

Adieu, my much honoured and beloved brother.

I remain your's.

Moscow, Feb. 29, 1786

I left my coach at St. Petersburgh, and hired for myself and my small suite, the carriages of the country, called Kibitkas; they are exactly like cradles, the head having windows to the front which let down; I can sit or lay down, and feel in one like a great child, very comfortably defended from the cold by pillows and blankets. These carriages are upon sledges, and where the road is good, this conveyance is comfortable and not fatiguing; but from the incredible quantity of sledges that go constantly upon the track of snow, it is worn in tracks like a road; and from the shaking and violent thumps the carriage receives, I am convinced the hardest head might be broken. I was overturned twice; the postillions I fancy are used to such accidents; for they get quietly off their horse, set the carriage up again, and never ask if the traveler is hurt... Their method of driving is singular; they sit behind the horses that are harnessed abreast ... a shrill whistling noise, or a savage kind of shriek is the signal for the horses to set off, which they do full gallop; and when their pace slackens, the driver waves his right-hand, shrieks or whistles, and the horses obey.

I would never advise a traveler to set out from Petersburgh as I have, just at the end of the carnival; he might with some reason suppose it is a religious duty for the Russian peasant to be drunk; in most villages I saw a sledge loaded with young men and women in such a manner, that four horses would have been more proper to draw it than one, which wretched beast was obliged to fly with the noisy company up and down the village, which is generally composed of houses in straight rows on each side of the public road. The girls are dressed in their holiday-clothes, and some are beautiful, and do not look less so from various coloured handkerchiefs tied over their forehead, in a becoming and *pittoresque* manner.

The Russian peasant is a fine, stout, straight, well-looking man; some of the women, as I said before are uncommonly pretty; but the general whiteness of their teeth is something that cannot be conceived; it frequently happened that all the men of the village were in a circle around my carriages ... and rows of the most beautiful oriental pearl cannot be more regular and white than their teeth. ... It is a matter of great astonishment to me, how the infants outlive the treatment they receive, till they are able to crawl in the air; there is a kind of space or *entresol* over every stove, in which the husband, wife, and children lie the greatest part of the day, and where they sleep at night ... the heat appeared to me so great that I have no conception how they bear it; but they were as much surprised at me for seeking a door or window in every house I was obliged to go into, as I could possibly be at their living in a manner without air. The children look all pale and sickly, till they are five or six years old. The houses and dresses of the peasants are by no mean uncomfortable; the first is generally composed of wood, the latter of sheep-skins; but trees laid horizontally one upon another makes a very strong wall, and the climate requires a warm skin for clothing. It might appear to English minds, that a people who are in a manner the property of their lord, suffer many of the afflictions that attend slavery; but the very circumstance of their persons being the property insures them the indulgence of their master for the preservation of their lives. Before, my dear Sir, the invaluable advantage which these peasants have, as in paying annually a very small sum each, and cultivating as many acres of land as he thinks fit, his fortune depends entirely upon his own industry; each man only pays about the value of half-a-guinea a year ... if his lord would raise this tax too high, or make their vassals suffer ... misery and desertion would ruin his fortune, not theirs; it is true, that a lord is obliged to give one man as a recruit yearly out of such number; but it is one out of three or four hundred; so that notwithstanding this great empire is said not to be populated in proportion to the extent of it; when you reflect what a number of troops the Empress has, and these kept up by this method; the Russian people must be more numerous than strangers may imagine, in travelling through this country—It is very amusing to me to reflect, without prejudices of any kind, upon the ridiculous ideas of liberty and property that our English common people have; for_____

And now, my most honoured and dear brother that I have given you so pretty a picture of English liberty... I shall wish you a good night, and remain

Your's affectionately__

E.C_____

Moscow, March 3, 1786

I believe I have not told you, that I am possessed of all the instructions to proceed upon this new journey in a very pleasant manner. The commanders at Krementchouck and at Cherson are informed of my intention to proceed to Perckop, where I shall enter into that peninsula called the Tauride, which, from the climate and situation I look upon to be a delicious country; and an acquisition to Russia which she should never relinquish.

The Crimea was for a long time a formidable power to the Russians and Poles, till these nations became improved in military science. Until the peace of Karlowitz, both the nations were obliged to pay the Khan to the amount of 1000,000 six dollars, to insure their countries from the incursion of the Tartars. Russia has gained ground by degrees, and by arms and policy is become masters of the peninsula; the last Khan has a pension from the Empress, and is retired to live as a private gentleman; long before he resigned his sovereignty; the Turkish cabinet on one side; the crafty policy of the Russians on the other, left him no peace; even some hordes of Tartars insulted his tottering power. I am proceeding to, in which there is at present about thirty thousand of the Empress's troops, including five thousand Cossacks in her pay; which I am very curious to see ... notwithstanding all that has been said to deter me from continuing my tour, I shall certainly go on, and if I am not poisoned by the waters in Tartary, or drowned in my passage by the Black Sea to Constantinople, I shall, I hope, afford you some amusement in the geographical descriptions I shall give you and variety of military figures; who though not versed in tactics like your Prussian troops, may always entertain any person, who, like you, are a good soldier by inheritance, example, and practice; I am going to dine at my banker's, who insists on showing me his very fine hot-houses and having the honour of giving me a good dinner.

I remain unalterably

Your affectionate sister,

E.C___

Cherson, March 12, 1786

I was obliged to put my kibitkas on wheels at a vile little town called Soumi, before I arrived at Pultawa—notwithstanding there might have been many things worth stopping to look at in the immense town of Moscow, I was so impatient to meet the spring, that I would not send my name to any person whose civilities would have obliged me to stay. I cannot say that Moscow gives me any other idea than of a large village, or many villages joined, as the houses stand at such a distance, and it is such a terrible way to go to visit things or people that I should have made as many long journeys in a week, as there are days in one, had I staid. ... What is particularly gaudy and ugly at Moscow are the steeples—square lumps of different coloured bricks and gilt spires or ovals; they make a very Gothic appearance but it is thought a public beauty there; a widow lady was just dead, who having outlived all the people she loved, she left an immense sum of money to gild with the purest gold, the top of one of the steeples.

At Pultawa I was shown the ground on which the armies moved ... a memorable check to the wild spirit of Charles the Twelfth. A private person, one Paul Budenkof, has, at his own expense, erected a monument in remembrance of that event; it is a plate of brass, on which is represented the battle in a good engraving the plate is fixed into a pillar. At Soumi I conversed with a brother of Prince Kourakin's and a Mr. Lanskoy, both officers quartered there; and to whom I was indebted for a lodging: they obliged a Jew to give me up a new little house he was upon the point of inhabiting. The thaw had come on so quickly that I was obliged to stay two days while my carriages were taken off the sledges.

Mr Lanskoy has a little of the beauty and sweetness of countenance of his cousin who died; the favourite of the Empress; and who, if his pictures and the medal do not flatter him, was perfectly beautiful. Both Prince Kourakin and Lanskoy are very impatient to quit such dismal quarters, and seem to desire some event in which they may display a military ardour, very natural to soldiers, and increased in them, by having no polished people to converse with—as I found, upon asking what society they had, their account of the country nobles thereabout was truly laughable.

There is no gentleman's house at Pultawa; I slept at my banker's and walked all about the skirts of the town.

At Chrementchouk, the general who commands has a very pretty well-bred wife who did the honours of her house and the place perfectly well. Prince Potemkin has a large house just out of the town, which I went to see: at the Governors I assisted at a dinner where there was such a number of people, and so much company after dinner that I was heartily tired. An English woman, married to a Russian who was there, came to my lodging, and looked earnestly at me, said are you an English lady: I smiled and said, quite so: she flung her arms round my neck, and almost smothered me with kisses—Forgive me, said she: I, too, was born in England and have never had the happiness of seeing a country-woman since I left it: I am married, have children here, and probably shall never see England again. I was intreated to stay by all the ladies at least some days; but I cannot defer too long letting know what is become of me; I concealed from ___ and ___ my intended journey, and only wrote word from Petersburgh, that I was going to make a little tour to a warmer part of that country and I mean not to let either of them know where I am till I get safe to Constantinople.

I am going to see the Dock-Yard here and the fortifications, which are to be new done by a Colonel Korsakof, a very civil spirited young man here, who seems to have the welfare of this place, and the honour of his nation very much at heart. I shall give you an account of what I have seen to-morrow.

I remain with respect,

Your affectionate sister,

E.C___

Cherson, March 9, 1786

This place is situated upon the Dneiper, called by the ancients, the Boristhenes; which falls into the Black Sea; the only inconvenience of the Docks here is that the ships, when built, are obliged to be taken with camels into that part of the channel deep enough to receive them. The town is not at present very large, though there are many new houses and a church built after pretty models; good architecture of white stone. There are no trees near this place; korsakof is trying to make large plantations; the town is entirely furnished with fuel by reeds, of which there is an inexhaustible forest in the shallows of the Boristhenes, just facing Cherson_Rails, and even temporary houses are made of them. These reeds are strong and tall, and are a harbor for birds of various kind particularly aquatics; of which there are such a number, and of such beautiful kinds, that I can conceive nothing so entertaining as shooting parties in boats here. ___ Korsakof, and a Captain Mordwinof, who both have been educated in England, will, I have no doubt, make a distinguished figure in the military annals of Russia; Mordwinof is a sea-officer, and superintends the ship-building here—there are some pretty frigates on the stocks. Repninskai is the governor's name, and he has a young wife, who is very civil; my lodging is a large house built for a Greek Archbishop—but being empty, was appropriated to my life: I have remonstrated here, but in vain, against having sentinels, and the guard turning out as I pass through the gates. I hate all kind of ceremony and honours, particularly such as I am not accustomed to—but I am told here I must content myself with not refusing the orders that are given. The Emperor's Consul has a wife who wears a Greek dress here; I think it by no means becoming. Cherson may in time become a very beautiful town, and furnish the borders of the Boristhenes with examples of commerce; that inestimable and only real source of greatness to an empire. I am not soldier enough to know what fault there was in the fortifications, so that they are entirely to be done anew by the active and studious spirit of Korsakof, I have no doubt that they will be executed in a masterly manner.

I can conceive nothing so pleasant to a young soldier, as to be employed in places where his talents must create the defence and stability of newly acquired possessions. I leave this place in two days, dear Sir; and will do myself the honour of writing from the first town where I can sit down again for a few days.

I have nothing but maps and plans of various forts in my head at present, having looked over all such as my curiosity could induce me to ask for. The fortifications and plantations are executed here by malefactors, whose chains and fierce looks struck horror in my heart, as I walked over them, particularly when I was informed there are between three and four thousand. Yet I must confess, I think this method of treating criminals much more rational than that of shutting them up; and rendering them useless members of the society by which they must be maintained.

Mordwinof informs me, the frigate which is to convey me to Constantinople is prepared, and is to wait my pleasure at one of the seaports in the Crimea, and that the Comte de Wynowitch, who commands at Sevastopol has directions to accommodate me in the best manner. Mordwinof and Korsakof both are much more like Englishmen than any foreigners I ever met with, except one ... whom you are assured is the person upon earth I honour and esteem the most; and to whom I subscribe myself with all respect,

His most affectionate sister,

E.C_____

Karasbayer, April 3, 1786

I went in a barge for about two hours down the Boristhenes, and landed on the shore opposite to that on which Cherson stands. A carriage and horses belonging to a Major who commands a post about two hours drive from the place where I landed were waiting, and these conveyed me to his house, where I found a great dinner prepared, and he gave me some excellent fresh-butter made of Buffalo's milk; this poor man has just lost a wife he loved, and who was the only delight he could possess in a most disagreeable spot, marshy, low, and where he can have no other amusement but the troops... From thence I crossed the plains of Perekop, on which nothing but a large coarse grass grows, which is burnt at certain periods of the year. ... All this country, like that between Cherson and Chrementchouck, is called Steps. ... I should call it desert; except where the post-horses are found, not a tree not a habitation is to be seen. ... But one thing which delighted me much, for several miles after I had quitted Cherson, was the immense flocks of birds— buzzards, which I took at a certain distance for herds of calves—and millions of a small bird about the size of a pigeon, cinnamon colour and white ... droves of a kind of wild small goose, cinnamon colour, brown and white; As I went farther on, these multitudes decreased, not choosing I suppose to go too far from their shelter, the reeds.

Perekop is situated upon an eminence ... the ditch of it seems rather calculated for the lodgment of an enemy than a defence. ... The governor did every thing he could to detain me a few hours; but, as there was nothing to see, I went on. Just without the fortress of Perekop I was obliged to send one of my servants to a Tartar village to get a pass; the servent whom I sent, whose ridiculous fears through the whole journey have not a little amused me, came back as pale as death. ... He told me the chiefs were sitting in a circle smoking, that they were very ill black-looking people. I looked at the pass, it was in Turkish or Tartarian characters. I saw there two camels drawing a cart. This village gave me no great opinion of Tartarian cleanliness, a more dirty miserable looking place I never saw. The land at Perekop is but six miles across from the sea of Asoph, or rather an arm of it called the Suash, to the Black Sea. ... The Crimea might with great ease be made an island; after leaving Perekop, the country is exactly like what we call downs in England, and the turf is like the finest green velvet. ... The horses flew along; and though there was not a horse in the stables of the post-houses, I did not wait long to have them harnessed; the Cossacks have the furnishing of the horses ... and versts or mile-stones are put up; the horses were all grazing on the plain at some distance, but the instant they see their Cossacks come out with a little corn the whole herd surrounds him, and he take those he pleases. The posts were sometimes in a deserted Tartarian village, and sometimes the only habitation for the stable-keeper was a hut made under ground, a common habitation in this country, where the sun is extremely hot, and there is no shade of any sort. To the left of Perekop I saw several salt lakes about the third post—it was a most beautiful sight. About sun-set, I arrived at a Tartarian village of houses or rather huts straggling in a circle without fence of any kind. ... At different spots upon the downs, large herds of horses, cows, and sheep were approaching, with a slow pace, the village ... making at once a simple and majestic landscape, full of that peace and plenty which possessions in the primitive state of the world might have enjoyed.

I stopped there and made tea; that I might go on, as far as I could that night. ... You must not suppose, my dear Sir, though I have left my coach and harp at Petersburgh, that I have not all my little necessaries even in a Kibitka ... a tin kettle in a basket holds my tea equipage, and I have my English side-saddle tied behind my carriage. ... What I have chiefly lived upon is new milk, in which I melt a little chocolate. At every place I have stopped at I asked to taste the water from curiosity, I have always found it perfectly good.

I can easily suppose people jealous of Prince Potemkin's merit; his having the government of the Tauride, or commanding the troops in it, may have caused the invention of a thousand ill-natured lies about this new country, in order to lessen the share of praise which is his due, in the attainment or preservation of it ... but I see nothing at present which can justify the idea of the country's being unwholesome. To-morrow I shall have the honour of giving you an account of my arrival and reception here, and what sort of place it is.

I remain yours affectionately,

E.C___

CHAPTER TWO

~

Elisabeth Vigée Le Brun

An Artist in Russia

Elisabeth Vigée Le Brun was a noted French portrait painter of the late eighteenth and early nineteenth centuries. She was born in Paris in 1755, the daughter of Louis Vigée, an artist and painter from whom she received her first instruction. Elisabeth showed great talent at an early age and developed such skills that by the time she was in her teens, she was painting professionally. In 1776, at age nineteen, she married Jean-Baptiste-Pierre Le Brun, also a painter, and he exhibited her work at various salons, thus gaining recognition for her. Through him she made connections with the connoisseurs of

Elisabeth Vigée Le Brun
Public Domain

the art world and members of the aristocracy, maéy of whom she painted, including Queen Marie Antoinette.

In 1780, Elisabeth gave birth to a daughter, Jeanne Lucie Louise, whom she called Julie. She had another daughter who died young. In 1783, Elisabeth Vigée Le Brun was inducted into the Acadèmie Royale de Peinture et de Sculpture, only to have her membership retracted after the French Revolution.

Elisabeth was a consummate portraitist, but she was also a consummate traveler. She traveled to see the European world, visiting the art museums, the churches, the sculpture, the statuary, the countryside, and the works of other artists whose styles and techniques she appreciated and valued. Both she and her husband went to Flanders and the Netherlands in 1781 to see the works of Flemish masters.

The French Revolution in 1789 disrupted both the art world and Elisabeth's world. Fearing for her life, she fled Paris with her daughter and her daughter's governess to Italy, leaving her husband behind. She would live in exile for the next twelve years. She arrived in Italy and stayed in Rome for eight months, where she gained clients and painted the nobility, then spent six months in Naples where she painted the Queen of Naples and Lady Emma Hamilton. The proceeds she gained from her work were sent to her husband to pay off his gambling debts. Elisabeth enjoyed wandering through the streets of the city and had a love for nature and the natural world. She hiked Mount Vesuvius, sailed the bay of Naples, and admitted she would have liked to paint the scenery in Italy rather than the people. Elisabeth continued her travels through Italy, visiting the famous hill towns and stopping at Florence, Venice, and Turin before entering Austria.

Elisabeth spent two and a half years in Vienna. She had many commissions in the city from prominent individuals, including Princess Lichtenstein, Princess d'Esterhazy, and Baron Stroganoff. In every major capital that she visited, Elisabeth attended dinners, balls, and parties sponsored by the elite; she never lacked for company or invitations. It was in Vienna that she met the Russian ambassador who encouraged her to go to Russia to recoup her fortune; he assured her that she would be welcomed by Catherine the Great; hence she left Vienna in 1795 for Russia.

Elisabeth arrived in Saint Petersburg in July 1795 and stayed in Russia for the next six years. She did well financially, painting the granddaughters of Catherine the Great, the Grand Duchesses Alexandra and Helen; the Grand Duchess Elizabeth, the wife of Tsar Alexander I; the Grand Duchess Anne, wife of the Grand Duke Constantine; and Prince Stanislaus Poniatowski, former king of Poland. Elisabeth did not paint Empress Catherine for she died in 1796.

Elisabeth Vigée Le Brun and Daughter
Library of Congress

Elisabeth became very fond of the Russian people and was well liked by those in society. She led an active social life and was invited to balls and dinners at the great mansions of the aristocracy. She also worked very hard and was inducted in the St. Petersburg Academy. In October 1800, shortly after her daughter's marriage to Gaetan Bernard Nigris, a man she disapproved of, she traveled to Moscow to paint a member of the Stroganoff family and Prince Kourakin, who lived there. She stayed in Moscow for five months and returned to St. Petersburg where she made preparations to leave for France. Elisabeth loved Russia and the Russian people and was loath to leave the country, but her health and personal concerns caused her to return to her own country, then under the dictatorship of Napoleon, in 1802.

Elisabeth returned to Paris, where she was welcomed by family and friends and invited to many social events; however, she had a touch of melancholy and moved to the countryside. Thoughts of travel often improved her mood, and she decided to go to England in 1803. She visited London and the countryside but did not neglect painting, as she painted the Prince of Wales, Lord Byron, and Lady Elizabeth Craven, now the Margravine of Anspach, and her son Richard Keppel. After a stay of three years, Elisabeth returned to France, where she painted Mme. Murat, Napoleon's sister.

Travel beckoned again, and Elisabeth visited Switzerland in 1808 and 1809. She reveled in the beauties of nature, the mountains, ravines, and waterfalls, doing two hundred paintings of the natural world there. Ever the wanderer, she visited Bordeaux and the Chateau country in the Loire valley when she returned.

In her old age, Elisabeth lived in Paris in the winter and in the summer in Louveciennes, where she had purchased a house. Her husband died in 1813, her daughter in 1819, and her brother in 1820; she was left with two nieces who looked after her. She died on May 29, 1842, in Paris and is buried in her beloved Louveciennes. Since the Louvre did not have any of her works at her death, her nieces presented two of her portraits to the museum: one of Elisabeth and her daughter, the other of a young girl with a muff. Today, her delicate and exquisite portraits, many of women, are in major European and American museums.

Elisabeth wrote her memoirs entitled *Souvenirs* that were first published in three volumes in Paris in 1835. A translation of *The Memoirs of Elisabeth Vigée Le Brun* was published by the Indiana University Press in 1989. Her memoirs give a delightful account of her life, one of a sensitive, introspective artist who was honored by membership in the leading European Academies and was esteemed by her fellow artists.

The following selections are from *Souvenirs of Madame Vigée Le Brun.*

⟿

Souvenirs of Madame Elisabeth Vigée Le Brun

Meeting Catherine the Great

Tremblingly I arrived at the palace, and a few moments afterwards was *téte-à-téte* with the autocrat of all the Russias. M. d'Esterhazy had informed me that I must kiss her hand, and in consequence of this custom she had taken off one of her gloves, which ought to have reminded me of it; but I entirely forgot. It is true that the appearance of this celebrated woman made such an impression on me, that it was impossible to think of anything else but looking at her. I was at first extremely surprised to find her very short; I had fancied her prodigiously tall, as high as her grandeur. She was very stout, but had still a handsome face, beautifully set off by her white curly hair. Genius seemed seated on her high white forehead. Her eyes were soft and sweet, her nose quite Grecian, her complexion florid, and her features very animated.

She at once said in a voice of much sweetness: "I am charmed to see you here, Madame; your reputation has preceded you. I greatly love the arts; and above all painting. I am not a connoisseur, only an amateur."

Everything she said during this interview, which was rather long, was the hope that I should be so well pleased with Russia, that I should remain in the country some time, and her whole conversation showed so much true benevolence, that timidity disappeared, and when I took leave of Her Majesty I was entirely reassured. Only I could not forgive myself for having forgotten to kiss her beautiful white hand, and I was still more vexed because M. d'Esterhazy reproached me for it. As for my dress, she did not appear to have paid the least attention to it, and perhaps she was less scrupulous than our ambassadress.

Shortly after my reception, Her Majesty expressed her intention of allowing me to pass the summer in this beautiful country place. She ordered her Controllers of the Household to give me apartments in the chateau, desiring to have me near her in order to see me paint. But I have since heard that these gentlemen did not wish to see me placed so near the Empress; and not withstanding reiterated orders they persisted in saying that there were no available rooms to be had. What much surprised me was to hear that these courtiers, believing me to be of the party of Comte d'Artois, feared that through my influence I might succeed in replacing M. d'Esterhazy by another ambassador. It is highly probable that M. d'Esterhazy was quite aware of their proceedings; but he knew me very little not to understand that I was far too occupied with my painting to give my time to political matters.

The welcome which I received in Russia was sufficiently good to console me for a petty court intrigue. My letters of introduction became quite useless to me; not only was I invited to pass my life in the best and most agreeable houses, but I met again at St. Petersburg many old friends and acquaintances. First of all the Comte Stroganoff, a true lover of the arts, whose portrait I first took in Paris, when I was very young. He possessed, at St. Petersburgh, a splendid collection of pictures, and near the city, at Raminostroff, a charming Italian casino, where every Sunday he gave great dinner parties.

Painting the Grand-Duchesses Alexandrine and Hélène, daughters of Paul I

As soon as Her Majesty had returned to St. Petersburg from Czarskoiesiolo, the Comte Stroganoff brought me an order from her to paint the two Grand-Duchesses Alexandrine and Hélène. These princesses were about thirteen and fourteen years of age, and their countenances were really lovely, though with totally different expressions. Their complexion was so fine and delicate, you would have thought they lived on ambrosia. The eldest, Alexandrine, was of the Grecian type; but Hélène's face expressed much more refinement. I grouped them together, holding and looking at a portrait of the Empress; the costume was slightly Greek, but very simple and modest. I was therefore greatly surprised when Zouboff, the favourite, told me that Her Majesty was scandalized at the manner I had dressed the two Grand-Duchesses in my picture. I so entirely believed this unkind remark, that I speedily replaced my tunics by the dresses the princesses ordinarily wore, and covered their arms with long sleeves. The truth is the Empress had said nothing of the kind; for she had the goodness to assure me of this the very next time I saw her.

Painting the Grand Duchess Elizabeth

As soon as I had finished the portraits of the Grand-Duchesses, the Empress commanded me to take that of the Grand-Duchess Elizabeth, recently married to Alexander. I have already said what an enchanting person this Princess was; I should have preferred to paint her according to my imagination, instead of the ordinary costume of the day; but since this was not to be, I painted her full length, in court dress, arranging flowers in a basket. I went to her for the sitting and was shown into her divan; this *salon* was hung in pale blue velvet, edged with silver fringe. The Grand-Duchess speedily appeared, dressed in a white robe, such as she wore the first time I saw her; it was still Psyche, and her manner so sweet, so gracious, joined to her charming face, made me admire her doubly.

When I finished her large portrait, she made me make another for her mother, in which I painted her with a transparent violet shawl, leaning against a cushion. I can say the more I saw of her, the more I found her kind and loveable. One morning, when she was giving me a sitting, a sudden giddiness seized me, my eyes seemed to be full of sparks; she became much alarmed, and ran herself to fetch me water, and bathed my eyes, caring for me with the greatest solicitude, and on my return home sent at once to inquire how I was.

Painting the Grand Duchess Anne

I also at the same time made the portrait of the Grand-Duchesse Anne, wife of the Grand-Duke Constantine. She was a Princess of Coburg, and though not possessing such a heavenly face as that of her sister-in-law, was not less lovely and bewitching. She might have been sixteen years of age, and the liveliest gaiety reigned in all her features. The Princess, however, had not known much happiness in Russia.

Shortly after his marriage, [Constantine] became very jealous of his brother Alexander, which created violent quarrels between himself and the Duchess Anne, who was indignant at his suspicions. These differences got to such a point, that it resulted at last in a divorce. The Princess returned at first to her parents, but later on, when I was in Switzerland, I found her settled there.

There is every reason to believe, that the Grand Duchess Elizabeth, that angel of beauty, was not more happy than her sister-in-law, in retaining the heart of her husband. The love of Alexander for a charming Pole whom he married to Prince Narischkin, is known to all of Europe. ... Madame Narischkin was the most regularly beautiful; her figure was fine and supple, her face was purely Greek, which made her extremely remarkable; but she had not to my mind the exquisite charm of the Grand-Duchess Elizabeth.

Dinner in St. Petersburg

The dinner hour at St. Petersburg at all houses is from two to half-past; my daughter accompanied me. We were shown into a gloomy room, without my being able to discover any signs of dinner. One o'clock, two o'clock passed, still nothing appeared, at last two servants entered and arranged some card tables, shortly afterwards, guests arrived and at once sat down to cards.

Towards six o'clock, my poor child and myself became so famished that on looking at ourselves in glass we were really pitiable objects. I felt as though I was dying, and it was only half-past seven that dinner was announced; but our poor stomachs had suffered so much, it was impossible to eat. I learnt afterwards that the Comtesse D was intimately acquainted with Lord Wilford, and dined to please him at the hour they dine in London.

In general, nothing annoyed me more than dining out; I was, nevertheless, sometimes obliged to do so, above all in Russia, as I should have given much offence if I had invariably refused. The greatest magnificence presided at these repasts; the cooks were nearly always French, and the fare exquisite. A quarter of an hour before dinner, a servant always brought in a tray of liqueurs, and slices of thin bread and butter. No one takes liqueur after dinner; but always excellent Malaga.

Winter in Russia

If one stayed indoors all day, no one would know that winter had arrived, to such a perfection have the Russians carried the art of heating their apartments. From the hall door, every part is heated by the most excellent stoves, so that the open fires kept up are merely a luxury. The staircases and the corridors are of the same temperature as the rooms, where the doors remain open as in summer. It is said that when the Emperor Paul, then Grand-Duke, visited France, under the name of the Prince du Nord, he said to the Parisians: "At St. Petersburg we see the cold, but here we feel it." Also, when I had passed seven years in Russia and had returned to Paris, where I found the Princess Dolgorouki, I recollect one day we felt so dreadfully cold sitting close to a fire, that we said; "We must go and spend a winter in Russia to get warm."

The Russians

The Russian people are as a rule ugly; but they have a straightforward honest bearing, and are the best people in the world. You never meet a drunken man, though their habitual drink is the strongest brandy. The greater number of the Russians live on potatoes and garlic mixed with oil, and they smell of it, notwithstanding that they bathe every Saturday. This poor food does not prevent them from singing at the top of their voices, whilst working or rowing their boats.

The Russians are skillful and intelligent, for they learn all sorts of handicraft with amazing facility; many even obtain success in the arts. One day at the Count Stroganoff's I met a young man, his architect, who had once been his serf; this man had shown so much talent that the Comte presented him to the Emperor Paul, who made him one of his architects, and ordered him to build a theatre from the plans he had made and submitted to him. I did not see the theatre finished, but I am told it was very fine.

The domestics are remarkable for their intelligence. I had one who did not know a word of French, and I did not know a word of Russian; but we understood each other perfectly without the help of speech. I could ask for anything by raising my hand, and he was never at a loss, and served me admirably. Another precious quality that I discovered in him, was a thoroughly conscientious fidelity; I was frequently paid for my pictures in bank notes, and when I was occupied painting, I would place them by me on the table. On leaving my work, I constantly forgot to take them away, and they remained often three or four days there, without losing one. The good servant was named Peter; he wept when I left St. Petersburg, and I have always regretted him. The Russian people are in general very honest and gentle. At St. Petersburg and Moscow, I never heard of a great crime or even a theft. The honest and peaceful conduct is surprising in men who are still not far from being barbarians, and many people attribute it to the state of serfdom which exists in Russia; for my own part I attribute their honesty and other good qualities to their being extremely religious.

Evenings in St. Petersburg

Every evening I went out. Not only the balls, concerts, theatres, were frequent, but I delighted in the evening parties, where I found all the urbanity and grace of French society; for to use an expression of the Princesse Dolgorouki, it appeared as though good taste had bounded from Paris to St. Petersburg. The houses regularly open to visitors were numerous, and in all of them I was received in the most amiable manner. People met about eight o'clock, and supper at ten. In the interval I had tea; but tea in Russia is so excellent that, though I could not drink it myself, I was scented with its perfume.

Catherine the Great's Accomplishments

The People lived so happily during the reign of Catherine that I can positively affirm having heard her blest by both small and great, as one to whom the nation owed so much of its glory and well being. I shall not write about the conquests which flattered the nation's pride so prodigiously, but of the real and lasting good done by this Sovereign to her people.

During the space of thirty-four years, the time she reigned, her benevolent genius created or protected all that was useful and glorious. In memory of Peter I, she built an imperishable monument of two hundred and thirty-seven stone towns, saying that the wooden villages, which were so easily destroyed by fire, cost her much more. She covered the sea by her fleet; established everywhere manufactories and banks, so essential to the commerce of St. Petersburg, Moscow, and Tobolsk. She accorded new privileges to the Academy; founded schools in all the towns and country districts; built canals and raised granite quays; formed a new code of laws; created an establishment for foundlings; and finally she introduced in her Empire the blessing of vaccination, which her powerful will alone was capable of imposing on the Russian people, and the better to obtain this result she was inoculated first herself.

Funeral of Catherine the Great

The body of the Empress remained exposed for six weeks in a large saloon in the château, which was illuminated day and night, and splendidly decorated. Catherine lay on a couch, surrounded by escutcheons, bearing the arms of all the cities of the Empire. Her face was uncovered, her beautiful hand was placed on the bed. All the ladies, of whom some took turns to watch by the body, all kissed this hand or pretended to do so; as for me, I had never done so when she was alive, and I could not do so after death. I avoided looking at the face of Catherine II even, for it would have been so sadly present in my imagination afterwards.

The time arrived for the funerals, the coffin of Peter III, on which his son had placed a crown, was transported near that of Catherine, and both were taken to the citadel, that of Peter first; for Paul wished to cast a slight upon his mother's remains. I watched the mournful spectacle from my window, as one might watch a play. The coffin of the defunct Emperor was preceded by a guardsman, clad in gold armour from head to foot. The one who walked in front of the Empress's coffin wore only steel armour, and the assassins of Peter III, were compelled, by command of his son, to carry the ends of the pall which covered him. Paul followed the procession on foot, bareheaded, with his wife and the whole Court, who were very numerous and in deep mourning. The ladies had long trains and huge black veils falling around them. They had to walk thus, in the snow in fearfully cold weather, from the Palace to the fortress, which is some distance on the other side of the Neva. I saw several ladies looking nearly dead of cold and fatigue on their return.

Mourning was worn six months. The women had pointed caps coming low on their forehead, which did not improve their appearance at all; but the slight annoyance was as nothing compared to the alarm felt throughout the Empire at the death of Catherine II.

My Work in St. Petersburg

If my father's old friend (Doyen, a painter), was pleased with his fortune at St. Petersburg, I was the none the less pleased with mine. I worked unceasingly from morning to evening. Only on Sundays I lost two hours, which I was obliged to give to those who wished to visit my studio; amongst the number were often the Grand-Dukes and Grand-Duchesses. Besides the paintings of which I have spoken and numerous portraits, I had procured from Paris the picture of Queen Marie Antoinette, the one in which I painted her in a blue velvet dress—the interest it caused gave me great pleasure.

Painting the Empress Marie

Having been ordered by the Emperor to paint a portrait of the Empress, his wife, I represented her on foot, wearing a court dress and a crown of diamonds. I do not care to paint diamonds, the brush cannot give them sufficient brilliancy. But by making a background of a crimson velvet curtain, which brought out the crown into relief, I managed to make it as brilliant as it was possible to do. When I had the painting in my own rooms to finish it, they wished to lend me the court dress with the diamonds as well, but I refused that mark of confidence which would have made me live in a state of terror; I preferred to paint them at the Palace, and had my painting carried back accordingly.

The Empress Marie was a handsome woman; and from being rather stout, looked still fresh. She was tall, and commanding, with splendid fair hair. I remember seeing her once at a ball with her beautiful curly locks falling each side of her shoulders, surmounted by a coronet of diamonds; this tall and stately figure rose majestically by the side of Paul, forming a striking contrast. A noble disposition was added to so much beauty; the Empress Marie was really like the woman spoken of in the Bible, and her virtues were so well known that she was perhaps the only instance of a woman whom calumny dared not attack. I confess that I felt proud at being honoured by her notice, and the nice ways in which she always showed her kindness.

Our sittings always took place after the Court dinner, so that the Emperor and his sons, Alexander and Constantine, were often present. These august personages did not make me feel embarrassed, as the Emperor, the only one I feared, was always good to me. One day he brought me my cup of coffee himself, as I was standing at my easel, waited till I had finished it and took it away again.

During one of my sittings, the Empress brought her two younger sons, the Grand-Duke Nicholas and the Grand-Duke Michael. I never saw a finer grandchild than the Grand-Duke Nicholas, afterwards Emperor. I could almost paint him from memory even now, so much did I admire his lovely face, quite Grecian in its character.

Reception in the St. Petersburg Academy

One of the pleasantest memories I have is that of my reception as Member of the St. Petersburg Academy. I was informed by Count Stroganoff, then director, of the day fixed on for my reception. I had ordered for myself the Academy uniform, a riding habit with a little violet waistcoat, yellow petticoat, and black hat and feathers.

At one o'clock I entered a salon preceding a long gallery, at the end of which I distinguished Count Stroganoff, seated at a table. I was asked to go towards him. In order to do so, I had to cross this long gallery filled with spectators, but as, fortunately, I knew many people amongst this crowd, I did not feel very nervous. The Count made me a very complimentary little discourse, and then gave me from the Emperor a diploma which made me a Member of the Academy. In the evening, I met several persons who had been present at the spectacle. I was applauded for my courage in crossing the gallery full of people. "I could not have done so," I replied, "had I not known how kindly disposed they all were to me."

Death of Emperor Paul

On the 12th of March, 1801, halfway between Moscow and St. Petersburg, I learned the death of Paul I. I saw before the post-house numbers of couriers, who were going to spread the news through the Empire, and as they took all the horses, I was unable to procure any for myself. I was compelled to remain in my carriage by the road-side all night. There was an icy wind and I was nearly frozen. At last I procured some horses and did not arrive at St. Petersburg till eight or nine o'clock the following day.

I found the city in transports of delight; people were singing and dancing in the streets. Many of my acquaintances rushed to my carriage and shook my hands, saying, "What a deliverance!" The evening before the houses were illuminated. In fact, the death of this unfortunate prince was a most joyful event for the public.

Farewell to Russia

Neither these two sovereigns, or the people who showed such a flattering interest in me during my stay at St. Petersburg and at my departure, ever knew with what grief I left that city. When I passed the Russian frontier, I burst into tears, and made up my mind to revisit those who had for so long shown me every mark of friendliness and affection; but it was my destiny, or fate, never to see again the land which I still consider as my second country.

CHAPTER THREE

~

Martha Wilmot

An Irish Lady in Russia

Martha Wilmot of Glanmire, County Cork, Ireland, never imagined during her growing up years that she would spend eight years in Russia as a guest of Princess Catherine Daschkova. Born in 1775 to Edward and Martha Wilmot, she was of Anglo-Irish ancestry and was educated at home. Her residence in Russia came about through her cousin, Lady Catherine Hamilton, who befriended Princess Daschkova when she traveled through Ireland on a European tour.

Through her cousin's friendship with Daschkova, Martha was invited to visit the princess. In 1803, at age twenty-eight, she left alone on a four-month journey by ship to St. Petersburgh, then by coach to Moscow and Troitskoe, the country estate of the princess.

Princess Catherine Daschkova was an intimate of Catherine II (the Great) of Russia and was instrumental in securing the throne for her. She was the first woman to head the Imperial Academy of Arts and Sciences, a prolific writer and translator of foreign works, the first woman to hold a government office in Europe, and the first woman to become a member of the American Philosophical Society, though an invitation from Benjamin Franklin. In 1783, she was head of the Russian Academy and was instrumental in a project to create a dictionary of the Russian language.

Martha, during her years in Russia, kept a diary and wrote letters to her parents, sisters, and brothers. It is from these accounts that her life in Russia unfolds, one of travel to Moscow, St. Petersburgh, Poland, and White Russia, where the princess had an estate; of dinners and balls with the nobility; and

Catherine Dashkova
Hillwood Museum

of attendance at religious services of the Russian Orthodox Church. She had an opportunity as well to meet peasants, the Jewish community in Poland, and the merchant class. Martha seemed to blend seamlessly in her new environment, so vastly different from her life in Ireland. Though the princess spoke English and French, and they could communicate, Martha studied the difficult Russian language.

On a personal level, Martha and the princess had a maternal relationship. Both were exceedingly fond of each other, Martha calling the princess her beloved Russian Mother. She was showered with gifts from the princess, including jewels, clothes, decorative boxes, and even a young Russian maid, all her own. Martha encouraged the princess to write her memoirs, and she translated them from French into English. When Martha left Russia in 1808, she took a copy of the memoirs and some letters of Catherine II with her but had to burn the copy of the memoirs before being subject to search by customs. Fortunately, her sister Catherine Wilmot had taken a copy with her when she left Russia in 1807.

Initially, Martha made an attempt to return home in February 1808, but she changed her mind as she knew the princess was in failing health and would be brokenhearted by her absence. Torn by her loyalty to the princess and her desire to leave, she made the final break, leaving Russia on October 26, 1808. After a hazardous voyage, including being marooned on the island of Stamieux after the ship *Maria* was wrecked, and then on the island of Aspo, where they waited for better weather, she arrived in Harwich, England, on December 26, 1808, and returned to Ireland in 1809.

Once she arrived in Ireland, she lived with her parents in Derbyshire. In 1812, Martha married Reverend William Bradford. The couple had one son and two daughters. Her husband was appointed chaplain to the British Embassy in Vienna, and the family lived there for ten years. From 1820 to 1821, they toured Italy, and Martha kept diaries of that trip. The couple returned to Storrington, England, in 1829, when her husband was appointed chaplain to King George IV.

In 1840, the Wilmot sisters' edition of Princess Dashkova's memoirs was published in English in two volumes. They were titled *Memoirs of the Princess Daschkaw, lady of honour to Catherine II, empress of all the Russias, written by herself; comprising letters of the empress, and other correspondence.* Subsequently, the memoirs were translated into French, German, Russian, and Czech.

Martha moved to Dublin, Ireland, after her husband died in 1857. She died there at age ninety-eight on December 18, 1873, and is buried in Storrington. In 1934, Martha and Catherine's letters and journal entries were published as *The Russian Journals of Martha and Catherine Wilmot* by H. Montgomery Hyde and the Marchioness of Londonderry.

The following selections are from Martha's portions of *The Russian Journals of Martha and Catherine Wilmot.*

⌒

The Russian Journals of Martha and Catherine Wilmot

Sights of St. Petersburgh

St. Petersburgh, Friday 22nd July

Here I am seated in the Neva right opposite to the Statue of Peter the Great, just cast anchor. ... I have been diverted beyond measure at the Bridge of Boats, over which such myriads of bearded Men and Dressy Women, Coaches drawn by six and eight Horses so distant as to give the idea of many more, with a thousand new appearances to distract my wondering Eyes, are continually passing. The weather is scorching; and not a woman that I have yet seen has had any sort of shade in her face. ... The Statue has not struck me as I expected, but it is very grand and I'll tell you more when I get nearer to it.

To Her Mother

St. Petersburgh, 31st July 1803
Yesterday evening we went to see an air balloon. I delight in sights, not for their own sakes but because they collect a Mob, and that exhibits so much of national character. We had two mobs yesterday, a genteel one and a vulgar one. The first was in the Gardens belonging to the Academy of the Cadet Corps. ... The Emperor and the Empress then arrived. He is a tall fair handsomish-looking Young Man—she tall, fair, and would be very pretty, only for a dreadful scurvy she has in her face.

Mon. Eveng 1st August
I am just returning from Walking to examine the celebrated Statue of Peter the Great. It is undoubtedly noble beyond what one could almost suppose possible in imitative art. ... It really is the finest Statue I ever beheld. ... However it is a glorious Monument and the Russians value it as such.

Ball at Peterhof

To Her Sister Harriet

Saturday, 6th August
We arrived at the Palace at seven o'clock, the rooms of which were all thrown open and we there met such a crowd of people that we cou'd scarcely advance. At length the Emperor and Empress etc. etc. appeared and a Polish Dance was begun, Emperor leading out my beautiful acquaintance Mdm Adadoroff and (follow'd by, I dare say, sixty couples) literally walk'd the figure of 8 to music. It was simply a Promenade by which I saw again and again every Grandee who pass'd successively as close to me as they could do. The Empress look'd charming and the affable manner which she and all the Imperial family possess are quite delightful.

The Countryside

To Her Father

Laminchenoff, 19th August 1803
I am very sorry to quit St. Petersburgh where I spent three weeks most agreeably and where I hope to spend more time.

The country does not present much Variety at present. Wooden Villages interrupt the long and generally strait Wooden roads; and at one of these Wooden Cottages you stop to refresh yourself with either their excellent milk and brown bread or your own store of provisions as often as you like. Now and then a Town, brilliant with the numerous gilded spires and Domes of Churches, produces an effect from contrast that is very curious. The Peasants one and all please me, from the frolicksome Variety of their Dresses, their grouping together in cheerful gay looking odd societys. ... They dance frequently, but the Sluggish Men Gossip in distinct partys and seldom join in any of the Village amusements. I think the Men handsomer than the Women in general, but I give you my word both are as superior to Irish people of the same class as one nation can be to another.

Meeting Princess Daschkaw

To Her Father

Troitska, August 25th 1803

Her reception of me was that of the kindest affection. She address'd me in English which she speaks fluently, and in the course of the Evening we had a good deal of conversation; ... Her appearance is milder than I expected from what I heard at St. Petersburgh. Her Dress a Man's night cap and black Hat with a sort of dark *robe de chamber*. Her manners are easy, and a certain something that distinguishes her not unpleasingly from the common herd. You must know I am in safety after all my Journeying by Sea and Land.

This place is splendid. Her English taste provides, and she has really created from a rather barren situation one of the most lovely and magnificent places that is to be found anywhere! The weather is scorching, but there are contrivances for cooling as well as for heating the rooms, and we eat Ice wherever we chuse.

The Daily Routine

To Her Mother

Troitska, September 5th 1803

I'll tell you pretty nearly how my day is divided. I rise at half after seven, breakfast on Coffee in my own room which is a most cheerful agreeable and well furnished apartment. At eleven or twelve I visit the Princess in hers and we chat, sometimes about Kings and Empresses and sometimes about Wheat and rye for half an hour or so. I then return to my own room and Dress, or not, just as I like etc. etc. etc. I read the Psalms etc. every day as such a thing as a Protestant Church is not known here—and at two we dine, our Dinner superb and well dress'd with cleaniness and delicacy. ... I am beginning to pick up some Russian words. ... From dinner we retire to the Drawing room till four, and then go out to Walk in the beautiful grounds of Troitska.

A mixture of familiarity and Pride appears to me to be a striking characteristic of this country. 'Tis by no means uncommon to see Masters and Slaves mingle in the same dance, and in visiting at a strange House I have been more than once puzzled to find out which was the Mistress and which the *femme de Chambre*. Another Custom is that of maintaining a Fool in many of the first Houses.

About eleven we retire for the night. I am wrap'd up in a black and yellow silk shawl from morning till night, because it is the fashion.

From Her Journal

23rd September

In the Eveg the Princess talk'd a little of the wonderful scenes of the revolution in which she acted *so* wonderful a part at the age of 18. The Empress Katherine was 16 years older than her. It is a curious circumstance that Peter 3rd was Godfather to Princess Dashkoff who as she says herself "I dethroned."

Customs

Letter to Her Father

Moscow, Jany 2nd 1804

Another custom but of a more agreeable nature I experience'd this morning. Whenever a person quits one Home to go to another all the friends and even acquaintances may and generally do send some useful present a piece of furniture, food, anything you please. Diamonds, for example, but whatever is the value of the present, tis a custom for ages past to call it by the name of Bread and Salt, emblems of Hospitality. Now you must know Dr Hollidays with whom I travell'd from St. Petersburgh to Moscow is in the very act of getting into a new habitation. He was paying us a visit this morning and happen'd to mention the circumstance. The Princess delights in the idea of my being a Good Russian and told him she knew Miss Wilmot had (according to the national custom) prepared some Bread and Salt for Mrs. Halliday and requested She wou'd send for it in half an hour. Accordingly when her porters arrived, a very elegant table with a marble top was ready to be sent and a note for Mrs. H. written in Rus. Here it goes in English. "I send you to get your new Establishment the Bread and Salt."

Dissipated Life

Letter to Mrs. Robert Wilmot

Moscow, January 24th 1804

We have been leading a very dissipated life. Balls without end; Dinner that ends after four hours uninterrupted cramming of every delicacy that Nature and Art can procure—Grapes freshly gather'd. Pine apples, ditto, asparagus ditto—I forgot to mention Oranges which are this moment clustering on thousands of Orange trees in different parts of Moscow. Roses too are blooming in the midst of the sharpest degrees of cold; tis only a proof of however that things are valued according to the difficulty of procuring them and not their intrinsic merit.

Last Wednesday at the Assembly my cambric Muslin Gown with the thin work'd border well known on the banks of the Lee excited a general sensation and its simplicity and beauty was echoed by people tottering under the weight of Diamonds and Pearls. I have latterly been dress'd in very pretty Crape dresses and yet that Evening my taste and judgement pass'd unnotic'd. But a very elegant necklace of Pearl, four rows, and a opal set in Diamonds, shone resplendent on my neck, both a gallantry of the Princess's who seems to know no pleasure (but that of) procuring me whatever she thinks useful and pretty or amusing.

I give you twenty guesses to find out what I am going to do. You cannot. Well, I'll tell you. To sit for four pictures. Only think, the Princess will have Miniature of this ridiculous face of mine in a snuff box. A second Miniature she intends to send to my Mother. The two others are to be painted in Oyles.

From Her Journal

Sat. 10th February

The Princess has begun to write her life. Her motive for so doing is friendship to me, as she says she will give me the manuscript & liberty to publish it. It will probably be a most interesting work.

Eveg.

The ring which she put on my finger is magnificent. Every moment marks her affection.

The Poor Have Abundance

To Her Mother

Moscow, 12th Febry 1804

Many a bad dinner I made from the mere fatigue of being offer'd fifty or sixty different Dishes by servants who come one aft the other and flourish ready arrv'd fish, flesh fowl, Vegetables, fruits, soups of fish etc. etc. before your eyes, wines, Liqueres etc. etc. in their turn. Serious the profusion is beyond anything I ever saw. Many a time I wish'd the wasted food of these fatiguing feasts transported to little Erin, which too often wants what is here despis'd. The very poorest people here have resources and likewise abun-dance which our poor know nothing of, and the peasantry of this country really and truly enjoy not only the necessarys but the comforts of life to an astonishing degree.

Lent

To Her Father

Moscow, 7th March 1804
The Carnival is to commence here in less than a week and to last an entire one during which time we are to dress as fine as Jack daws and jostle against each other in genteel crowds from morning to night. At 12 o'clock on the last day of the festivity, when a more tremendous assemblage and a merrier Ball than ever is to collect half the Town, the solemn sound of the great cathedral Bell is to announce the Midnight hour and the commence-ment of the great Fast. At the sound those who are engaged in eating their supper of substantial food drop their knives and forks. All are forsaken in a moment, and for six weeks not only meat is forbidden but also fish, butter, cream, even with tea and Coffee, and almost every description of nourishing Food except Bread. Every one repairs to the confessionals, old sins are wip'd off, new ones, no doubt are determined against, and every one is 'tis possible for their natures to be during the fast. Every Evening there is a Ball, and sometimes *five* in the evening.

Russian Culture Is Melancholy

To Her Mother

Troitska, 24th April 1804
Certainly gaiety is not the characteristic of this country. On the contrary, their Music, their Dance, their countenances, all have a tendency to the penseroso; and take them all in all they may be call'd extremely handsome. I speak only of the lower orders. As for the higher, I decidedly prefer our islanders. The same principle seems to pervade all—*Servility*. I don't know whether that is a just term. Certainly there is more of politeness in their manner, and consequently less.

Easter Sunday

To Her Father

Troitska, Sat 11th May

I must not forget Easter Sunday for fear another Sunday shoul'd arrive and swallow it up forever. I must however begin with Saturday Evening 10 o'clock when the service was performed here because it is the custom and because the Princess cou'd not attend Matins. I shall take you to church for the benefit of seeing the images. Otherwise the service is the same, and after it is over Easter Eggs are present painted and carv'd and decorated in a variety of ways. I have already mention'd the System of Presents in this Country. Every thing encourages it, and there are different periods when a present is indispensable. The Princess's Egg which she presented to me I am to wear at my Ear next winter. 'Tis a diamond and another to make into an Earring, one and not two being the fashion here. In presenting the offering one must say in Russ "Christ is risen." The person answers "Most certainly Christ is risen." The humblest Peasant has a right to kiss the hand of the greatest Personage in the Empire when he says those words, and even the Emperor cannot refuse his to any creature who asks it.

A Rich Peasant

From Her Journal

Sunday 2nd June

To-day we dined at the village of Gastechevo with a rich Peasant, the Patriarch of the Place whose family a few years ago amounted to 34 who sat down at the same table every day. 'Tis the custom for the Pesantry to live together as their riches consist in themselves, their own labour, etc. They farm the Ground which they have in abundance, and the more numerous a family is the richer they become. One or two learn a trade & go to town to practice it, making of white bread for examples which the Mujfics (Peasants) sell in small portions & large quantities in Moscow, first however obtaining a licence from the Magistrates & a passport from their Master.

The Princess Writes Her Memoirs

Sunday 25th August

The Princess is writing her History very diligently at present, but 'tis astonishing to see with how little trouble it goes forward. She settled long accounts with her steward, then writes half a page, then perhaps she settles a law suit between two peasants, then writes again. ... In short it would have been a million of sins if she had continued to withhold from the public the events of a life so interesting as hers or the sentiments of a heart so little known and so often misrepresented.

Pashinka

Monday 18th November

My little Pashinka is arriv'd this Eveg, and the dear princess assures me she is now my *own property* for ever. Poor little soul; she shall never find that word *property* abused by me. But I accept with pleasure a power which I *may use* to give *her* her liberty or take her to any part of the World where I go if she attaches herself to me.

Learning Russian

28th December Saturday

I am slaving at russ & seriously determin'd to learn it. My Master was with me last night & I am returning to the drudgery of a grammar of nouns, pronouns & verbs. Deuce take the tower of Babel!

The Beggars' Hospital

Wed. 23rd March

I have begg'd to be appointed by the Princess Governess to the Beggars' Hospital and am invested in my office.

Thursd 25th March

I visited the poor people yesterday. They are wretched specimens of old age & poverty rapacious yet I believe incapable of enjoying much comfort. The Princess had order'd an Arm Chair & some other conveniences to be made for them.

Monday 30th March

Still very cold, however I walk'd out & visited the Hospital. It appears to me that the few souls who take refuge there have so few wants that they are encapable of enjoying any thing beyond food, warmth & repose. I found more than half the number asleep on the top of the stove. A blind woman is the only one who attempts needlework or knitting etc., and the Cook of the Society is more than *half a fool.* These two are however the only useful members of the Community. There is an old Man & an old Woman who never fail to squabble when they are not sleeping and the remainder are Nonentity. Such is my young family (as the Princess calls them).

Dedication of the Princess's Memoirs

Saturday 8th November
The Princess Shew'd me this Eveg the dedication which she has just written for her History 'tis dedicated to me. I have been aware of her intention for some time past or else I'm sure I should have been quite overwhelmed by it. Dear respected Friend, may it be long before either dedication or book of Memories retrace to the public the scenes of that life which must be closed before they are publish'd.

Soldiers for the Crown

Wed. 12th November
Yesterday was the Melancholy day for giving up to Government the Recruits which the Princess was oblig'd to furnish. This year there are 4 men taken from every five hundred, last year there were only half the number. The Man who goes to Soldier is considered *Dead* to his family. In conformity to this idea little Paschinka has been in a flood of tears bewailing the loss of an Uncle who was amongst the number. This idea arises from the size of the Empire which (together with bad posts & little notion of reading or writing amongst that class) makes any news from a Soldier a thing scarcely possible. His friends are therefore inconsolable for a short time & then forget him entirely. 'Tis a cruel period thercfor for a good Master or Mistress who must notwithstanding supply the demands of the Crown.

Women and Their Fortunes

Sunday 17th August
The full & entire dominion which Russian Women have over their own fortunes gives them a very remarkable degree of liberty & a degree of independence of their Husbands unknown in England. Is this the reason that *Do-*

mestic happiness is more frequent here than there? I do not think it is. Morals are purer, and that's the real cause. Here a Woman's powers to dispose of her own wealth is a great check on her husband's inclination to forsake her or to tyrannize. If she dies without children her entire property returns to her family unless She makes it over by will to him or you or I as John or Molly which she has equal power to do. This is the reason that one so often hears two Ladies perhaps young pretty & coquettish talking to each other about the sale of Lands, purchase of *Souls* (slaves).

Superstitions of the Russians

Saturday 13th Febry
    This reminds me that I ought to note the excessive Superstition & Credulity of the Russians in general. 'Tis almost boundless. The lower orders believe *rigidly* in the power & influence of Fairys, Witches etc. etc. etc. The Higher Orders to a Man to a Woman play *la bonne avanture* on the Cards & are happy or miserable according to the good or bad Omens of the fortune telling Cards. Myriads of Nobles would not sleep in a room alone, nor remain five minutes in the dark for worlds.

Peace of Tilsit

Monday 18th July
    On Saturday the 16th the news of Peace between the Russians & French. The Peace is very unpopular. However M. de Tutelman has given orders that it should be celebrated magnificently and Sunday there was an illumination, ringing of all the bells till my ear ached, firing of Cannon, a Tedeum and Buonaparte named Emperour & King, instead of Buonaparte in all the Churches.
    I had a visit from Mrs. Halliday who tells me the English are universally blamed in this town by the Russians for not having sent troops to protect Dantzik & Konigsberg from falling into the power of the French. Perhaps they may have some reason. I never see a Newspaper & know *nothing* absolutely. However not content with blaming their delay on that affair they have had the absurdity to say that the war has been to *please the English* who have ended by betraying them. This is to throw from themselves all blame of having lost the late battle (fought near Friedland) and made an unpopular Peace at a Moment when even the Turks had cut off the head of their emperor, Changed their Government & that the politics of the Ottoman Porte would have favour'd Russia & Engl and according to all human calculation destroy'd Buonaparte's terrific power. The Russians shut their eyes to the

strides that little Hero (for he is one tho' I wish him 100 fathoms under ground & laid at peace) is making. Prussia is now in his power, what remains? A *Span* in comparison with what he had already overcome, & that in the country of the Poles who are in their hearts the bitterest enemys the Russians have.

Thursday 21st July
The entire conversation of the present moment is the Peace. The Emperour sent Prince Basil Dolgouruky to announce the event to the Town of Moscow thro' the Govr Genl & thro the Senate. ... The peace is, it seems, a very unpopular measure. ... So that the State of Warfare in which the World is, from Empires to Kingdoms, to Provinces, to Towns, to familys, to individuals, makes of Europe one great Convulsion from which no atom can escape.

In the late battle near Friedland 'tis well known that the Russians were often in a pityable State for want of provisions & ammunition. In the service there is a Corps apart for these two essential things. The latter is the Artillery branch. The Former is divided into two branches the *Provisiansky* depot is confided to officers of the highest distinction who have others under them from the Genl to the Ensign and a uniform apart. Their duty is to provide all sorts of Food, to have provisions made in the neighborhood of war so as to facilitate its transport in case of emergency. The other call'd *Commissariat* is just in the same style but providing Clothing for the troops in their affair. The Emperour since his return from the Army has publish'd a Ukase to deprive all Officers of their uniforms till the guilty are brought to punishment.

Russia and England

Thursday 19th November
Yesterday's post brought the news of a *suspension* of friendship between this Country & Engd! This is woeful news indeed, & heaven only knows what may be the consequence. A thousand fears Crowd upon my mind, & I feel completely in a Labyrinth. All intercourse by letter will be of course stopt, & in what state of misery will my family be to say nothing of what I shall suffer in ceasing to receive news from them. Great God in what a state is the World, & to what great event is this leading!

Rumors of the Plague

Saturday December 5th 1807
The news of last night's post was that there are strong suspicions of the plague's being at Moscow, that Police Officers go from House to House to see

that the familys fumigate with juniper berrys and other preservatives against this horrible Malady! ... I think that the news is powerfully exaggerated. The season is so unwholesome particularly for Russian constitutions, that it may naturally cause disease but after having escaped during the Summer with the return of so many diseased soldiers 'tis not improbable that the month of Decr should be the period for the Plague to shew itself.

Leaving the Princess

Saturday Morng, 23rd Septr

In a few hours we shall set out for Moscow, and in a few days my fate will be decided. I have felt so agitated ever since I recd Mr. H[aw]'s letter that I have done nothing but think & think of the best way of telling the news to my beloved Princess if the scheme can take place.

The grounds are now in high beauty, & were it not for the prospect of perhaps returning home I should be griev'd to the heart at quitting Troitskoe, its river, its fresh air, its quiet and my leisure which might all be enjoy'd for another Month. ... So adiēu Troitskoe I doat upon you during the fine Weather, and hate and fear you when the nights are long & the days are gloomy for many a reason which I will not confide to this journal.

Thursday 28th September

All arrang'd, & in three days I shall be gone. Great God how agitated I feel & how griev'd at parting with my beloved princess. No it is inexplicable the kind of feeling I have. ... I instantly wrote a letter to my beloved princess and she rec'd the news better than I expected and as a thing she had some suspicion of.

The dear princess is so affecting in her tears that there's no looking at her without feeling one's heart & soul wrung to the quick.

Tuesday 17th October

I am in continual hot water on the subject of my passport. ... Mr. Halliday has found out a ship at Cronstadt & we shall probably sail tomorrow Night. I was a Stouter Sailor years ago, but my heart is heavy as lead quitting the Country of my Russian Mother. Great God how low spirited I feel; indeed I am far from well.

CHAPTER FOUR

~

Catherine Wilmot

An Irish Lady in Russia

Catherine, the sister of Martha Wilmot, was the oldest of six daughters of Edward and Martha Wilmot. She was born in Drogheda, County Louth, Ireland, in 1773. Later, the family moved to County Cork and then Glanmire, where she grew up.

Before going to Russia in 1805 to bring her sister Martha home, she traveled with the Earl of Mountcashell and his wife through Europe, visiting Italy and France, where she met Napoleon and Talleyrand, then to Germany and Denmark. Wilmot's journey to Russia took two months; she arrived in August 1805 at Princess Catherine Dashkova's estate, Troitskoe.

For the next two years, Catherine lived with her sister and the princess at her estate. She kept a journal and wrote letters home describing their social life, Russian customs, the serfs, her presentation to the Empress Elizabeth, the beautiful city of St. Petersburgh, the character of the princess, women's rights over their property, military power, intermarriage of the nobility, and the rising merchant class. She was of the opinion that Russia was a despotism. Fortunately, she took a copy of the princess's memoirs with her when she left in 1807, as the original was later burned by Martha, who feared its confiscation by the authorities when she departed a year later.

Catherine returned to Ireland without her sister, who could not bear to leave the princess yet. Catherine never married, and, with her health declining, she left Ireland to move to a warmer climate. She lived in Moulins, France, then moved to Paris, where she died on March 28, 1824.

Empress Elizabeth
Public Domain

Catherine's letters are included in *The Russian Journals of Martha and Catherine Wilmot*, published in 1934. *The Grand Tours of Katherine Wilmot, France, 1801-1803 and Russia, 1805-1807* was published in 1992. Her papers are in the Royal Irish Academy.

The following selections are from Catherine's portions of *The Russian Journals of Martha and Catherine Wilmot*.

⌒

The Russian Journals of Martha and Catherine Wilmot

Impression of St. Petersburgh

St. Petersburgh, at Mr Raikes's

Wednesday (7th August)

We then drove on to Petersburgh which was a little journey of 30 versts, & I protest so lovely a drive I never beheld; it is in the Style of that from

Paris to Versailles. Palaces of the most astonishing beauty rising up at either side clothed in Forests & sweetly cultivated in pleasure grounds & Lawns to the front. Two of 3 are Imperial residences, and the road which is broad & superexcellent full of all descriptions of Equipages, mostly driving 4 Horses abreast & 2 to the end of the Shafts. ... The moon rose as yellow as gold over the black forests & conducted us on to Petersburgh where we arriv'd at near 11 o'clock. I was in perfect extacy with all I had seen!

I am to delay therefore for a fortnight at Petersburgh & then proceed to Moscow. Trusty servants & travelling Carriages are to be provided for me. In short, my way is strewed with flowers, for what with the affection of the Pss & her influence everything is *smack smooth* & I only have to repel politeness. ... Already a Fox fur pelisse of the rarest kind is provided for my bones & sundry pieces of satin together with a sarsenett dress for my Squire! ... I expect this Year to be a Fairy tale.

Presented to the Empress Elizabeth

St. Petersburgh, Chez Mme De Poliansky

August 26th

After having waited three quarters of an hour, at length an opposite door open'd, & thence came the Empress Elizabeth follow'd by the *fat* Countess Protassoff at her heels. The Empress is the loveliest creature I almost ever saw & in both face & figure excessively like the print of *Cordelia*, King Lear's daughter. At her entry the Ladys rose & the Gentlemen retired. She was dress'd in white embroidery & immense pearls in her beautiful brown hair. She has the humility, modesty and sweetness of an Engel in her demeanour, & when we were presented & would fain have kiss'd her hand she struggled from the Ceremony & in her turn stooped down & kiss'd our cheeks! She spoke French to all, excepting one Russian lady to whom she spoke Rus. Her voice is sweet & low. ... Appropriate *trifles* were all of course she utter'd. She ask'd me how I liked Petersburgh & hoped it had given me a good impression. I said, *it had* (was not that witty). She said she had heard of my Sister at Moscow, & that she understood I intended to take a long Journey for the gratification of seeing her. I said, *yes!* And that I only delay'd at Petersb. for the honor of being presented to her Imperial Majesty.

The Lower Orders

Sunday 27ᵗʰ August
  The lower orders of people astonish me by their grotesque appearance &
the great unmerciful *Patriarchal Beards* that the Men wear! T'is impossible
to conceive that they were *not* born before the Flood, or that their names
are *not* Jacob, Benjeman & Manassus. At the rising & setting of the Sun &
on other occasions they begin to cross themselves, but so *obstreperously* that
the operations do not finish under qrtr of an hour. They bow their heads
down almost to the ground & then not only *recover their balance* but throw
themselves proportionately back again, crossing themselves at arms length.

Daily Routine at Princess Daschkaw's Estate

Letter to Anna Chetwood

Sept 24th, Troitskoe
  We assemble at 9 in the Morn to drink our Coffee attended by *Filles de
Chambres*, & then what with lounging or talking of music or walking most
frequently a couple of hours are spent Lord knows how! Then instead of pick-
ing up lost time from that till 5 o'clock, the thunder of the dinner Bell sounds
at ½ past one or 2 o'clock at farthest, & we assemble to solemnize our long
repast where each several dish of 2 courses & a dessert are not only carved
on another Table & handed to you but you are expected to eat of them all
without mercy. This is one of the Princess's particularities. Everything is better dress'd & done than anywhere else & she prides herself on the produce
of her Farm, Dairy, Gardens, Hot Houses, Pineries, etc.etc. I have acquired
a passion for the drink of the country call'd *Quass* which is intolerable to
everywhere but here but which I like better than Champaigne. Honey with
fresh cumbers is a favorite dish, preserved Dates, Apple bread, young pig &
Cold Cream, Egg Patties eat with Soup, another Soup made of Fish & every
sort of Sallad & eat Cold. In fact there is no end to the Whimsical varieties
that a Russian Kitchen furnishes peculiar to itself together with imitations
from every other in the World.

Russians Are Francophiles

Letter to Anna

Setpr 24th, Troitskoe

Russia is yet barbarous enough to be distinguish'd for her Hospitablity. She has many other Nationalities no doubt, but my experience has not been able to distinguish any excepting amongst the lower orders of People, for with respect to the higher I am sorry to say they imitate the French in everything! And tho' the French manners are appropriate to themselves I can't endure the *singerie of Bruin* when he frolicks with the Monkey on his back! Instead of the dignified Salutation of former times you are kiss'd on both your cheeks with the appearance of transport & are told mechanically how enchanted they are to make your acquaintance etc.etc.etc. The dress too is a bad imitation of the French & they have universally adopted their Language! One is more surprised at finding this the case at Moscow than at Petersburgh, for in fact Petersburgh is a medley of foreigners; but Fashion does the same in one place that commercial necessity occasions in the other, & in the midst of this adoption of manners, customs & language there is something childishly Silly in their reprobating Buonaparte when they can't eat their dinners without a French Cook to dress it, when they can't educate their Children without unprincipled adventurers from Paris to act as Tutors and Governesses, when every House of some consequence (that I have seen at least) has an outcast Frenchman to instruct the Heir apparent—in a word, when every association of fashion luxury, elegance, & fascination is drawn from France; & in this obliteration of themselves a dying squeak against Buonaparte redeems them in their own Eyes from their Political Suicide! Such arrant folly! What I have seen therefore has been a superstructure from France—the Monkey rampant on the Bear's back!

Gifts of Princess Daschkaw to Martha Wilmot

Since I am on the subject of presents I must mention a gorgeous gold snuff Box with the Empress's Picture emboss'd which Matty was obliged to accept, a collection of gems in the line of Natural History, a collection of Coins, a collection of Medals, and little *odd come dods* from Herculaneum, a two gold lion headed clasps taken from the golden hoards of Tartars (conquer'd many years ago by the Russians and exterminated by John the Terrible), also a full suit of Russian Costumes worn at Court by Princess Daschkaw, Agate snuff Box, blood stone ditto, a comb, broach, band for the head, necklace and three rings of Turquoise. This set of ornaments are sentimentally arranged in pearls and topas's in a wreath so as to resemble the little flowers call'd *Forget me not*. She has also given her a lovely watch (tho' she had one of her own) gold Venetian chains and myriads of Seals, a gold comb, a gold and pearl crescent, eighteen different rings, exquisite cornelian earrings like bunches of red currants, pearl necklace and bracelets, beautiful ones, coral ones, amber ones, etc.etc. a small Pianoforte, a beautiful guitar, quantities of music, silver cups, boxes without end etc.etc. Then as to cloaths I literally believe she has satin dresses of every colour under the sun, mock lace dresses, a real black lace veil, which covers her from head to foot, velvet dresses, crape ones, muffs, pelisses etc.etc. and a library of more than 150 valuable books, maps, etc.etc.

The Princess's Estate Troitska

Oct 1st

I believe I never mentioned Troitska. It is a fine place, the Princess has made it herself, and situated in the midst of 16 Villages belonging to her. Three Thousand Peasants (my subjects, as she calls them) live most happily under her power; and of all the blessed hearted beings that ever existed on that subject she is the most blessed (excepting Your Mother). There are two hundred servants, taking in all denominations inside and outside, in this establishment, more than a hundred horses, two hundred stock of cows, and everything else in proportion. The Church establishment belongs to her, and is built at the back of the House. A lovely wood belonging to the estate 9 miles long and 4 broad is within a few yards of the place inhabited by Wolves, and in it the Princess and I lost our way yesterday even for an hour and half. A beautiful river winds all through the ground and serpentines amidst the entire estate. However Troitska is dead flat almost, and to the cultivation alone its beauty is attributable. An immense quantity of ground is laid out under shrubberies and all sorts of pleasure grounds completely in the English stile. The House is enormous with wings on either side which are only connected by balconies raised on iron railings up to the 2nd story.

In the midst of this immense Establishment and in the center of riches and honours I wish you were to see the Princess go out to take a walk, or rather to look over her subjects! An old brown great coat and a silk handkerchief about her neck worn to rags is her dress, & well may it be worn to rags for she has worn it 18 years and will continue to do so as long as she lives because it belong'd to Mrs. Hamilton. Her originality, her appearance, her manner of speaking, her doing every description of thing (for she helps the masons to build walls, she assists with her own hands in making the roads, She feeds the cows, she composes music, she sings, plays, she writes for the press, she shells her corn, she talks outloud in church, and corrects the Priest if he is not devout, she talks out loud in her little Theatre and puts in the Performers when they are out in their parts, she is a Doctor, an Apothecary, a Surgeon, a Farrier, a Carpenter, A Magistrate, a Lawyer; in short she hourly practices every species of incongruity, corresponds with her brother, who holds the first post in the Empire, on his trade, with Authors, with Philosophers, with Jews, with Poets, with her Son, with all her Relations and yet appears as if she had her time a burthen on her hands) altogether gives me eternally the idea of her being a Fairy.

The Character of Princess Daschkaw

Letter to her sister Alicia

Monday, December 8th

I have since I came here often thought what a task it would be to attempt to draw the Character of the Princess Daschkaw! I for my part think it would be absolutely impossible. Such are her peculiarities & inextricable varietys that the result would only appear like a Wisp of Human Contradictions. For my part I think she would be most in her element at the *Helm of State*, or Generalissimo of the Army, or Farmer General of the Empire. In fact she was born for business on a large scale which is not irreconcilable with the Life of a Woman who at 18 headed a Revolution & who for 12 years afterward govern'd an Academy of Arts and Sciences.

The State of Russia

Letter to Anna Chetwood

23rd March

As I conjured you up to the top of Ivan Veleka, so let me spirit you down again amongst us at Troitskoe to repose a little with us in this Feudal State, for if you will have my opinion of the matter Russia is but in the 12th Century. Yes! I know all about the luxury of Moscow & the civilization of Petersburgh, but have you ever seen a clumsy romping ignorant Girl of 12 years old with a fine Parisian Cap upon her head? So seems to my eye this Imperial Realm. The cloister'd ignorance not only the 12th but of the 11th Century is the groundwork of this colossal Region and 5 or 6 Centurys will no doubt produce the same effects here they have in other parts of Europe; but Time must disengage the ligaments which bind the plant before it strengthens & expands into a self supported standard. More sudden means would bend it to the Earth & so Russian political liberty & civilization.

Agreeable Things

Let us talk rather of what is agreeable; & do you know, in spight of what I say there exists a thousand *agremens*, even in the way of amusements which recompence one for the hollowness of societys. For example, the dryness of the Climate, the elasticity of the Air, the extraordinary diversion of the Ice Mountains, the Traineau Courses, the Stoves, the Baths, the warmth of cloathing, & the habit of breakfasting in one's own room. All these things I delight in tho' I do not often practice the exposure to Air as absolutely one is looked upon as Mad for not subscribing to the National Confinement.

Moscow in the Summer

Letter to the Rev. John Chetwood

October 14th, Troitskoe

At Moscow however I must pause a moment where in reality we remained 8 days to familiarize ourselves to its Novelties during the Summer Season, for of all Towns I believe it least resembles itself in Winter when the sparkling Frost shone on from the eternal bright Stars of the Northern Constellation makes one fancy the World cut in Diamonds. Literally it appear'd so to us as we used to drive in the Snow by the Whitest Moonlight from our Winter Orgies. Not so in the Yellow Rays of perpetual Sunshine which from a thousand gilded domes & balls & spires reflected an eternal dazzle thro' the livelong day.

Its Boulevards & public walks of a Summer's Evening are enchanting, & you may form some idea how much it deserves the title of *Rus in Urbe* when I tell you amongst various other Spacious Gardens attach'd to the residences of private individuals no less than 14 English Acres are laid out in the Vaux Hall stile to the House of the Grand Chancellor Count Ostrowman in the very centre of the Town. The Flower Markets too may for the luxuriance of every blossoming plant very well vie with Covent Garden; and as to fruits, there is display beyond every thing I have seen elsewhere of the Kind which is not surprising when one recollects that Hot Houses are a necessary of life here. ...

The Archbishop of Moscow

The present Archbishop Plato, who is esteem'd one of the most Singular men in Russia, is the superior of this Establishment. He is a mixture of everything opposite to the Religion & Constitution of his Country, & yet keeps up to all the outward forms so as to awe the populace like a demi-god. He is thought of so much consequence from his influence and cleverness that he is held in dread at Court & universally esteem'd, an Iron Wheel in the political Machine of State.

Women's Rights

Letter to her sister Harriet Troitskoe

21st October 1806

You must know that every Woman has the right over her own Fortune totally independent of her Husband, & he is as independent of his Wife. Marriage therefore is no union of interests whatsoever, & the Wife if she has a large Estate and happens to marry a poor Man is still consider'd rich while the Husband may go to Jail without one farthing of her possessions being responsible for him!

Nobles and Merchants

And this brings me to one general observation which is that the Landed property of this Imperial Realm is from unconscientious extravagance of the Nobles passing like Wild-fire to the Merchants who are in Russia neither more nor less than Pedlars & Shopkeepers; and, exactly as they did in France before the Revolution, the Princes of the Country are breaking down all ideal Barriers & marrying the daughters of the Merchants as fast as they can!

Peace between Russia and France

Letter to Anna Chetwood

Petersburgh, July 15th

Yesterday the Peace between the Emperors & Bonaparte was announced. This House is just opposite the Fortress from whence the Cannon roar'd all day & illuminations blazed all night through the Town. Heaven knows whether these are to be taken as demonstrations of real joy. If they are, they are only a proof that amongst the Miracles of the Day *old Bruin* is transform'd into an Ass! But I shall be chain'd in a Kibitka & sent to Siberia if I don't hold my tongue. ... Tis the general observation here that the Illumination last Night for the Peace was demonstrative of the public *sensation*, & if so no great approbation can be augur'd for it was as shabby as possible, and as we drove through the streets it gave me the idea of *Death* in Milton when he "grin'd horribly a ghastly smile"; but Russia is a mere blubber cheek'd boy who to get a Holyday will risk a thrashing. This Peace I look upon as no better, & in my opinion Buonaparte has the rod in his own hands. Everyone rails against the English for being such dilatory Allies. The Ignoramuses (who are 99 to one) snarl against England, the other attribute it to the opposition principles which were at the Helm, but all the Bears to a Cub grumble against us.

CHAPTER FIVE

~

Mary Holderness

A Farmer's Wife in the Crimea

Little is known of Mary Holderness's early life in England. Her husband was involved in a farming venture in the Crimea, whereby he would purchase or sublet land on an estate for development. The owner of the estate, the Reverend Arthur Young, sought farmers to answer the call, and the Holderness family sailed from Gravesend in September 1815 and arrived in Riga in early November. From there, they journeyed by coach to Kiev and southward to the Crimea, which they reached in February 1816. The family lived in Karagoss (now Pervomaiske) until March 1820, when Mary, presumably without her husband, left Karagross, stopping in Nikolayeff and Odessa before returning to England.

Mary kept copious notes about her travels, the post stations, the towns they passed through, a visit to Kiev, and, when settled in the Crimea, the peoples who inhabited the region: Great Russians, Little Russians, Greeks, Germans, Bulgarians, Armenians, and Nogay Tatars and their customs, religion, dress, food, and occupations. Not neglecting the women of the region, she highlighted their status and role in society. Once home, she first published *Notes relating to the Crim Tartars* in 1821, followed by a more extensive work, *New Russia: Journey from Riga to the Crimea, by way of Kiev: With some account of the Colonization and the Manners and Customs of the Colonists of New Russia. To which are added notes relating to the Crim Tartars*. The latter was published in 1823. Her goal in writing these books was to give readers an accurate description of the Crimea and its people, from one who lived among them.

Once she returned home, her literary work provided some income; however, she supplemented it by taking in boarders at her home in Pentonville, England. Unfortunately, after this, Mary Holderness drops out of the historical record.

The following selections are from *New Russia.*

∽

New Russia: A Journey

Kiev

We entered Kiev very late in the evening, but had the comfort of getting into very good quarters. Its situation is remarkably fine; one part of the town is on a bold and rocky eminence; in going to it, we passed up a hill of more than a mile in length, with rocks towering above, and precipices below us. The hill between the upper and lower town commands a most extensive and beautiful prospect, taking in the old town, or city of Kiev that is in the valley, which is called the Podole, the Castle of Pestcherskey, a stately monastery, churches,

Steppe
Library of Congress

barracks, and the river, which is broad, and must in summer be a magnificent addition to this estate.

It is the best town we have seen, and of far greater extent than any except Riga. The shops are very superior, and many things are to be bought cheaper here than many other parts of the country which we previously passed.

The Stepp

On leaving Balta we entered upon a country the very reverse of what we had passed; a rich black soil said to be most luxuriantly fertile. This, which is called Stepp, was a few years ago nearly the whole of it uninhabited; for the sake of increasing population, and its consequent advantageous results, the Emperor has to some persons made grants of land on this Stepp; to others he has sold land at a low rate, and it is now, in many parts, getting thickly peopled.

Odessa

The town of Odessa is a very flourishing seaport, and a most astonishing place, if it be remembered that about twenty years ago a few fishing huts had comprised the whole of its inhabitants, and that in 1812 a third of its population was destroyed by the plague. It was founded in 1796, and to the Duke de Richelieu, Odessa owes whatever of prosperity it now enjoys, or whatever pre-eminence as a city it may hereafter attain. It is situated on a rock, and is very extensive, the style in which it is built making it cover a large quantity of ground: the streets run in parallel lines.

The bazars, or markets, occupy two large squares at the eastern and western extremity of the town. The merchants have their warehouses attached to their houses, which are many of them only one story high, others one floor above the ground. As no part of the town is paved, it is in wet weather the dirtiest place I ever saw, except Balta; and in summer the dust was as intolerable as the dirt in winter. Here is a pretty theatre, but the different manner of lighting it makes it much less gay and pleasing than ours; the stage only is well illuminated, and the rest of the theatre almost dark. Italian operas, and Russian and French plays, are got up in pretty good style.

But that which is most worthy of remark at Odessa is a very fine institution for the education of the young nobility, called the Lyceum. All the languages are taught here by different professors, and the various accomplishments required. It is considered a military establishment and the students intended for the service, either in the navy or the army, have the rank of cadet given them on their entrance. A part of the institution is adapted for girls.

The gardens of Odessa, though requiring much care in their infancy, yet are afterwards very productive; the dryness of the soil and climate makes a long preparation requisite for the planting of trees; but have once taken root, they soon begin to bear, and yield abundantly.

Sympheropol to Karagoss

From Sympheropol we soon journeyed on to Karasubazar. This is the first Tatar town, and is much more singular than pleasing; narrow and irregular streets, presenting a most extraordinary number of shops, occupied by Tatars, Jews, Armenians, Russians, and Greeks. For the sale of fruit alone, there are said to be one hundred shops; there are about the same number for the sale of Tatar shoes. Every article of sale brought into the Crimea is to be had cheaper here than elsewhere. We staid a day and two nights, and made purchases of provisions, etc., to carry with us to Karagoss, and reached that place in the afternoon of the third of February, most thankful to have completed our undertaking, and arrived at our long-wished-for destination.

The Taurida (Greek for the Crimea)

The whole of the government of the Taurida, with the exception of the Crimea, is one united mass of colonization. Of course, in point of numbers, the Russians rank first, and occupy by far the greatest part of this vast space, which, previously to its conquest from the Tartars, was a flat and fertile waste of interminable extent of pasture land, over which the Nomadic nation of Nogay Tatars wandered with their flocks and herds. It is now colonized by 1st, Little Russians; 2nd, Great Russians; 3rd, Nogay Tatars; 4th, Greeks; 5th, Germans; 6th, Armenians; and 7th, Bulgarians. The two latter are comparatively few in number to the others.

The boundary line of colonization might be extended to the Danube, including Bessarabia and Moldavia, which assuredly form a most material part of this immense colony, which is twice as large as Great Britain, and its soil certainly thrice as fertile as that of England in general. ... But in this country we are describing, Nature reigns in her greatest luxuriance of vegetation, and varies little in the fertility of the soil. From the Don to the Danube, from Poland to the Black Sea, the soil is, with few exceptions, a dark putrid loam of great depth. The great colony likewise possesses the advantage of being traversed in almost every direction by some of the largest rivers in Europe—the Danube, the Dneister, the Bog, the Dnieper, the Don, and the Kuban.

Emperor Alexander Visits the Crimea

In an empire so extensive as that of Russia, whatever be the efforts, whatever the wishes of him who governs, it is scarcely to be expected their influence, so powerfully felt at the centre, can extend with equal force to those distant provinces, which his smile seldom visits, his presence rarely cheers. Yet here, though depravity marks so many individuals, and they mar the endeavours which the Emperor is continually making for the universal benefit of his subjects, even here, he is beloved and respected, reverenced and obeyed.

His visit to the Crimea was a subject of joyful expectation before it took place; and the mild and conciliating manners of this most powerful monarch won the hearts of the humblest of his subjects: few there are who do not boast of having seen the Emperor Alexander, and not a few who had the honour to converse with him. Divested of the parade of state, he travelled without any military escort, and won, or secured the confidence of his people, by that he evinced in them.

The Tatars of the Crimea

The male population of the Tatars inhabiting the Crimea amounts of one hundred and eighty-six thousand souls; of these about six hundred only are Murzas (noblemen), the number of noble families being so materially reduced, that they are not supposed to exceed sixty.

Notwithstanding the Tatars of the different villages in the Crimea plough, in fact, wherever they please, and as much as they like, upon payment of the aforesaid tithe, and are liable to very few our-going (labour excepted), yet so great is their natural aversion to industry, that multitudes of them, rather than plough and sow, will buy corn to feed their families; others grow enough only for a part of the year, and exchange the rest for wool, sheep, etc.

In the simple life of the Tatars, much may be traced of similarity with those recorded in the earliest ages of Scripture history. Their riches consist now, as was usual then, in flocks and herds, and in the number of their families. Exchange is still the medium of purchase, and money is but seldom required or produced in bargains made between one Tatar and another. ...

The Tatars of the Crimea may be divided into three classes: the Murzas, or noblemen; the Mullas, or priests; and the peasantry; the latter paying great deference to both the former. The Mulla is considered the head of every parish, and nothing of consequence to the community is undertaken without his consent.

Tatar Women

A Tatar wife is most completely the slave of her husband, and that the men consider her such, I had from the mouth of one of the most respectable of them. Thus she is only desirable as she serves to gratify his passions, or to connect him with some Tatar of better family or greater riches than himself. Among the peasantry, however, who are less bound by rigid forms, or less observant than their superiors, I have often seen sincere affection displayed.

At the birth of a child, it is universally the custom for the other females of the village to visit the lying-in woman, each bringing some present, either of food, clothes, or money. However trifling their gifts may be, they are accepted, while the not giving would be considered a disgrace. How far this custom extends among the rich Tatars, I cannot say, but among the poor it is very general.

The Tatar women suckle their children from two to three years, and think us barbarous for weaning ours so early. For the first half year they are seldom carried in the arms, but are commonly laid on their backs in a kind of cradle, in which they are bound so as not to roll out. To the top of this, immediately over heads, are attached coloured beads, bits of glass, or money, in order to attract their notice. ... A Tatar child is swathed from head to foot with no other clothes than a few rags for the first two or three months, but after that it is habited in the same stiff and formal manner as the mother; and its dress, the ugliness of its features, and, more than all, the scorbutic humours which almost invariably cover it from a very short time after its birth, makes it, of all the infants I ever saw, the most disgusting and uninteresting.

A Tatar woman can rarely read, and the whole of the instruction thought requisite for girls is that of embroidery, which is the chief and almost only occupation of those above the rank of peasantry. Spinning and weaving, which they also sometimes perform, are more generally the work of their servants. This employment, and some small share in the domestic concerns (the more important of which devolve on the elders of the family), fill up the dull and monotonous round of a Tatar life.

In the villages of the plain, the priest is the parish schoolmaster; and it sometimes happens that his wife can also read. In this case, while the husband superintends the boys, she teaches the girls of the village, or rather the very small number of them who are desirous of learning.

The dancing of the women is very ridiculous; two only dance at a time, extending the hands, turning the head towards one shoulder, and bending the eyes continually on the ground with affected bashfulness. The step is somewhat like the slow movements of the English hornpipe, and the dance finishes at the option of the performers. ... The men are allowed to dance in the court-yard of the women's apartments, who look at them from their latticed gallery.

Swinging is a favourite amusement with them, and the love of it is by no means confined to children. The ladies seemed surprised when I told them that I had for some time left off this diversion, though I liked it much when a child. I cannot wonder, however, that they continue to be fond of the pastimes of early life, since they continue always to be children in understanding; and there is something reasonable in their love of this exercise, since it is the only one which they are permitted to take, and that only at the seasons of their two great holidays.

The women's apartments of the richer Tatars are situated within an inclosure, through the gates of which none but servants of the family, and female visitors, are admitted. Of the former, only one or two have the privilege of entering the rooms themselves. The master has another house, distinct from this building in which he receives his guests.

It is well known that the Mahometan law admits of a plurality of wives. Four are allowed; but few Tatars are found to have more than one. As long as they continue to live in unity with the first, it very seldom happens that they take a second; for the women, though brought up in such perfect subservience and submission have still the same passions and feelings as ourselves, and can as ill brook to share with another the affections of their husbands. Whether or not the existence of the law, and the knowledge of the right which it confers may stimulate them to a more attentive observance of their duties, and more constant endeavours to maintain undivided the regard of their lords, I will not venture to say, but I think it by no means an improbable effect; certain it is, that though a Tatar husband is supreme and absolute, and though he considers his wife most perfectly his slave, still is he affectionate and kind to her, and instances of unhappy marriages are few.

Infidelity

The highest points of excellence in the Tatar character are their sobriety and chastity, for both of which they are universally remarkable and praiseworthy. The Tatar law, I have been told, in cases of infidelity, sentences the offender to be placed in a grave dug for the purpose when, the whole neighbourhood being assembled from many versts round, each person present flings a stone, and the delinquent is thus sacrificed to the rage of offended feelings.

The Crim Tatars, however, now living under the Russian government, and subject to Russian laws, are no longer able to exercise their own customs, and this, among the rest, has fallen into disuse.

Superstitions

It is a very common custom in the Crimea, with the Tatars as well as the Bulgarian settlers, to stick up a horse's skull near their houses in order to preserve them from witchcraft. It appears, I am told, from ancient authority, that a somewhat similar superstition prevailed among the earliest known inhabitants of this country (the Taurians), who however made use of a human skull for this purpose.

A Tatar, who was hired to go from Karagoss to Odessa, refused to set out on a Tuesday, considering it an unlucky day: "for," said he, "I once began a journey on that day, and lost two horses by it, so that I would not again run the risk for one thousand rubles."

Beggars

Mendicants are very rare among the Tatars; their mode of life is so simple, and the few wants they have beyond what their own labour gives them are supplied at so little cost that the son finds his parents, when advanced in life, no burden to him; and his children are an addition of wealth to his store. In the few cases which occur of the old being reduced to beg, I am told that they never enter a Tatar cottage to ask charity and meet with a denial; money, clothes, bread, or some sort of food is given to them, and a Tatar would be ashamed who would refuse to listen to this call upon his humanity.

Tatar Agriculture

The habits and modes of agriculture of the Tatars are rude and simple. They have not industry sufficient to induce them to labour hard for the acquirement of wealth, and even wealth itself, from the jealousy which it excites among them, can scarcely be considered a desirable possession. The enjoyment of ease and indolence, on any terms, is the summit of their happiness, and he who can command these blessings has no further motive or stimulant to exertion.

Horses

The horse is the constant companion of the Crim Tatar, who will never walk two hundred yards from his own door if he has a horse to ride on. The accumulation of live stock seems to be the universal system of those among them who can afford it; and accordingly the *taboons*, or studs, possessed by some of the Murzas are considerable. That belonging to Yie Yie Murzal in our immediate neighborhood consists of no less than five hundred mares.

They appear to have no idea of deriving any fixed revenue from breeding these animals, nor indeed any advantage, that I could understand, from keeping so many.

On Leaving the Crimea

From what has been premised, it will readily be seen, that the routine of a country life amidst such a primitive race as the Tatars, though it was occasionally enlivened by visits to the towns, or neighboring proprietors, or made interesting by the means of serving our poorer neighbours, yet could have been little of anecdote, while it afforded much of observation and abundance of employment.

The moral character of the peasantry of the Crimea is exceedingly de praved and vicious; and, excepting the Tatars, I never found it possible, by any good offices or kindness to excite any attachment in them that the sight of a glass of brandy would not instantly surmount; and amongst the servants we have had, from gross immorality and inveterate love of drunkenness, were almost invariably the leading traits.

The different modes by which they manifested their regret at the time of my leaving Karagoss were thus evinced: my Tatar neighbours were with me throughout the day previous to my departure, either sitting silent in my room, or assisting in the arrangement of the journey; but on the day of my departure few could see me; and when the children went to bid good bye to the women; they found them shut up, and really grieving. My two servants, one a Pole, the other a German, busily and attentively assisted me throughout the preceding day; but when their duty was done, they took care to drown their sorrow in large libations of wine and brandy which they had previously promised me they would not do. On the morning of my departure, they felt still more strongly the necessity of repeating that, which the preceding night had produced exhilaration; and I fear, if not the ostensible, I was at least the nominal cause of a repetition of the same offence the following evening; and well was it if the evil stopped here.

CHAPTER SIX

~

Lady Elizabeth Eastlake

An Art Critic in Russia

Lady Elizabeth Eastlake was an art historian and critic. Born Elizabeth Rigby in Norwich, England, in 1809, her parents were intellectuals, and she was educated at home by private tutors. Fond of drawing, she studied art during her youth, and after a move to Germany to convalesce from an illness, she wrote articles on writers and artists. After a visit to Revel, Estonia, in 1838, where her married sister lived, and to St. Petersburg, she published a two-volume work entitled *Letters from the Shores of the Baltic* in 1841. She later returned to Revel several times.

In 1842, her mother, now a widow, moved to Edinburgh, Scotland, where Elizabeth frequented social circles among the literati, meeting prominent artists and photographers. In 1849, at age forty, Elizabeth married Sir Charles Locke Eastlake, Director of the National Gallery in London and president of the Photographic Society. Their social life in London included the leading lights of the day. The couple toured Europe seeking acquisitions for the National Gallery.

German and Italian art were Elizabeth's academic interests, and she wrote books and articles on those topics. She was an esteemed art critic by her contemporaries. The arrival of photography and its popularity with the masses led her to write an article on the subject.

Lady Eastlake died in 1893 and is buried in Kensal Cemetery, Kensington, Greater London. Two years later, in 1895, her *Letters and Correspondence* were edited by her nephew Charles Eastlake Smith and published as *Journals and Correspondence of Lady Eastlake* in London. Lady Elizabeth found much to dislike in Russia: society, education, the language and literature,

Elizabeth Eastlake
Library of Congress

church architecture, the pavement, the dreariness of St. Petersburg, customs (especially that of kissing), ranks, the civil service, and the power of the tsar in whom the country's fate was entrusted. Despite her indictments, she had genuine interest in the country's destiny and future.

The following selections are from Volumes I and II of *Letters from the Shores of the Baltic*.

⌢

Letters from the Baltic, Volume I

Arrival in St. Petersburg

My letters of introduction soon procured their bearer much kind attention; and first and foremost among those who exercised these courtesies towards a stranger was Baron S., aide-de-camp to the Emperor, and Fort-major of Petersburg—a pale young man, seemingly sinking beneath the weight of a gorgeous uniform, who introduced himself with the utmost simplicity and kindness, and put at my immediate disposal his house, his horses, and everything he could command. These were soothing sounds after the irritation of the Douane. As an earnest of his intentions he further begged to leave at my disposal for the present, and for as long a time as I should think fit to retain—a soldier. As he evidently attached no more importance to this proposition, and perhaps less, than if he had offered me an extra pair of walking shoes, all scruple on my part would have been misplaced; nevertheless, it was with undisguised amusement that I saw one of these military machines mount immovable guard at my door. He was a brow-beat, rusty-moustached, middle-sized man, with hard lines of toil on his sunburnt face. ... I found my poor sentinel a willing, swift, and most useful messenger in this city of scanty population and enormous distances. ... it may be added he also found me a kind mistress, for the tyrannical, inhuman mode in which inferiors are here addressed is the first trait in the upper classes which cannot fail to disgust the English traveler. Our communication was restricted nevertheless to a smile on my side, as my orders were interpreted to him, and to "Sluschouss" ("I hear") upon his receiving the same.

Russian Churches

Having thus taken the aggregate of a Russian church interior, for the rest are mere repetitions of the same barbaric splendor, unsanctified by true art, we proceed to the Academy of Arts on the Wassili-Ostrof. This is one of those outwardly splendid piles, with ten times more space than in England would be allowed for the same object, ten times more out of repair, and ten thousand times dirtier. At the ceremony of Russian baptism the sign of the cross is made on the lips to say nothing bad, on the eyes to see nothing bad, on the ears to hear nothing bad—and, it must be supposed, on the nose to smell nothing bad—for the Russians do not seem inconvenienced by the trials to which this organ is exposed on entering their dwellings.

Buildings in St. Petersburg

I hardly passed a building that did not in some way lay claim to my admiration. So much, and most justly so, in praise of the masonry of St. Petersburg, that any further comment on my part is superfluous. On the other hand, considering how our English feelings have been wounded in the reflection that most of the beautiful edifices of the olden time which adorn our capital, are placed where they neither can be approached or appreciated, while those of the modern are allowed space and air, as if only to expose their defects, I consider that a little conscientious detraction of these northern upstarts may be more acceptable. The buildings, it is true, are with rare exception magnificent or graceful, and generally consistent in style; but as they are built so they are left; and as neither a Russian sun nor a Russian frost can be trusted for gentle treatment, the stucco falls off, the paint blisters up, the wood-work decays, and none of these items being renewed, the edifice soon exhibits a want of finish which an English eye must lose some of its home recollections to overlook. But, habituated to the sight, no Russian eye is offended by this mixture of shabbiness and grandeur. Added to this their houses are wretchedly *glazed* and wretchedly *shod*. Except an occasional square of plate glass, every where beautiful, not a pane is seen through which a beauty would care to be criticized; nor, beyond the Nevski, which is laid with a level mosaic pavement of wood, is there a foot of pavement in St Petersburg which would allow you to converse in an open carriage with this same beauty in comfort. Around the winter palace it is execrable—such holes as an infant Zarovitch might be lost in.

Petersburg Not a Gay Capital

No one can assert, however, that this is a gay capital; its population is one of wheels more than men, without whose restless whirl the streets would be as lifeless as London at four o'clock in the morning. Here are no busy, noisy pedestrians, that mainspring of gaiety in other cities; and of the few who do tred her huge squares and drawn-out streets not above one woman is seen to four men. It is true the court and beau monde were still at their summer haunts, but these only contribute an artificial effervescence during the fashionable part of the day, and cannot be classified as a characteristic of activity.

The English in St. Petersburg

In truth, nowhere can England be seen to better advantage than in the person of the British Factory—a body of English merchants who settled here in the middle of last century—as soon, indeed, as this new capital afforded any commercial advantages, and who have firmly transplanted to this northern soil the fairest blossoms from the parent tree. Every charitable custom is perpetuated—every hospitable anniversary celebrated—and every public rejoicing or mourning observed with jealous loyalty. The families, most of them highly aristocratic in descent, keep carefully aloof from all Russian society, and an intermarriage with a Russian is a circumstance of the rarest occurrence. At the same time this very adherence to national forms—prejudices if you will—has procured them universal respect. It is a mistake to suppose that foreigners like us the better for imitating them. The Emperor know that his sixteen hundred English children will always respect the existing laws, and wishes, perhaps, that the rest of his family were as peaceable. It is true they grumble a little at a new Ukase, but this is their prerogative whether home or abroad. Owing to the English habits of business—their punctuality, exactness, and probity—many a practical, useful institution has arisen of which the Russians equally benefit. It will be easily imagined that the straightforward English merchant, equally accustomed and compelled to trust his dependents in the various responsibilities of a counting-house, found but a slippery colleague in the merry, lay, thieving Russian; at the same time the wags of the English to their inferiors being as much higher as their treatment was more humane, it became the interest of both parties to reform an evil which gave the one a bad servant, and deprived the other of a good master.

Why St. Petersburg Is an Unloveable Residence

What is there about this capital which renders it so unloveable as a residence? I had experienced within its walls kindness as much beyond my expectation as my deserts—not only courtesy and hospitality, but real genuine Christian goodness, and I turned away with a feeling of thankfulness that my life was not destined to be there. It seems as if the soil, revenging itself for having been taken by force, and appropriated to a purpose Nature never intended, inspires a sense of dreariness and loneliness which can hardly be rationally accounted for. I never read or heard of the English traveler, sojourning beyond a few days, who did not quit Petersburg with a sentiment of release from bondage; and many a Russian, long-time resident abroad, whose darling vision by day and night it has been to retire to his native capital with the fruits of his expatriation, has, upon experiment, owned the disappointment, and ended his days elsewhere. "*Je deteste* Petersbourgh" is the thankless sentence you hear from every mouth.

～

Letters from the Baltic, Volume II

Russian Language and Literature

The native Russian may borrow technicalities from others, but morally, feelingly, or imaginatively, he has an infinitely greater variety of terms at his disposal than any of the nations who may consider themselves his creditors. At once florid and concise—pliable and vigorous, tender and stern—redundant in imagery, laconic in axiom, graceful in courtesy, strong in argument, soothing in feeling, and tremendous in denunciation, the latent energies of the language are a prophetic guarantee of the destinies of nations.

The grammar is excessively verbose and intricate, and, though many have essayed, no modern grammarian has yet succeeded in reducing it to a compass of any encouragement to a learner. Articles the Russian grammar has none, but these are amply indemnified by three genders and eight varyingly terminated cases, which are brought into active requisition by an unusual abundance of preposition and conjunction. The declension of all parts of speech is highly irregular, the construction of words particularly synthetic. The language is profusely strewn with proverbs, phrases of courtesy, and other Orientalisms which occur in daily use. For instance, every nation has some mode, more or less characteristic, of recommending themselves to the memory of distant friends: the French send friendship; the Germans, greeting; The English, love; the Estonians, health; but with Oriental gravity the Russians, even in the most intimate relations of life, send only a *Pohlan*—literally, an obeisance, or salaam.

With regard to the literature of Russia, it is neither sufficient in volume nor nationality to warrant an opinion. Lomonosoff is the etymologist of the empire; Karamsin, the historian; Pouschkin and Derjavine, the poets; Gretsch and Bestucheff, its prose writers and novelists.

Ranks in Russia

Russia has only two ranks—the highest and the lowest; consequently it exhibits all those rudenesses of social life which must be attendant on these two extreme positions of power and dependence. It is vain therefore to look for those qualities which equally restrain the one and protect the other, and which alone take root in that half-way class called forth in the progress of nations equally for the interest of both. For in this light it is impossible to view the scanty and broken-linked portion of Russian society which a sanguine and too hasty policy has forced, not nourished, into existence, and which at present rather acts as the depression and not the foundation of that most important body denominated the middle ranks of a nation. To study the real destinies of Russia the philosopher of mankind must descend to a class still in bondage, and not yet ripe for freedom, but where the elements of political stability and commercial energy are already glaringly apparent.

The Custom of Kissing

Fathers and sons kiss—old generals with rusty moustachios kiss—whole regiments kiss. The Emperor kisses his officers. On a reviewing day there are almost as many kisses as shots exchanged. If the Emperor reprimands an officer unjustly, the sign of restoration to favour as well as the best atonement is—a kiss. One of the bridges in Petersburg is to this day called the *Potzalui Most*, or Bridge of Kisses (not of Sighs), in commemoration of Peter the Great, who, having in a fit of passion unjustly degraded an officer in face of his whole regiment, kissed the poor man in the same open way upon the next public occasion on this very bridge.

On a holiday or *jour de fête* the young and delicate mistress of a house will not only kiss all her maid-servants but all her men-servants too; and, as I mentioned before, if the gentleman venture not above her hand, she will stoop and kiss his cheek.

Daily Routine of a Russian Family

The daily routine of a Russian family of this rank is easily complied with. Breakfast no visitor is expected to join; the family usually assembling for this meal in too deep a négligé for a stranger to witness. By noon the lady of the house is seated at her writing-table or embroidery-frame. Lunch is not served, but each orders a hot cutlet as he may feel inclined. Then visitors throng in, or the carriage and four awaits you. ... Dinner is generally at four—at least this is the Imperial hour. After dinner the more intimate friends of the family drop uninvited in, and make up the whist-table; and then some depart for the theatre, or later for balls, and so the days go round.

Arrival of Emperor Nicholas I

This was the Emperor—the plainest dressed, but the most magnificent figure present, wanting no outward token to declare the majesty of his presence. He passed slowly on, accommodating his manly movements to the short feeble steps of the Empress, who arrayed in a blaze of jewels, dragged a heavy train of orange-coloured velvet after her, and seemed hardly able to support her own weight. To the Imperial pair succeeded the *Naslednik*, or *Heritier*, the slender prototype of his father's grand proportions. Portly ladies and graceful maids of honour, with grey-haired generals, were seen in glistening train behind.

The display of diamonds here is immense. Every woman of rank has a glass case, or a succession of glass cases, like those on a jeweller's counter, where her jewels are spread out on purple velvet, under lock and key, in her own bedroom; and as it is here that she often receives her morning guests, for nothing is seen of sleeping or dressing apparatus save the superb mirrors and a gorgeous screen, her wealth of brilliants and other jewels is displayed to advantage.

Nicholas I (Lady Elizabeth Eastlake)
Library of Congress

Epiphany

On the 6th of January, O.S., the fête of the three kings, this court ceremony was renewed, with the addition of a procession of priests. After which the Emperor proceeded to bless the waters of the Neva, which are supposed to be gifted with supernatural virtues; on which occasion himself and every body present is bare-headed.

Description of the Emperor

The person of the Emperor is that of a colossal man, in the full prime of life and health; forty-two years of age, about six feet two inches high, and well filled out, without any approach to corpulency—the head magnificently carried, a splendid breadth of shoulder and chest, great length and symmetry of limb, with finely formed hands and feet. His face is strictly Grecian—forehead and nose in one grand line; the eyes finely lined, large, open and blue, with a calmness, a coldness, a freezing dignity, which can equally quell an insurrection, daunt an assassin, or paralyze a petitioner; with dark moustache and small whiskers, but not a sympathy on his face! His mouth sometimes smiled, his eyes never. There was that in his look which no monarch's subject could meet. His eye seeks every one's gaze, but none can confront his.

The Heritier now also took his station at our pillar. He inherits his father's majestic person and somewhat of the regularity of his face, but with the utter absence of the Emperor's unsympathizing grandeur. On the contrary, the son has a face of much sentiment and feeling; the lips full—the eyelids pensive—more of kindness than of character in his expression.

Rivalry among Russian High Society

At this time all the noble and wealthy houses in Petersburg are vying with one another in the number and splendor of their entertainments—endeavoring to compress as much pleasure as possible into the few remaining weeks before Lent, when balls, theatres, and masquerades are denied them, and their only passe-temps reduced to soirées, concerts, and tableaux.

The Emperor, who, as Grand Duke Nicholas, was noted for the simplicity of his tastes, and could hardly be induced to enter a place of amusement, now resorts to them with an increasing pleasure from which some augur no auspicious results—frequents the houses of the nobility and generals, who would spend to their last kopeck, and often go beyond it, to entertain him suitably—while the Empress's love of amusement and dress, besides inoculating her august spouse, has fixed a standard of merit, and exacted a rate of expenditure, which, to say the least, was not required to stimulate the already too-expensively disposed Russian.

Wherever the Imperial family appear, however great their affability, their desire to please and be pleased, the mere fact of their presence throws a restraint, a *gêne* over the whole assembly, who are depressed rather than exhilarated by the cold glaze of the Imperial eye, and who feel that the whole attention of these hosts is concentrated on one object.

The young military are in apprehension lest their uniform should not be found in strict accordance, to the shape of a button or the length of a spur, with the latest regulation—the young ladies, and equally their chaperones, are in anxiety lest any awkwardness of dress or manner should incur the censure, however pleasantly expressed.

In Russia, therefore, where the Zar is *"la loi vivante"*—the constitution in person—no etiquette can exist, or rather only such as he pleases for the time being. Whatever he does is right—he cannot demean himself. His rank takes care of itself.

Intellectual Life

Here it is absolute *mauvais genre* to discuss a rational subject—mere *pedanterie* to be caught upon any topics beyond dressing, dancing and a *jolie tournoure*. The superficial accomplishments are so superficialised as scarcely considered to exist—Russia has no literature, or rather none to attract a frivolous woman—and political subjects, with all this incidental chit-chat which the observances, anniversaries, etc., of a constitutional government bring more or less into every private family, it is needless to observe, exist not. Sad to say, nothing absolutely nothing, for old and young, man and woman, save the description, discussion, appreciation or depreciation of *toilette*—varied by a little *cuisine* and the witless wit called *l'esprit du salon*.

Added to this wearying theme, it is the bad taste of the day to indulge in any indelicacy of language which some aver to proceed from the example of the court of Prussia, and which renders at times even the trumperies of toilet or jewellery rather a grateful change of subject.

It is not from lack of education that frivolity of the Russian women is derived, for their tuition is generally conducted with great care by those placed as preceptresses over them; but such is the withering spell of fashion, that a young woman entering society is as anxious to hide the acquirements as any other *gaucheries* of the school-room, and it must be said generally succeeds.

Languages, which they imbibe in childhood, are the only demonstrations of acquirement permitted. English is heard on all sides, though it is little gratifying to hear our sober tongue applied to ideas by no means corresponding.

Emperor Paul

The death of Emperor Paul is a subject now discussed without any great reserve. Owing to his tyrannical, or, it may better be said, insane excesses, beneath which no individual in the empire would be considered safe, it was agreed upon for the public safety, and with the connivance of his eldest son, the late Alexander, to depose him from the government and imprison him for life. His immense personal strength frustrated, however, all possibility of capture while his recognition of the assailants rendered his murder necessary. Count Pahlen was the individual who strangled him with his pocket-handkerchief, and bore ever the sobriquet of *Schnupftuch Pahlen.*

The Empress at the Theater

It was here that the only opportunity of seeing the Empress occurred—her Majesty's state of health forbidding her all other participation in the amusements of the season. And even here, in order to avoid the risk of exposure to the air, her Majesty arrived in her morning dress, being preceded by her waiting-women with several cartons which were visible in the withdrawing-room behind the Imperial box, and where her Majesty attired herself for the evening. The theatres are all heated, and sometimes to an excessive degree—the thermometer in our box standing at 82. Her Majesty's malady appeared to be of a highly nervous nature, with an incessant restlessness of person and change of position. Her Majesty's person bore traces of symmetry, but in her present debilitated and emaciated state it was impossible to judge of her former personal attractions.

The Stability of Russia

From careful observation, and the judgement of those longer experienced, it would appear that the guarantees for the continued stability of Russia lie exclusively in the person of the monarch and in the body of the people. In the nobility, whose elements of national character fall far beneath those of his serf, the monarch finds no efficient help. Foreign education and contact has, with a few brilliant exceptions, rendered them adepts in the luxury and frivolity rather than in the humanity of civilization, or grafted them with democratic Utopian ideas that in no state, and least of all in Russia, can bring forth good fruit. The Emperor, therefore, has full ground for the double mistrust with which he views money taken out of the empire and pernicious ideas brought in.

Again, in the so-called middle class—here the mean excrescence of a partial civilization, who have renounced all of their nationality save its barbarity—all real support to the Crown seems still further removed. These occupy the lower departments of the state, clogging all straightforward dealing, perverting the real intention of the laws, and intercepting every humane Imperial act by the most cunning and unprincipled dishonesty.

Despised by the nobles, this class retaliates by a species of persecution which it is impossible to guard against. No lion's mouth, or familiars of the Inquisition, are needed in a state of things where, ere a false denunciation can be sifted and dismissed, the denounced is equally ruined in purse and worn out with constant care; and nowhere sad to say, are denunciations of this kind so frequent as at this time in Russia.

The Zar and the People

By a providential adaptation which surpasses all speculation of legislative philosophy, the people of Russia venerate their sovereign simply because he is absolute. With them respect for the anointed sovereign is a religion; and to restrict him by human ordinances would be to strip him of his divine credentials. What Zar has yet been dethroned or murdered by an act of the people?

What a magnificent engine, thus weighted, is the power of a Russian sovereign! With the mind filled by the absoluteness of his sway, and the eye possessed by the magnificence of his person, Nicholas I seems too grand a combination for mortal ken.

But it seems a prevailing principle with the Crown to interpose its presence, or an earnest of its presence, in every circumstance of life, whether usual or accidental—to prove to its subjects the indispensability of its help—to maintain literally the relation of parent to child—and by retaining its hold over every department, and making that a favour which we should consider a right, to facilitate the immediate exertion of its power.

Farewell to Russia

And with the vanished gaieties of this gayest and dullest of all capitals the sober writer of these letters must also pass away—to retain a sincere admiration for the intrinsic elements of Russia—the deepest interest in its welfare—the highest faith in its destiny—but also the reluctant conviction that, at this present time, Russia is the country where the learned man wastes his time, the patriot breaks his heart, and the rogue prospers.

CHAPTER SEVEN

Mary Alsop King Waddington

A Guest at the Coronation of Alexander III

Mary Alsop King Waddington spent most of her adult life in France. She was born in New York City on April 28, 1833, from a distinguished lineage. Her paternal grandfather, Rufus King, of the Federalist Party, was a United States Senator and a candidate both for vice president and president of the United States. Her maternal grandfather, Nicholas Low of New York, was a successful businessman; his daughter, Henrietta, was her mother. Her father, Charles King, was president of Columbia College and had been a newspaper editor and a politician.

The Kings moved to France in 1871, and Mary lived there the rest of her life. At the age of forty-one, she married William Henry Waddington in Paris. He was the son of Thomas and Janet Chisholm Waddington of England, who, like her parents, settled in France. Waddington served the government of France as prime minister in 1879 and as ambassador to Great Britain from 1883 to 1893. The couple had one son, Francis Richard. William Henry Waddington died in 1894.

Mary Alsop King Waddington wrote four books about her life in France and her years as a diplomat's wife. *Letters of a Diplomat's Wife* was published in 1902, describing her attendance at the coronation of Alexander III in May 1883 in Moscow and a trip to St. Petersburg that followed. Two years later, in 1904, *Italian Letters of a Diplomat's Wife* was in print, followed by *Chateau and Country Life in France* (1909) and *My First Years as a Frenchwoman* (1914).

Mary died in Paris on June 30, 1923.

The following selections are from *Letters of a Diplomat's Wife*.

⁓

Ambassade de France à Moscou

Maison Klein, Malaia Dimitrofska

Mardi, May 22d, 1883

How shall I ever begin to describe to you, Dear, the wonderful life we are leading. Everything is unlike anything I have ever seen. I suppose it is the beginning of the real far-off East. This morning I am sitting at the window reading and writing, and looking out into the court-yard, which is a never-failing interest—such quantities of people always there. The first thing I hear in the morning is Pontécoulant's voice. He is there every day at eight o'clock, conferring with Leroy and Hubert, examining the horses and carriages, deciding which ones are to be used, and giving orders for the day.

Then arrive the two Russian landaus which go all day, and very different they look from our beautiful equipages and big important servants. Then comes Lhermite, rattling off, in a low pony cart with the boy from the Consulate along-side of him. He goes to market every day and nearly has a fit because he can't talk himself, and he knows they are all lying, and stealing, and imposing upon him generally. In one corner there is a group of little Russian horses tied to the stable doors, with Russian soldiers fussing over them. They have been sent from one of the cavalry barracks for the gentlemen to ride. In every direction men are cleaning carriages, saddles, harness, liveries; and with such little noise—they are extraordinarily quiet.

May 22d, 5:30

We have just got back from the Governor's palace; and to-night the Emperor is safe in the Kremlin. It was a marvelous day. We started (the whole Mission) at 10:30 this morning, W and I alone in the d'Orsay, which looked very handsome. It is dark blue with white stripes, like all our carriages, and lined with blue satin of rather a lighter shade. The men were in demi-gala, blue plush breeches, white silk stockings, and high hats (not tricornes), with silver bands and cords. Thornton, the English coachman, looked very smart and handled his big black horses perfectly. The gentlemen told us he used very strong language when he got back to the stables over the abomination of the Moscow pavement. We were preceded as usual by Richard and Benckendorff in a light carriage. I wore one of Philippe's dresses, brown gauze embroidered in velvet flowers, all the front ecru lace, and an ecru straw bonnet with a vieux rose velvet crown.

I was much amused while I was dressing to hear various members of the party in the lingerie, "Madame, voulez-vous me coudre un bouton; les plumes de mon chapeau ne tiennent pas," [Madame, do you want me to sew on a button; the feathers of my hat don't hold] etc., even Thornton came in to have his lace cravat tied. We were a long time getting to Prince Dolgourouky's palace; not that it is far away but the streets are barricaded in every direction, however I didn't mind—the crowd was so interesting, packed tight; they had been standing for hours, they told us, such pale, patient faces but so unjoyous; no jokes, nor bits of songs nor good-natured scuffling; so unlike our Paris crowd on a great fete day, laughing and chaffing, and commenting freely on everything; and certainly very much unlike the American-Irish crowd at home in New York, on the 4th of July or St Patrick's day. I remember quite well putting boxes of firecrackers in a tin pail to frighten the horses, and throwing numerous little petards under people's feet, but no fire-crackers exploding anywhere in Moscow to-day. The tribunes covered with red cloth, or red and gold, crammed; and armies of soldiers mounted and on foot, in every direction; and yet we were only in the side streets. The real crowd was in the Tverskaya where the cortége was to pass.

When we finally arrived we were received by the Governor's two nieces, Madame Mansouroff and Princess Obolenski. The Prince, like all the other Russian noblemen, took part in the cortege. All our colleagues were there, but the Duc de Montpensier was the only special envoy. All the other foreign Princes were riding with the Emperor's suite. It was almost a female gathering, though of course all the men of the Corps Diplomatique were there. We waited some little time in the large drawing-room, where many presentations were made; and then had a very handsome breakfast, people talking very easily, but the Russians visibly nervous and preoccupied. As soon as it was over we went out on the balconies, where we remained until the cortége arrived. They brought us tea at intervals, but I never stirred from my chair until the end.

It was a beautiful sight as we looked down—as far as one could see, right and left, flags, draperies, principally red and gold, green wreaths, flowers and uniforms—the crowd of people well kept back behind a triple row of soldiers, the middle of the street perfectly clear, always a distant sound of bells, trumpets, and music. A salute of cannon was to let us know when the Emperor left Petrofski, the small palace just outside the walls where he has been all these days. As the time drew near one felt the anxiety of the Russians, and when the first coup sounded, all of them in the street crossed themselves. As the procession drew near the tension was intense. The Governor's Palace is about half way between the gate by which the Emperor entered the Kremlin. He had all that long street to follow at a foot's pace. As soon as he entered the Kremlin another cannon would tell his people he was safe inside.

At last the head of the gorgeous procession appeared. It was magnificent, but I can't begin to tell you the details. I don't even remember all I saw, but you will read it all in the papers, as of course all their correspondents are here. There were quantities of troops of all descriptions, the splendid chevaliers-guardes looked very imposing with their white tunics and silver *cuirasses*; both horse and men enormous. What I liked best were the red Cossacks (even their long lances red). They looked perfectly wild and uncivilized and their little horses equally so, prancing and plunging all the time.

The most interesting thing to me was the deputations from all the provinces of this vast Empire—Kirghis, Moguls, Tartars, Kalmucks, etc. There was a magnificent chief from the Caucase, all in white, with jeweled sword and high cap (even from where we were, so high above the crowd, we saw the flash of diamonds): the Khan of Khiva, and the Emir of Bokhara, both with high fur caps, also with jewels on cap and belt. A young fellow, cousin I think of Prince Dolgorouky, came and stood near me, and told me as well as he could who the most important people were. Bells going all the time (and the Moscow bells have a deep, beautiful sound) music, the steady tramp of soldiers, and the curious, dull noise of great crowd of people.

Then a break in the troops and a long procession of gala court carriages passed, with six horses and six runners, a man to each horse, with all the grand-maitres and high officials of the Court, each man covered with gold lace and embroidery, and holding his staff of office, white with a jewel at the top. After that more troops, the Emperor's body-guard, and then the Emperor himself. He was in full uniform, riding quite alone in front on his little white horse which he had ridden in the Turkish campaign. He looked quite composed and smiling, not a trace of nervousness (perhaps a little pale), returned all the salutations most graciously, and looked up, bowed and smiled to our balcony. A little distance behind him rode his two sons, and close up to him on the left rode the Duke of Edinburgh in red; any bomb thrown at the Emperor must have killed the English Prince.

Then followed a suite of princes—some of their uniforms, Austrian, Greek and Montenegrian standing out well. From that moment there was almost silence on the balcony; as the Emperor disappeared again all crossed themselves, and everyone waited for the welcome sound from the Kremlin.

After a long interval, always troops passing, came the Empress. She was with her daughter, the little Grand Duchess Xenia, both in Russian dress. The carriage was short, a coupé, but half glass, so we saw them perfectly, and the high head-dress (kakoshnik) and white veil, spangled with silver was very becoming. The carriage was very handsome, all gold and paintings; six white horses led, and running footmen. The Empress and her daughter were seated side by side, and on a curious sort of *outside* seat, on one side of the coup, was a page, dressed in red and yellow, a sort of cloth of gold, with high feathers in his cap. The Empress looked grave and very pale, but she smiled and bowed all the time. It must have been an awful day for her, for she was so far behind the Emperor, and such masses of troops in between, that he might have been assassinated easily, she knowing nothing of it.

There was again a great sound of bells and music when the Empress passed, all the people crossing themselves, but the great interest of course was far ahead with the Emperor. A great procession of Court carriages followed with all the Princesses, Grandes-Maitresses, etc., and endless troops still, but no one paid much attention; every ear was strained to hear the first sound from the Kremlin. When the cannon boomed out the effect was indescribable. All the Russians embraced each other, some with tears running down their cheeks, everybody shook hands with everybody, and for a moment the emotion was contagious—I felt rather a choke in my throat. The extraordinary reaction showed what the tension had been.

After a whirl of felicitations we went into the dressing-room for a few minutes, had tea (of course), and I talked to some of the people whom I had not seen before. Montpensier came up, and was very civil and nice. He is here as a Spanish Prince. He told me he had been frightfully nervous for the Emperor. They all knew that so many Nihilists were about—he added, "*Il était superbe, leur Empereur, si crane!*" [He was superb, their emperor, so bold!]

We had to wait a few moments for the carriage and we got home about 5, having been standing a long time. We were almost as long getting back to the Embassy as we were coming. There was a dense crowd everywhere, and the same little detachments of Cossacks galloping hard into the midst of people, and apparently doing no harm to anyone.

I will finish now before going to bed—happily all our dissipations finish early. We dined quietly with only our own Embassy and Benckendorff, and then drove about for an hour or so looking at the illuminations, which were not very wonderful. We met all our colleagues doing the same thing. W. has just had his report from the detective. He said all the Nihilists were scattered along the route to-day, but evidently had no intention of doing anything. It seems curious they should be allowed to remain, as of course the Russian police know them quite as well as our man does.

I have just had a notice that the Empress will receive me to-morrow. I will try and write a few lines always late before going to bed, and while the whole thing is still fresh in my memory. If this letter is slightly incoherent it is because I have had so many interruptions. The maids can hardly undress me, they are so anxious to tell me all they have seen. It certainly was a magnificent sight to-day, and the fears for the Emperor gave such a dramatic note to the whole thing. My eyes are rather tired, looking so hard, I suppose.

Wednesday, May 23d

Well, dear, I have had my audience. It was most interesting. I started at 11 o'clock in the gala carriage, Hubert driving me, as he wanted to go once to the Kremlin with the carriage before the day of the Coronation. It seems there is a slight rise in the road just as one gets to the gate, which is also narrow. I wore the blue brocade with bunches of cherries, the front of moussé velvet, and a light blue crêpe bonnet, neither gloves nor veil. Benckendorff and Richard, as "officer de service," went ahead in a small carriage. Benckendorff said I must have one of my own Embassy, and Richard thought it would amuse him to come. W. rather demurred—was afraid we wouldn't be serious enough, but we promised him to be absolutely *dignes*. Do you remember at the first official reception at the Instruction Publique he never would let you and Pauline stand behind me—he was afraid we would make unseemly jokes, or laugh at some of the dresses.

Our progress to the Kremlin was slow. The carriage is heavy, goes always at a foot's pace, and has a swinging motion which is very disagreeable. I felt rather shy, sitting up there alone, as of course there is a great deal of glass, so that I was much "*en évidence*." Everybody looked, and the people in the street crowded close up to the carriage. We found grand preparations when we got to the Palace—the great staircase covered with a red cloth, and every variety of chamberlain, page, usher, and officer on the stairs and at the door. Benckendorff and Richard helped me out of my carriage, and Richard's impulse was to give me his arm to go upstairs, but he was waved back imperatively, and a magnificent gentleman in a velvet coat, all lace and embroidery, advanced, and conducted me up the grand staircase, always a little behind me. I passed through a hedge of uniforms and costumes. When we came to the landing where there was a piquet of soldiers my attendant said—"La France," and they presented arms.

At the top of the staircase, at the door of the first of a long enfilade of salons, I was handed over, with a very long bow, from my first gentleman to another of the same description, equally all gold lace, and embroidery; and so I passed through all the rooms, always meeting a new chamberlain in each one. The rooms are large and high, with vaulted roofs like a cathedral, little or no furniture (I believe the Russian court never sits down except at meals). We made a halt in one of the salons, where we found several maids of honour of the Empress, who were presented to me. They were all dressed much alike in long, light dresses, and wore their badge—the Empress's chiffre in diamonds on a blue ribbon. While I was talking to them, a procession of diplomats and special envoys passed through the room. They had just been received by the Empress.

Presently appeared Prince Galitzin—Grand Maitre des Cérémonies, attired in red velvet and lace and embroidery, who said, "*Sa Majesté sera bientôt prête.*" [Her Majesty will be ready soon.] I continued my progress with the same ceremonial, passed through the salle du trône, which is handsome, white and gold; and came to a standstill in the next salon, evidently the ante-chamber of the room where I was to be received, as the two colossal negroes who always accompany the Emperor and Empress were standing at the door. They were dressed in a sort of Asiatic costume, cashmeres, turbans, scimitars, etc. I was received by the Princess Kotchoubey and Count Palen, Arch Grand Matre des Cérémonies. The Princess K is the mother of Princess Lise Troubetzkoi (whom you will remember in Paris as having a salon the first days of the Republic where political men of all opinions assembled— Thiers was her great friend). She was a little old lady dressed entirely in white, with a jewel low on her forehead. Count Pahlen was dressed in blue velvet and embroidery, and carried his staff of office, white, with a large sapphire on the top.

We talked a few minutes, when apparently there came a signal from the Empress. The doors flew open, and the Princess advanced to the threshold, making a beautiful curtsey (I am sure mine was not half so good), she seemed to go straight down to the ground, said, "*J'ai l'honneur d'annoncer l'Ambassadrice de France.*" [I have the honor of announcing the ambassadress from France.] She then withdrew to one side-I made a curtsey at the door, which was instantly shut, another, a little farther on (the regulation is 3), but hadn't time for my third, as the Empress, who was standing in the middle of the room, advanced a few steps, shook hands and begged me to sit down. I hadn't seen her for some years, since she came to Paris with her husband then Grand Duke Héritier (his father was still alive), and I didn't find her changed. She recalls the Princess of Wales but is not so tall; has beautiful dark eyes, and a very gracious manner. She was dressed almost as I was, but in a different color, yellow brocade with bunches of plums, splendid lace in front, and a beautiful pearl necklace three rows of large stones (my one row of fairly large ones was nowhere). I think I stayed about 20 minutes.

We talked easily enough. She said the long day yesterday had been very fatiguing, the going at a foot's pace all that long distance with the peculiar swinging motion of the heavy gala carriage had tired her very much; also the constant bowing right and left, and the quantities of flags and draperies waving under her eyes. She didn't say anything about being nervous, so of course I didn't. She gave me the impression of having extra-ordinary self-control. I asked her what the little Grand Duchess thought of it all. She said that she really didn't know—that she didn't speak, but looked at everything and bowed to all the people exactly as she did.

She said the day of the *sacre* would be very long and tiring, particularly beginning so early in the morning; that she was very *matinale*, quite accustomed to getting up early—was I? "Fairly—but I hadn't often been up and dressed in full dress and diamonds at seven in the morning." "You would prefer a ceremony by candlelight." "I think we should all look better at 9 o'clock in the evening." She laughed, and then we talked a little; Paris, chiffons, etc. She said some of her best dresses had come from Philippe. We talked a little about Moscow and the Kremlin. She asked me what I had seen. When I spoke of the church and the tribunes for the Corps Diplomatique with no seats and a very long ceremony, she was quite indifferent; evidently didn't think it was of the slightest consequence whether we were tired or not; and I don't suppose it is.

When she *congêdied* me the door flew open (she evidently had a bell under her chair which she touched with her feet); she shook hands, and walked immediately to a door at the other end of the room; so I didn't have to back out all the way. Princess Kotchoubey and Count Pahlen were waiting for me. The Princess said, "*Sa Majesté vous a gardé bien longtemps, Madame l'Ambassadrice. J'espère que vous avez été content.*" [Her Majesty has kept you a long time, Madame Ambassadress. I hope you are happy.] Pahlen also made me a polite phrase. They both accompanied me across the room, and then the door opened, and another chamberlain took possession of me. Just as we got to the door, the Princess was saying something about her daughter "*devenue absolument une Parisienne*" [she has become a Parisienne], when it opened; she stopped short in the middle of her phrase, and made me a little curtsey—her function was over once I passed into the other room. It was too funny.

I was conducted through all the rooms and down the great staircase with the same ceremony. I found Richard waiting in one of the big rooms, with the "Dames du portrait," but this time he didn't venture to offer his arm to the Ambassadress, and followed with Benckendorff at a respectful distance.

I found my carriage surrounded by an admiring crowd. The horses are handsome and enormous, particularly here where the race is small, also the French gala liveries are unlike anything else. Hubert, my own coachman, sits up so straight and pompous on his box, and looks so correct I hardly know him. The movement of the gala carriage is something awful, makes me really ill.

May 23d, 10 o'clock
We have had a quiet evening—some of the gentlemen have gone off to hear the famous Bohémiennes in one of the public gardens. They have been leaving cards all day on the special envoys, Princes, etc. W. and Pontécoulant are having a conference, and I have got into my tea-gown, and am reading a little, writing a little and being generally lazy. W. and I also did a round of visits this afternoon.

As naturally none of our servants know either a word of Russian, or the streets of Moscow, we took with us the little polyglot youth from the Consulate, who knows equally well French, Russian, and German. We gave him our list, and he went ahead in a drosky.

We found no one but the Princess Oblenski, who spoke at once about the Emperor's *entrée*; said no one could imagine the relief it was to all of them to know that he was actually safe in the Kremlin. They had evidently all dreaded that day and of course notwithstanding all the precautions a bomb could have been thrown. The thrower, *par exemple*, would have been torn to pieces by the crowd; but what makes the strength of the Nihilists is that they all count their lives as nothing in what they consider the great cause.

How hideous the life of the Emperor and the Empress must be. They say they find letters on their tables, in their carriages, coming from no one knows where, telling them all the horrors in store for them and their children.

Ambassade de France à Moscou

Maison Klein, Malaia Dimitrofska

Thursday, 24 Mai, 1883
I am having a quiet morning. We have no particular function to-day. Madame Jaurès is coming to get me after breakfast, and we are going to do a little sight-seeing. The first thing I hear in the morning always is Pontécoulant's voice in the court talking to Leroy and Hubert, and examining the horses. The pair we had in the gala carriage yesterday went beautifully. Hubert was rather nervous, as there is a steep little bit just as one passes through the gates of the Kremlin—it is also narrow, and those big, unwieldy carriages are not easily handled. The pavement is so rough that I was actually a little sick yesterday after I came in. I was called off by a visit from Prince Orloff (Russia Ambassador in France). He comes almost every day, and is much interested

in all our doings—said the carriage and general style of everything was much admired yesterday. About two Madame Jaurès came, and we started off sight-seeing. The admiral, Jaurès, and one or two of the young men met us at the Kremlin, and we went over the two palaces—new and old. The old one is most curious; small, dark, low rooms, vaulted ceilings, all most elaborately or-namented in Byzantine style; a small steep, twisting staircase; large porcelain stoves, and absolutely uncomfortable. We saw the dining room where the Emperor and Empress will dine in state the day of the Coronation. The new palace is quite different—high, light, large rooms, white, which must look beautiful at night lighted by thousands of wax candles. In the great ballroom the two Throne chairs are on a gold dais with great curtains of purple velvet and ermine—very royal looking. (I wonder if the sight of all this splendor will destroy my mental equilibrium—I assure you I felt rather like a queen myself yesterday, seated up alone in the great gala carriage, with everybody bowing and gaping.)

There is a splendid view over the Kremlin, the river and the town from all the palace windows. We went again to the church of the Assumption, where we found Count Pahlen superintending. He showed us some of the famous paintings—among others a Madonna with a black face, a splendid diamond necklace, and large sapphires and emeralds disposed about her person. There are jewels almost everywhere; on pictures, brackets, etc. Pahlen told me, when I was noticing them, that the Russian Court was famous for colored stones, particularly emeralds and sapphires—told me to notice the Grand Duchess Constantine's emeralds, and the Empress's sapphires. I will, if ever I get time to go into details, but everything is on such an enormous scale here. He also asked me if I was accustomed to standing three or four hours, and if not he would suggest a pliant (stool) "*dissmulé sous les plis de la traine*" [hidden under the pleats of the train], and showed me with pride the rails, covered with red velvet, in our tribune, which he had had put there so we should be comfortable! It will really be an awful day, particularly as we have to begin it early, but I suppose we shan't die of it.

I came back about 4, changed my dress for something more *élégant* (the blue silk with long blue redingote and white lace), and started off again in the d'Orsay for some visits (the little boy in the drosky going in front). I found the Princess Radziwill in two small rooms (she received me in her bed-room), all she could find for herself and her husband in Moscow and that at an awful price (and she is Russian born). I also found Countess Pahlen, wife of the Grand Master, who was very smiling, and suggested that we should have an evening reception, which would be much appreciated. Of course we shall be delighted, and had even thought of a ball, but all those things had been settled in Russia before we left Paris. The Russian Court wished to have one ball only, as the Coronation Functions were numerous and fatiguing and that is to be at General Schweinitz's (Doyen of the Corps Diplomatique).

After leaving Countess Pahlen I went again to the Kremlin, the d'Orsay always exciting much attention. I had the greatest difficulty in finding the Duchesse d'Edinbourgh, for whom I had to write myself down, and could find no servant who spoke either German, French or English. The crowd and confusion was something awful; apparently the whole of Moscow was going wherever I was—Ambassadors, Generals, Chamberlains, maids-of-honor, servants with tea, crowding in all the corridors. You never saw such a sight, and just many more in the court-yards—carriages, soldiers, workmen, people, carpenters, bales of stuffs, and planks for stands, and all in that beautiful cadre—the old gray walls looked so soft, and the marvelous effects of colour everywhere. I was well shaken up, such a pavement. I met the Duc de Mont-pensier at every turn, sight-seeing too. We had a quiet dinner, the personnel only with Benckendorff. The gentlemen had been going all around too all the afternoon playing cards. They all say the pavement is most trying.

W. and Pontécoulant have come in late as usual for a last little talk. I told them what Countess Pahlen had said about an evening reception. W. had had the same idea. I think the house is large enough—the ballroom ought to light well, all white with yellow satin furniture. We must have a talk with Lhermite about flowers; he says there are none here, his come from Paris.

To H.L.K.

Saturday, May 26, 1883

Well, Dear, I am just alive, but nothing more, having performed 5 Grand Duchesses. The gentlemen all went off in full uniform at 11 to begin their au-diences. I followed later alone (they always go *en bande*) with Richard going in the small carriage in front as *officier de service* (which amuses us perfectly). I wore the white soft silk with Valenciennes that you liked, and the flower hat. Benckendorff complimented me on my toilette. It was a long affair getting to our different Princesses. They are all lodged in the Kremlin, and the various palaces connect with all sorts of passages and staircases, but the corridors are narrow and the block something awful. My first audience was with the Grand Duchess Michel. Her husband is an uncle of the Emperor, and was for a long time Governor of the Caucasus. When we finally got to the door of the apartments I was received by 2 Chamberlains (all gold and embroidery), who never left me until they deposited me in the carriage at 5 o'clock—I had started at 1:30. The ceremonial was always exactly the same, one or two ladies-in-waiting were in the room communicating with the one in which the Grand Duchess was waiting. They announced "*L'Ambassadrice de France*," I got through as many of the three regulation curtseys as I could— I never really had time to make the third, as they all advanced a few steps and shook hands. The Grand Duchess Michel is a Baden Princess, tall, slight, very intelligent, simply dressed in black velvet and of course a pearl necklace. She spoke to me in English, French, and German, but the conversation was mostly in French. She seemed well up in French literature, and asked me what I thought of Zola's "*L'Assommoir*," was really surprised when I said I hadn't read it, nor in fact scarcely anything he wrote. She considered it a marvel, and couldn't understand any French woman not reading every word that came from "*un des plus puissants cerveaux du siècle.*" [one of the most influential intellects of the century]. She knew too all the *pièces de théâtre*, and when expressed surprise that she had had time to read so much, said her life in the Caucasus was so lonely—no society of any kind, and no resources outside of her own palace. I should think she was a *maîtresse femme*.

After leaving her I was taken in hand again by my two chamberlains, and walked some distance across one or two courts, always meeting more chamberlains escorting colleagues, principally men, all in uniforms and orders, doing the same thing, and trying to get on as fast as they could. My next visit was to the Grand Duchesse Constantine. When we got to the anteroom and small salon we found them full of gentlemen, who proved to be our Mission, who had arrived a few minutes before. That made a slight change of programme, as the Grand Duke decided to receive W. and me together with the Duchess—accordingly we were received first, alone, in a small room. The Grand Duke was standing close to the door; the Grand Duchess in the centre of the room. He is a sailor, looks very intelligent. She has been very handsome, carries herself beautifully, and has a splendid figure. He was in uniform—she in red velvet (she didn't have on her emeralds—I suppose we shall see them all tomorrow). They both talked very easily about all sorts of things; Greece, of course and the Schuylers, of whom she spoke very warmly. Her daughter is the Queen of Greece—I hope we shall see her, as I have heard Gert talk so much about her. The Grand Duchess said she was tired already, and the Ceremonies haven't begun yet. She had received yesterday 100 ladies of Moscow. They came in groups of 10, and she had to find something to say to each one.

As soon as the audience was over W. asked permission, as usual, to present the rest of the Mission. I remained in the outer salon talking to the ladies-in-waiting. The apartment is high, with a splendid view over Moscow. They pointed me out several churches and curious roofs—were much interested in all my visits and my clothes, supposed I had quantities of trunks.

After that I departed again alone, and saw the Grand Duchess Catherine, who was very amiable, but kept me a few minutes only, as she had so many people to receive. Then I took another long walk, and up several flights of narrow turning stairs (the chamberlains in front and Richard behind) to the Duchesse d'Oldenburg. The Belgian Mission was being received, so I waited in the outer salon, and again W. and the gentleman arrived. And he and I were received together. Evidently they like it better when we can go together, as it saves time for them—and if we are tired, think what they must be.

I went off again alone, and was received by the Grand Duchess Wladimir, who is charming—a German Princess. She is young, a pretty figure, very well dressed in white. She looked rather delicate, having just got over a rather bad attack of measles. She dreads the fatigue very much to-morrow, and has asked the Empress if she might have a folding-chair, a pliant of some kind, but her "*demande n'a pas été accueillie favorablement* [request was not granted]. *L'imperatrice elle-même sera debout tout le temps.* [The empress herself will be standing all the time.] *Il faudrait absolument que nous fassions comme elle.*" [We must do exactly as she does.] I didn't mention my pliant, as I am quite sure no one will notice to-morrow anything I do.

That finished me, and, as I had been standing or walking since I left the Embassy, so I was glad to find the carriage, which was by no means easy. There were quantities at the Kremlin, and as we never by any chance came out at the same door by which we went in, and the coachman was told to follow, he naturally had some difficulty in getting it. Also it is raining hard, which complicates matters. There are carpets down to the doors, but so many people have passed over them that they are just as wet and muddy as the streets. We met all the rest of the Mission at the Embassy door, and then there was a general détente, the men all calling for their servants to get them out of their uniforms, and to bring beer and cigars.

W. came in to tea. He looked really done up—he had been at it steadily since 12. There are so many Princes and Grand Dukes without any wives. I am writing in bits, but will finish as usual the last thing. We have had a small dinner—the other French Embassy (permanent), Lagrené, Consul, and Orloff. Benckendorff of course. They all went away early, as our day to-morrow is an awful one.

It is pouring still, and we are rather melancholy at the thought of our gala carriages and blue and silver liveries in heavy rain. Just before dinner I had a visit from Philippe, and he made various *essais* with my diadem and feathers. He is to be here at six to-morrow to *coiffer* me. He also requested that he might see my dress so as to make his coiffure *"harmoniser avec l'ensemble"* [go with the dress]. I wanted to see it too, so as to be sure that everything was right, and the flowers well sewn on. It is now reposing on one of the big arm-chairs in the dressing-room, covered with a sheet. My eyes are shutting of themselves, so I will stop.

Please send all my letters on to America, as I never can write two accounts of our life here.

To H.L.K.

Ambassade de France à Moscou, Maison Klein, Malaia Dimitrovska

Dimanche, 27 Mai, 1883

I am perfectly exhausted, Dear, after the most beautiful, bewildering, exhausting day I have ever gone through. We got home at 4:30. I rested a little, had tea as usual in my boudoir with W. and Richard, and will write as much as I can while I am still under the impression of all I have seen.

I was up at 5:30, as we had to leave here at 7. Philippe was very punctual—put on diadem and feathers very well. Happily it was all blue, rather dark (as my dress too was blue), and he remarked pleasantly, to put me at my ease I think, and make me feel as comfortable as I could at that hour of the morning, *"Le bleu c'est le fard de Madame"* [blue is Madame's color]. He couldn't understand that I wouldn't let him *maquiller* my face—said all the princesses were painted—but I really couldn't do that.

When I appeared in the drawing-room, the men of the Embassy were very complimentary about my dress. We went in our three carriages (I had the white moirè cloak, trimmed with dark feathers over me), W. and I and Pontécoulant in the first gala carriage drive by Leroy (I wish you could have seen him, as much taken up with *his dress* as I was with mine). He stood giving directions to a quantity of understrappers, but never touching harness, not even whip, until we appeared, then got on his box as we got into the carriage, settled himself in a fine pose, and we started.

The second gala carriage drive by Hubert (who looked very well) came next, and then the d'Orsay. It really was a very pretty *cortége*, and we were much looked at and admired, as we drove very slowly, and jolting very much, to the German Embassy. All our colleagues came up about the same time. Some of the gala carriages were very good, the Austrian, but ours out and out the best. No one else had three.

We assembled in one of the large rooms of the palace, and then walked through numerous rooms, galleries, and finally through an open court, entirely covered with a red carpet, and lined with soldiers and officers—every description of uniform. The Chevalier-Guardes, magnificent in their white tunics, silver *cuirasses* and helmets. Happily it was fine—I don't know what we should have done in the rain and also so early in the morning the sun was not *gênant* (as it was later in the day). The long procession, the men in uniform and decorations, the women in full dress, feathers and diadems, was most effective.

I left my cloak in the carriage, and didn't feel chilly, but some of the women were uncomfortable, and had little lace and fur tippets. We filed into the church (which is small), and into the Diplomatic Tribune, and settled ourselves quite easily—there was plenty of room. The effect inside was dazzling: tapers, flowers, pictures, jewels, quantities of women already seated, all in the Kakoshnik, and a general impression of red and gold in their costumes. All the Empress's ladies wear red velvet trains embroidered in gold. People seemed to be coming in all the time. Deputations from the provinces, officials of Moscow, officers, chamberlains, a moving mass of colour. The costume of the Popes was gorgeous—cloth of gold with very high jeweled *mitres*.

We waited some time before the ceremony began, but there was so much to see that we didn't mind, and from time to time one of the officials came and stood with us a little, explaining who all the people were. The whole church was hung with red, and red carpets everywhere. Just in the middle there was a high *estrade*, covered with red velvet, and a great gold *baldaquin* with Imperial eagles embroidered on it. It was all surrounded by a gold balustrade, and on it were two thrones. A little lower on the same *estrade* were the places of the Princes of the family, and the Foreign Princes.

A little before 9 the Imperial family began to arrive. Almost all the Grand Duchesses in *trains of d'argent* bordered with sable, and magnificent jewels. Then there was a great sound of trumpets, and cheering outside (those curious, suppressed Russian cheers), and they told us the Emperor and Empress were coming. They were proceeded by an officer of the Chevalier-Guardes, with *sabre-à-nu*. The Emperor was in full uniform with the blue ribbon of St. André. The Empress quite simple in white and silver, the Imperial eagles embroidered on the front of her dress; no diadem, no veil, nor jewels; her train carried by 4 pages, her hair quite simply done—she looked so young, quite like a school-girl. Then followed a glittering suite of Princes, officers, etc.

The service was very long, the chanting quite fine; the men have beautiful, deep voices—I cared less for the intoning, they all end on such a peculiar high note. I didn't like the looks of the Popes either—the long beards worried me. Of course the real interest was when the Emperor took the crown from the hands of the Pope (kneeling before him) and put it on his own head. He looked like a magnificent figure, towering over everybody, as he stood there in his Imperial robes, cloth of gold lined with ermine, and a splendid jeweled collar. The crown looked high and heavy—made entirely of jewels.

His two brothers, Grand Dukes Wladimir and Alexis, put on his robes. The Grand Duke Wladimir always stands close behind his brother. He has a stern, keen face. He would be the regent if anything should happen to the Emperor, and I think his would be an iron rule.

As soon as the Emperor was crowned the Empress left her seat, came to the middle of the platform, made a deep curtsey to the Emperor, and knelt. Her court ladies then gathered around her, and put on the Imperial mantle, also in cloth of gold lined with ermine, and the same jeweled collar like the Emperor's. When she was dressed, the Emperor, stooping low over her, put on her crown, a small one made entirely in diamonds, raised her and kissed her. As she stood a moment she almost staggered back under the weight of the mantle—the 4 pages could hardly hold it.

Then the long procession of Princes and Princesses left their seats on the *estrade* and passed before the Sovereigns. First came his two brothers, Wladimir and Alexis. They kissed the Emperor, then bent low before the Empress, kissing her hand. She kissed them each on the forehead. Next came the two young Princes, in uniform like their father, wearing also the blue ribbon of St. André, and the little Grand Duchess (aged 10) in a short white dress, but the Kakoshnik.

It was a pretty sight to see the children bowing and curtseying low to their parents. Some the ladies' curtseys were wonderful—the Arch Duchess Charles Louis extraordinarily graceful (I wonder how I ever shall get through mine—I am certainly much less souple than these ladies). When they had all passed the Emperor went alone into the chapel to *communier* and receive the sacred oil—the Empress remained kneeling outside.

We had various incidents in our tribune—one or two ladies fainted, but couldn't get out, they had to be propped up against the rail, and brought round with fans, salts, etc. We stood for three hours and a half.

The Emperor and Empress left the church with the same ceremony (we all following), and then there was a curious function. Under a dais, still in their court robes, their trains carried by six or eight officers, they walked around the *enceinte*, going into three or four churches to make their devotions, all of us and all the other Princes following, all their suites, and an accompaniment of bells, cannon, music, and cheers. (I forgot to say that when the Emperor put his crown on his head in the church, the cannon announced to his people that their sovereign was crowned.)

We had a few drops of rain, then the sun came out strong, and I was rather wretched—however Général Pittié came to my rescue, and shaded me with his hat (all the men were bareheaded). There were tribunes all along the route for the people who hadn't been able to get into the church; in one of them all the younger members of the Embassies, as of course *all* couldn't be got inside. These two were all gold and red, filled with women, mostly in white, and men in uniform. You can't imagine what a gorgeous sight it was, and the crowd below packed tight, all gasping at the spectacle.

We didn't dirty our dresses (the trains of course we carried in our arms), I don't know why, as the red carpet was decidedly damp and muddyish in places. We finally arrived at the Vieux Palais, where we were to breakfast, and the Emperor and Empress were also to have a little respite before dining in state with their people.

We had a handsome breakfast, quantities of gold and silver plate, and many Russian dishes. I didn't much like the looks of the soup, which was clear, but had various things floating about on it—uncooked fish, little black balls, which I thought might be caviar, which I don't ever like; and I was rather wondering what I should eat (I was very hungry), when my neighbor, Nigra, the Italian Ambassador, suggested I should share his meal. He didn't like Russian cookery either, so he had intrigued with a friendly official, who was going to bring him a cold chicken and a bottle of good red wine. I accepted joyfully, and we had a very good breakfast.

I think we were about three-quarters of an hour at table, and it was very pleasant to sit down after those hours of standing. When the breakfast was over, a little after two, we were conducted to the Imperial dining-room, a square, low room in the old Kremlin with a vaulted ceiling and heavy Byzantine decorations; quantities of paintings on a gold ground, bright coloured frescoes, most elaborate. There were great buffets and tables covered with splendid gold and silver plates, flagons, vases, etc. At the end of the room was a square, raised platform covered with red, and a splendid dais, all purple velvet ermine and gold embroidery where the Imperial couple were to dine with their faithful subjects.

We strangers were merely admitted for a few minutes to see the beginning of the meal, and then we retired, and the Emperor remained alone with his people. Of course officers and officials of all descriptions were standing close around the platform. There was a large table to the left as we came in, where almost all the Russians were already assembled—all the women in the national dress, high Kakoshnik, long white lace spangled veil, and sort of loose hanging sleeve which was very effective.

Presently we heard a sound of music, and trumpets, which told the Royalties were approaching, and as they came near the familiar strains of the polonaise from Glinka's opera *"La Vie Pour le Czar,"* which is always played when the Emperor and Empress appear. They came with the usual escort of officers and chamberlains smiling and bowing graciously to all of us. They seated themselves (always in their cloth of gold mantles, and crowns on their heads) on the two throne chairs; a small table was placed in front of them, and then the dinner began.

The *soupière* was preceded by a chamberlain in gold lace; held by a Master of ceremonies and flanked on each side by a gigantic *Chevalier-garde*, *sabre-à-nu*. There was always a collection of officials, chamberlains, pages, etc., bringing up the rear of the *cortége*, so that at each entrée a little procession appeared. We saw three dishes brought in with the same ceremony—the fish was so large on a large silver dish that *two* Masters of Ceremonies held that.

It was really a wonderful sight, like a picture in some old history of the Moyen Age. As soon as the Sovereigns had taken their places on the thrones all the Russians at their table sat down too. We couldn't, because we had nothing to sit upon, so we remained standing at the end of the room, facing the estrade. They told us that when the Emperor raised his glass and asked for wine that was the signal for us to retire; and that it would be after the roast. (All our instructions were most carefully given to us by Benckendorff, who felt his responsibility.) Think what his position would have been if any member of *his* Embassy had made a "gaffe." Accordingly as soon as the roast made its appearance all our eyes were riveted upon the Emperor. He raised his glass slowly (very high) to give us time. General Schweinitz, as Doyen, stepped well forward, and made a very low bow. We all bowed and curtseyed low (my knees are becoming more supple) and got ourselves out backwards. It wasn't very difficult as we had our trains in our arms.

I don't think we shall see anything more curious than that state banquet. I certainly shall never see again a soup tureen guarded by soldiers with drawn swords.

10 o'clock

We dined quietly, everyone giving his experiences—of course the younger members of the Embassy, who had no places in church, had a better impression of the ensemble than we had. They said the excitement and emotion of the crowd in the square before the church was extraordinary. All crossed themselves, and many cried, when the cannon told them that the Emperor was crowned. They seemed to be an emotional, superstitious race. They also said the procession around the courts, when the Emperor and Empress were going to the various churches was wonderful—a moving mass of feathers, jewels, banners, bright helmets, and *cuirasses*, all glittering in the sun.

After dinner we drove about a little, seeing all the illuminations, but the crowd was so dense we could hardly move, though the soldiers did all they could, and battered the people about. Then it began to rain a little, so I begged to come home. It is raining quite hard now—I hear it on the marquise. Heavens how tired I am, but the papers will keep you quite *au courant*.

Ambassade de France à Moscou

Maison Klein, Malalia Dimitrofska

Monday, May 28th, 1883.

We are all again in Court dress at 11 this morning to go to the Palace and present our *felicitations* to the Imperial couple. It seems there was some misunderstanding about our being received this morning, so some of our colleagues had come, and gone, rather put out at the vagueness of the instructions. We decided to remain, as we had arrived in all our finery, particularly as one of the chamberlains told us it would be most interesting. Deputations from the provinces were to present addresses of *felicitations* and we would see all the national costumes.

As we had some time to wait, the Greek chamberlain suggested that we should take advantage of the opportunity to be presented to the Queen of Greece. He thought he could arrange it, so he went off to her rooms, and presently appeared with a maid of honour, Mlle. Colocotroni (a friend of Gertrude's), and we were taken at once to the Queen, who was standing in a small salon overlooking the river. She is young and handsome, fair, stoutish, but tall enough to carry it off well, and was chatty and sympathetic—said she supposed I was quite tired after yesterday, that it certainly was very trying; that the person who was the least tired was the Empress.

As soon as our audience was over we returned to the large audience hall, where we found Benckendorff tearing his hair out, in a wild state, because we were late—all our colleagues had taken their places. However we were in time, and arranged ourselves, the ladies all together on the right, the men opposite. I was the Doyenne, and stood at the head of the column. All about the room were groups of people from the provinces waiting their turn, but there was such a crowd of uniforms and costumes that one could hardly distinguish anything.

Presently, the Court appeared—the Emperor always in uniform, the Empress in a very handsome train, blue velvet, embroidered in gold, and a splendid tiara, necklace and front of sapphires. They had the usual train of Princes, chamberlains, aides-de camp, etc. As soon as they had taken their places on the platform all the Missions (men) advanced according to their rank, the Ambassador made a few steps forward, said a few words of *felicitation* to the Emperor (the Mission remaining at a respectful distance behind), then made a low bow, and all retired *reculons*.

As soon as all the men of the Corps Diplomatique had passed the Empress left her place and came to us. Her train was carried by 4 pages, a high official, red velvet and gold lace, carrying the extreme end. She passed down the line of ladies, saying something to each one. I heard her speak three languages—English, French, and German—quite easily.

We waited until the Court retired, and then there was the usual stampede for the carriages. I have not been out this afternoon. We start for our Court ball at 8:45, and of course dine early.

To H.L.K.

Ambassade de France à Moscou, Maison Klein, Malaia Dimitrofska

Mardi, 29 Mai, 1883.

I will begin my letter while I am waiting to go with some of the gentlemen and Benckendorff to see the preparations for the great people's *fête*. I couldn't write last night, I was so tired out. Two court dresses and functions, and hours of standing is a good deal for one day. We started early, at a quarter to 9. We assembled in the same room in the old Kremlin where the Imperial couple had dined this afternoon. Almost all our colleagues and some of the swell Russians were already there, and everyone moved about, talking and looking until the welcome strains of the march told us the Emperor and Empress were coming.

The Court appeared always with the same brilliant suite—the Empress looked charming in a pink velvet train, embroidered in silver. All the Grand Duchesses in *drap d'argent*, bordered with beautiful black sable.

As soon as the Court arrived the polonaise began; the Emperor making the first with Queen of Greece, the Empress with Schweinitz. It was a charming sight. All the trains were *étalées* their full length. The gentleman takes his partner's hand, holding it very high, and they make stately progress through the rooms. I didn't dance the first one. We had a very good view of the whole thing. It was a beautiful sight—the men all in uniform, with orders, and broad ribbons; and the women with their trains down the full length. The Russian trains, of white and silver bordered with fur, made a great effect.

The Emperor danced with the Queen of Greece, Arch Duchess Charles Louis, and the Ambassadrices Lady Thornton, Mdme. Juarès, Countess Dudzeele, and me—the Empress with the six Ambassadors. I danced the second polonaise with the Grand Duke Wladimir, who is handsome and spirited looking. He told me who many of the people were. In one of the rooms were all the Russian women, not in costume, but in ordinary ball dress, all however, wearing the Kokoshnik studded with jewels, and most becoming it was.

I rather enjoyed my polonaise with the Emperor. He showed me quantities of people—a splendid man from some part of Asia dressed in white, with jewels, coloured stones mostly, all down the front of his coat, and pistols in his belt with jeweled hilts. Also the Khan of Khiva, with all the front of his high fur cap covered with jewels, also his belt, which seemed made entirely of diamonds and rubies.

The music was always the march from Glinka's opera; each band in turn taking it up as the *cortége* passed though the rooms. The last polonaise finished about 11:30, and the Court immediately retired. We had no refreshments of any kind and made the same rush for our carriages.

5 o'clock

We had rather an interesting afternoon. We met one of the committee at the place, sort of great plain, or meadow, where the Fête Populaire is to be, near the Petrofski Palace, where the Emperor stayed before he made his public *entrée* into Moscow, who showed us everything. There are quantities of little sheds or *baraques*, where everybody (and there will be thousands, he tells us) will receive a basket with a meat paté, a paté of confitures, a cake, and a package of bonbons. There are also great barrels of beer where everyone can go with a mug and drink as much as he can hold.

We asked M. (I forget his name) how it was possible to take precautions with such a crowd of people, but he said they anticipated no danger, it was the "People's day," which sounded to us rather optimistic. It was rather nice driving about.

Now I have just been, at the request of Lhermite, to look at his table, as we have our first big dinner to-night (all Russians); all the flowers, "Roses de France," have just arrived from Paris—three nights on the road; they look quite fresh and beautiful—were packed alone in large hampers. I shall wear my blue tulle ball-dress to-night, as we go to the ball at the Governor's Palace after dinner.

Wednesday, 30th

Our dinner was pleasant last night. As it was entirely Russian we had the curious meal they all take just before dinner. A table was spread in the small salon opening into the dining-room, with smoked and salted fish, caviar, cucumbers, anchovies, etc. They all partook, and then we passed into the dining-room, where the real business began. I sat between M. de Giers, Foreign Minister, and Count Worontzoff, Ministre de la Cour. They were very pleasant, and rather amusing over the exigencies of the suits of the foreign Princes: the smaller the Power the more important the chamberlains, equerries, etc. ... Both gentlemen were very complimentary over the dinner and flowers—asked where in Moscow we had been able to find them, and could hardly believe they had arrived this morning, three nights and three days on the road.

The guests went off about 10; and we half an hour later to the great ball. I wore my light blue tulle with silver braid; the crowd and heat was something awful—the staircase was a regular *bousculade*, and I was thankful those big Russian spurs merely tore my flounces, and didn't penetrate any further. We finally arrived, struggling and already exhausted, in the ballroom, where we found all the Grand Dukes and Grand Duchesses already assembled to receive the Emperor.

We had some little time to wait, so they all came over and talked to us. The Queen of Greece is most attractive—so simple. ... We soon heard the sound of the March, and then there was a rush towards the door by which the Emperor and Empress were to enter that we quickly withdrew into the embrasure of the window and let the torrent pass. ... The crowd was dense. W. and I made our way quickly to the head of the stairs and waited there as they had told us the Emperor would not stay long—merely make a tour through the rooms.

They appeared very soon, shook hands with us both, and seemed very glad to get away. ... It is rather pretty to see the Grand Duke Wladimir *always* close to his brother to shield him from any danger. We were all rather cross when we got home.

This morning I have been shopping with W., Richard and Pontécoulant. It is rather an unsatisfactory performance, as we can't either speak or understand Russian. In the bazaars and real Moscow shops they know nothing but Russian. We take the little polygot boy with us but as he invariably announces "*la grande Ambassade*" we see the prices go up. Richard was quite fascinated with the Madonnas, with their black faces and wands, set in a handsome frame of gold, with light blue enamel. He bought two, one for Louise and one for me, which I am delighted to have. We bought various little boxes, some of lacquer, others in silver, rather prettily worked, and a variety of fancy spoons, buckles, etc.

I must stop now and dress. We dine at 6, so as to be at the Opéra at 9. We shall go "*en gala*," our three carriages, as it is a fine warm night. The detective is a little anxious for to-night (it would be such a good opportunity to get rid of all the Russian Princes, to say nothing of the foreigners). He and Pontécoulant suggested to W. that I should be left at home, but I protested vigorously. If they all go, I am going too. I don't feel very nervous, I wonder why; for it really is a little uncomfortable—unusual to hesitate about going to the Opéra because one might be blown up.

To H.L.K.

Jeudi, May 31st, 1883

I was too tired to write last night, though the opera was over fairly early. It was a beautiful sight, the house brilliantly lighted and crowded, nothing but uniforms, orders, and jewels. There was one dark box, which of course attracted much attention; the Americans—all the men in black, except the three naval officers (we were *acclamés* all along the route, and I must say Leroy and Hubert looked very well in their tricornes and powdered wigs). I wore the crème embroidered velvet with blue satin front, tiara, and blue feathers in my hair. ... I fancy Philippe had made a sort of tower on the top of my head, but he again assured me I must have a *"coiffure de circonstance."*

The square before the Opéra was brilliantly lighted (they certainly light most beautifully in Russia— thousands of candles everywhere), a red carpet down and quantities of palms and flowers—always also quantities of gilded gentlemen. We didn't wait very long for the Court to appear—about a quarter of an hour—and were much taken up looking at everything, and everybody, and trying to recognize our friends. A large box at one end of the house, opposite the stage, was reserved for the Royalties, all draped of course in red and gold.

Everyone rose when the Emperor and Empress arrived, always with their brilliant cortége of Princes. One of the most striking uniforms was the Prince of Montenegro's, but they all made a fine show, and a most effective background for the women—the orchestra playing the Russian Hymn, the chorus singing it, all the house applauding, and all eyes fixed on the Royal box.

It was really magnificent, and the Emperor looked pleased. They gave the first act of Glinka's opera *"La Vie Pour le Czar."* When the curtain fell the whole house rose again; and when the Emperor and Empress left their box, there was a general movement among the people, and some of our colleagues had come to pay us a visit when Count Worontzoff (Ministre de Cour) appeared and said, *"Sa Majesté,"* hoped we would come and have tea with her, and he would have the honour of showing us the way; so he gave me his arm and took me to the foyer, which was very well arranged with flowers, plants, and red carpets.

We stayed, I should think, about half an hour at the tea-table, and then went back to the theatre. The ballet was long, but interesting, all the mazurkas of the Empire were danced in costume. We got our carriages easily enough and the arrangements were good.

CHAPTER EIGHT

~

Isabel F. Hapgood

An American Tourist in Russia

Isabel Florence Hapgood was a linguist, author, editor, and translator of Russian and French works. She was an ecumenist and a lifelong Episcopalian with a consuming interest in Russian Orthodoxy, Russian liturgical music, and choral singing. That interest developed as a result of her many trips to Russia.

Isabel's father, Asa, was an inventor, and her mother's family were of English descent. The couple settled in Worcester, Massachusetts, where they raised their three children. Isabel and her twin brother, also named Asa, were born in Boston on November 21, 1851, and they had a younger brother named William. Isabel was educated at Worcester Collegiate Institute in 1863 and 1864 and then attended Miss Porter's School in Farmington, Connecticut, graduating in 1868. She had a flair for languages and over the years learned and spoke Russian, Polish, German, and several Romance languages. She also had knowledge of Church Slavonic, which was the language of the Orthodox Liturgy.

Fascinated with Russian history and the language, she traveled in Russia with her mother from 1887 to 1889. During this first long trip, she visited St. Petersburg, Tsarskoe Selo, Moscow, Kiev, Kazan, Niznhi Novgorod, and Yaroslavl and cruised the Volga River. The two women stayed at an estate of a prince in the countryside, visiting Count Leo Tolstoy at his home in Moscow and at his estate, Yasnaya Polyana, in the country during the summer. Isabel returned to Russia several times after her initial trip.

Once she returned to the United States, Isabel wrote articles for *The New York Evening Post*, *The Atlantic*, and the *Nation* for twenty-two years and translated and published Tolstoy's and Gogol's short stories. She also compiled *Epic Songs of Russia* and contributed to the *Book of Ballads* by Professor Francis James Child. In addition, she translated the works of Victor Hugo from French.

Continuing her interest in Russian Church music, Isabel began a project translating the Russian Orthodox Liturgy and acapella choral music for American listeners. She enlisted the support of Archbishop Tikhon of Alaska and the Aleutians Islands in this effort. After the archbishop returned to Russia, she was given a set of Church Slavonic texts by Archbishop Nicholas that she translated and published in 1906. During a trip to Russia in 1916–1917, Isabel visited Tikhon, now Patriarch, in Moscow and worked on a second edition of her work, but when the Russian Revolution happened, she was forced to leave the country. The second edition, endorsed by Patriarch Tikhon, was published in 1922, for which she received $500. This work was followed by a history of Russian Church music, which, unfortunately, was not published and was subsequently lost.

Isabel Hapgood died on June 16, 1928, in New York City and was buried in the family plot in Worcester, Massachusetts. She is commemorated by the Episcopal Church on June 26.

The following selections are from *Russian Rambles*.

〜

Russian Rambles

The Névsky Prospekt

The Prospekt wakes late. It has been up nearly all night, and there is but little inducement to early rising when the sun itself sets such a fashion as nine o'clock for its appearance on the horizon, like a pewter disk, with a well-defined hard rim when he makes his appearance at all. If we take the prospekt at different hours we may gain a fairly comprehensive view of many Russian ways and people, cosmopolitan as the city is.

At half past seven in the morning, the horse-cars which have been resting since ten o'clock in the evening, make a start, running always in groups of three, stopping only at turn abouts. The dvorniki retire from the entrance of the courtyards, where they have been sleeping all night with one eye open, wrapped up in their sheepskin coats. A few shabby izvóstchiks make their appearance somewhat later, in company with small schoolboys in their soldierly uniforms, knapsacks of books on back, and convoyed by servants. Earliest of all are the closed carriages of officials, evidently the most lofty in grade, since it was decided, two or three years ago, by one of the class, that his subordinates could not reasonably be expected to arrive at business before ten or eleven o'clock after they had sat up until daylight over their indispensable club vint—which is Russian whist.

Boots (*muzhiki*) in scarlet cotton blouses, and full trousers of black velveteen, tucked into tall wrinkled boots, dart about to bakery and dairy shop, preparing for their masters' morning tea. Venders of newspapers congregate at certain spots, and charge for their wares in inverse ration to the experience of their customer. By noon everyone is awake. The restaurants are full of breakfasters.

Mass is over, and a funeral passes down the Névsky Prospekt, on its way to the fashionable Alexander Névsky monastery or Novo-Dyevitche convent cemetery. The deceased may have been a minister of state, or a great officer of the Court, or a military man who is accompanied by a warlike pageant. The priests, clad in vestments of black velvet and silver, seem to find their long thick hair sufficient protection to their bare heads. ... The dead man's orders and decorations are borne in imposing state on velvet cushions, before the gorgeous funeral car, where the pall, of cloth of gold which will be made into a priest's vestment once the funeral is over, droops low among artistic wreaths and palms, of natural flowers, or beautifully executed in silver. Behind come the mourners on foot, a few women, many men, a Grand Duke or two among them, it may be ... the devout of the lower classes, catching sight of the train, cross themselves broadly, mutter a prayer, and find time to turn from their own affairs and follow for a little way, out of respect to the stranger corpse.

From noon onward the scene on the Prospekt increases constantly in vivacity. The sidewalks are crowded especially on Sundays and holidays, with a dense and varied throng, of so many nationalities and types that it is a valuable lesson in ethnography to sort them out. ...

The plain facades of the older buildings on this part of the Prospekt, which are but three or four stories in height—elevators are rare luxuries in Petersburg, and few buildings exceed five stories—are adorned, here and there, with gayly-colored pictorial representations of the wares for sale within. Most fascinating of all the shops are those of the furriers and goldsmiths, with their surprises and fresh lessons for foreigners; the treasures of Caucasian and Asian art in the Eastern bazaars; the "Colonial wares" establishments with their delicious game, cheeses, and odd *studena* (fishes in jelly), their tiny oysters from the Black Sea at twelve and a half cents apiece.

Enthralling as are the shop windows, the crowd on the sidewalk is more enthralling still. There are Kazaks, dragoons, cadets of the military schools, students so varied, though their gay uniforms are hidden by their coats. ... There are officers of every sort: officers with rough gray overcoats and round lambskin caps. ... There are civilians in black cape-coats of the military pattern, topped off with cold, uncomfortable, but fashionable chimneypot hats, or, more sensibly, with high caps of beaver.

Most of the ladies, on foot or in sledges, wear *bashlyks* or Orenburg shawls, over wadded fur caps, well pulled down to the brows.

The more fashionable people are driving, however, and that portion of the one hundred and fourteen feet of the Prospekt's width which is devoted to the roadway is, if possible, even more varied and interesting in its kaleidoscopic features than the sidewalks. It is admirably kept at all seasons. With the exception of the cobblestone roadbed for the tramway in the centre, it is laid with hexagonal wooden blocks, well spiked together and tarred, resting on tared beams and planks, and forming a pavement which is both elastic and fairly resistant to the volcanic action of the frost. Street sweepers, in red cotton blouses and clean white linen sweep on calmly in the icy chill. The police, with their *bashlyks* wrapped round their heads in a manner peculiar to themselves, stand always in the middle of the street and regulate traffic.

When spring comes with the magical suddenness which characterizes Northern lands, the gardens, quays, and the Névsky Prospekt still preserve their charms for a space, and are thronged far into the night with promenaders, who gaze at the imperial crowns, stars, monograms, and other devices temporarily applied to the street lanterns, and the fairy flames on the low curb-posts, with which man attempt, on the numerous royal festival days of early summer, to rival the illumination of the indescribably beautiful tints of river and sky.

Experiences with the Russian Censor

In spite of the advantage which I enjoyed in a preliminary knowledge of the Russian language and literature, I was imbued with various false ideas, the origin of which it is not necessary to trace on this occasion. I freed myself from some of them; among others, from my theory as to the working of the censorship in the case of foreign literature. My theory was the one commonly held by Americans, and, as I found to my surprise, by not a few Russians, viz., that books and periodicals which have been wholly or in part condemned by the censor are to be procured only in a mutilated condition, or by surreptitious means, or not at all. That this is not the case; I acquired ample proof through my personal experience.

"Do you really let people have these forbidden books?" "Certainly," was his half-surprised, half-indignant reply. "And what can one have?" "Anything," said he, "only we must, of course, have some knowledge of the person. What would you like?"

I could only express my regret that I felt no craving for any prohibited literature at that moment, but I told him I would endeavor to cultivate a taste in that direction to oblige him; and I suggested that, as his knowledge of me was confined to the last ten minutes, I did not quite understand how he could pass judgement as to what mental and moral food was suited to my constitution, and as to the use I might make of it. He laughed amicably, and said: "*Nitchevó*—that's all right; you may have whatever you please." I never had occasion to avail myself of the offer, but I know that Russians who are well posted do so, although I know that many Russians are not aware of their privileges in this direction. It is customary to require from Russians who receive literature of this sort a promise they will let no other person see it—an engagement which is as religiously observed as might be expected, as the authorities are doubtless aware.

During the whole of my stay in Russia, I received many books unread, apparently even unopened to see whether they belonged on the free list. In one case, at least, volumes which were posted before the official date of publication reached me by the next city delivery after the letter announcing their dispatch. Books which were addressed to me at the Legation, to assure delivery when my exact address was unknown or when my movements were uncertain, were, in every case but one, sent to me direct from the post-office. I have no reason to suppose that I was unusually favored in any way. I used no "influence"; I mentioned no influential names, though I had the right to do so.

I once asked a member of the censorship committee on foreign books on what principle of selection he proceeded. He said that disrespect to the Emperor and the Greek Church was officially prohibited; that he admitted everything which did not err too grossly in that direction, and, in fact, *everything* except French novels of the modern realistic school. He drew the line at these, as pernicious to both men and women.

Bargaining in Russia

In Russia one is expected to bargain and haggle over the price of everything, beginning with hotel accommodations, no matter how obtrusively large may be the type of the sign, *Prix Fixe*, or how strenuous may be the assertions that the bottom price is the first named. If one's nerves be too weak to play at this game of continental poker, he will probably share our fate, of which we were politely apprised by a word at our departure from a hotel where we had lived for three months—after due bargaining—at their price: "If you come back, you may have the corresponding apartments on the first floor below (the *bel étage*) for the same price." In view of the fact that there was no elevator, it will be perceived that we had been paying from one third to one half too much, which was reassuring as to the prospect for the future, when we should decide to return!

The next time I had occasion to hire quarters in a hotel for a sojourn of any length I resorted to stratagem, by way of giving myself an object lesson. I looked at the rooms, haggled them down, on principle, to what seemed to me really the very lowest notch of price; I was utterly worn out before this was accomplished. I even flattered myself that I had done nearly as well as a native could have done, and was satisfied. But I sternly carried out my experiment. I did not close the bargain. I asked Princess _____ to try her experienced hand. Result, she secured the best accommodations in the house for less than half the rate at which I had been so proud of obtaining inferior quarters! When we moved in, the landlord was surprised, but he grasped the point of the transaction, and seemed to regard it as a pleasant jest against him, and to respect us the more for having outwitted him. The Princess apologized for having made such bad terms for us, and meant it! I suspect that that was a very fair sample of the comparative terms obtained by natives and outsiders in all bargains.

From the zest with which I have beheld a shopman and a customer waste half an hour chaffering an article up and down five kopecks (two and a half cents or less), I am convinced that they enjoy the excitement of it, and that time is cheap enough with them to allow them to indulge in this exhilarating practice.

Any one who really likes bargaining will get his fill in Russia, every time he sets his foot out of doors, if he wishes merely to take a ride. There are days, it is true, when all the cabmen in town seem to have entered into a league and agreed to demand a ruble for a drive of a half a dozen blocks; and, again, though rarely, they will offer to carry one mile for one fifth of that sum, which is equally unreasonable in the other direction. In either case, one has his bargaining sport, at one end of the journey or the other.

Tsar Alexander III

So much has been said about the habits of the late Emperor Alexander III, in his capital, that a brief statement of them will not be out of place, especially as I had one or two experiences, in addition to the ordinary opportunities afforded by a long visit and knowledge of the language and manners of the people.

When the Emperor was in St Petersburg, he drove about freely every day like a private person. He was never escorted or attended by guards. In place of

Левицкій
на Мойкѣ, 30 С. Петербургъ.

Tsar Alexander III
Library of Congress

a lackey a Kazák orderly sat beside the coachman. The orderlies of no other
military men wore the Kazák uniform. Any one acquainted with this fact,
or with the Emperor's face, could recognize him as he passed. There was no
other sign; even the soldiers, policemen, and gendarmes gave him the same
salute which they gave to every general. At Peterhoff, in summer, he often

drove, equally unescorted, to listen to the music in the palace park, which was open to the public.

On the regular festivals and festivities, such as St. George's Day, New Year's Day, The Epiphany (the "Jordan," or Blessing of the Néva), the state balls, Easter, and so forth, every one knew where to look for the Emperor, and at what hour. The official notifications in the morning papers, informing members of the Court at what hour and place to present themselves, furnished a good guide to the Emperor's movements for any one who did not already know.

I was driving down the Névsky Prospékt on the afternoon of New Year's Day, 1889, when, just at the gate of the Anítchkoff Palace, a policeman raised his hand, and my sledge and the whole line behind me halted. I looked round to see the reason, and beheld the Emperor and Empress sitting beside me in the semi-state cream-colored carriage, painted with a big coat of arms, its black hood studded with golden doubleheaded eagles, which the present Emperor used on his wedding day. A coachman, postilion, and footman constituted the sole "guard," while the late prefect, General Gresser, in an open calash a quarter of a mile behind, constituted the "armed escort." ... When cabinet ministers or high functionaries of the Court died, the Emperor and Empress attended one of the services before the funeral, and the funeral. Thousands of people calculated the hour, and the best spot to see them with absolute accuracy. At one such funeral, just after rumors of a fresh "plot" had been rife, I saw the great crowd surge up with a cheer towards the Emperor's carriage, though the Russians are very quiet in public. The police who were guarding the route of the procession stood still and smiled approvingly.

A Russian Summer Resort

The spring was late and cold. I wore my fur-lined cloak (shúba) and wrapped up my ears, by Russian advice as well as by inclination, until late in May. But we were told that the summer heat would catch us suddenly, and that St. Petersburg would become malodorous and unhealthy. It was necessary, owing to circumstances, to find a healthy residence for the summer, which should not be too far removed from the capital. With a few exceptions, all the environs of St. Petersburg are damp. ... In Tzárskoe, as in Peterhoff, villa life is the only variety accepted by polite society. ... We decided in favor of Tzárskoe, as it is called in familiar conversation. As one approaches the imperial village, it rises like a green oasis from the plain. It is hedged in, like a true Russian village, but with trees and bushes well trained instead of with a wattled fence. ... It is situated sixteen miles from St. Petersburg, on the line of the first railway built in Russia, which to this day extends only a couple of miles beyond—for lack of the necessity of farther extension.

Before making acquaintance with the famous palaces and parks, we undertook to settle ourselves for the time being, at least. It appeared that "furnished" villas are so called in Tzárskoe, as elsewhere, because they require to be almost completely furnished by the occupant on a foundation of bare bones of furniture, consisting of a few bedsteads and tables. This was not convenient for travelers, so we determined to try to live in another way. But we had been told of an establishment which rejoiced in the proud title of *gostínnitza*, "hotel," in city fashion. It looked fairly good, and there we took up our abode, after due and inevitable chaffering. ... Its only recommendation was that it was situated near a very desirable gate into the Imperial Park.

The Market at Tzárskoe Seló

The scene at the market was always entertaining. Tzárskoe is surrounded by market gardens, where fruits and vegetables are raised in highly manured and excessively hilled-up beds. It sends tons of its products to the capital as well as to the local market. Everything was cheap and delicious. Eggs were dear when they reached a cent and a half apiece. Strawberries, huge and luscious, were dear at ten cents a pound, since in warm seasons they cost but five.

The native cherries, small and sour, make excellent preserves, with a spicy flavor much liked by the Russians in their tea. ... Pears do not thrive so far north, but in good years apples of fine sorts are raised, to a certain extent, in the vicinity of St. Petersburg. ... Apples, plums, grapes, and honey are not eaten—in theory—until after they have been blessed at the Feast of the Transfiguration, on August 18 (N.S.)—a very good scheme for giving them time to ripen fully for health.

When the mushroom season came in, the market assumed an aspect of half-subdued brilliancy with the many somber and high-colored varieties of that fungus. The poorer people indulge in numerous kinds which the rich do not eat, and they furnish precious sustenance during fasts, when so many viands are forbidden by the Russian Church and by poverty.

Pentecost in the Orthodox Church

One of the great festivals of the Russian Church is Whitsunday, the seventh Sunday after Easter; but it is called Trinity Sunday, and the next day is "the Day of the Spirits," or Pentecost. On this Pentecost Day, a curious sight was formerly to be seen in St. Petersburg. Mothers belonging to the merchant class arrayed their marriageable daughters in their best attire; hung about their necks not only all the jewels which formed a part of their dowries, but also, it is said, the silver ladles, forks, and spoons; and took them to the Summer Garden, to be inspected and proposed for by the young men.

But the place where this spectacle can be seen in the most charming way is Tzárskoe Seló. We were favored with superb weather on both the festal days. On Sunday morning every one went to church, as usual. The small church behind the Lyceum, where Pushkin was educated, with its un-Russian spire, ranks as a Court church; that in the Old Palace across the way being opened only on special occasions, now that the Court is not in residence. Outside, the choir sat under the golden rain of acacia blossoms and the hedge of fragrant lilacs until the last moment the sunshine throwing into relief their gold-laced black cloth vestments and crimson belts. They were singers from one of the regiments stationed in town, and crimson was the regimental color. The church is accessible to all classes, and it was crowded. As at Easter, every one was clad in white or light colors, even those who were in mourning having donned the bluish-gray which serves them for festive garb. In place of the Easter candle, each held a bunch of flowers. In the corners of the church stood young birch-trees, with their satin bark and feathery foliage, and boughs of the same decked the walls. There is a law now which forbids the annual destruction of young trees at Pentecost, but the practice continues, and the tradition is that one must shed as many tears for his sins as there are dewdrops on the birch bough which he carries, if it has no flowers. Peasant women in clean cotton gowns elbowed members of the Court in silk; fat merchants, with well-greased, odorous hair and boots in hot, long-skirted blue cloth coats, stood side by side with shabby invalid soldiers or smartly uniformed officers. Tiny peasant children seated themselves on the floor when their little legs refused further service, and imitated diligently all the low reverences and signs of the cross made by their parents. Those of larger growth stood with preternatural repose and dignity of the adult Russian peasant, and followed the liturgy independently. ... After the ever beautiful liturgy, finely expressed special prayers were offered, during which the priest also carried flowers.

Russian Children

What strikes one very forcibly about Russian children, when one sees them at play in the parks, is their quiet, self-possessed manners and their lack of boisterousness. If they were inclined to scream to fling themselves about wildly and be rude they would assuredly be checked promptly and effectually, since the rights of grown people to peace, respect, and the pursuit of happiness are still recognized in that land. But, from my observation of the same qualities in untutored peasant children, I am inclined to think that Russian children are born more agreeable than Western children; yet they seem to be as cheerful and lively as is necessary and in no way restricted.

A Meeting with Tolstoy in Moscow

I had been discussing matters with the count, while the others joined in from time to time. It began with the Moscow beggars.

"I understand them now, and what you wrote of them," I said. "I have neither the purse of Fortunatus nor a heart of flint. If I refuse their prayers, I feel wicked; if I give them five kopecks, I feel mean. It seems too little to help them to anything but *vódka*; and if I give ten kopecks, they hold it out at arm's length, look at it and me suspiciously; and then I feel so provoked that I give not a copper to any one for days. It seems to do no good."

Count Leo Tolstoy
Library of Congress

"No," said Count Tolstóy with a troubled look, "it does no good," Giving money to any one who asks is not doing good; it is a mere civility. If a beggar asks me for five kopecks, or five rubles, or five hundred rubles, I must give it to him as a politeness, nothing more, provided I have it about me. It probably always goes for *vódka*."

"But what is one to do? I have sometimes thought that I would buy my man some bread and see that he ate it when he specifies what the money is for. But, by a singular coincidence, they never ask for bread money within eye-shot of a bakery. I suppose that it would be better for me to take the trouble to hunt one up and give the bread."

"No. For you only buy the bread. It costs you no personal labor."

"But suppose I had made the bread? I can make capital bread, only I can-not make it here where I have no conveniences; so I give the money instead."

"If you had made the bread, still you would not have raised the grain—plowed, sowed, reaped, threshed, and ground it. It would not be your labor."

"If that is the case, then I have just done a very evil thing. I have made some caps for the Siberian exiles in the Forwarding Prison. It would have been better to let their shaved heads freeze."

"Why? You gave your labor, your time. In that time you could probably have done something that would have pleased you better."

"Certainly. But if one is to dig up the roots of one's deeds and motives, mine might be put thus: The caps were manufactured from remnants of wool which were of no use to me and only encumbered my trunk. I refused to go and deliver them myself. They were put with a lot of other caps made from scraps on equally vicious principles. And, moreover, I neither plowed the land, sowed the grass, fed the sheep, sheared him, and cleansed and spun the wool, and so on; neither did I manufacture the needle for the work."

The count retreated to his former argument, that one's personal labor is the only righteous thing which can be given to one's fellow-man; and that the labor must be given unquestioningly when asked for.

I am aware that it has become customary of late to call Count Tolstóy "crazy" or "not quite right in the head," etc. The inevitable conclusion of any one who talks much with him is that he is nothing of the sort; but simply a man with a hobby, or an idea. His idea happens to be one which, granting that it ought to be adopted by everybody, is still one which is very difficult of adoption by anybody—peculiarly different in his own case. And it is an uncomfortable theory of self-denial which very few people like to have preached to them in any form. Add to this that his philosophical expositions of his theory lack the clearness which generally—not always—results from a course of strict preparatory training, and we have more than sufficient foundation for the reports of his mental aberration. On personal acquaintance he proves to be a remarkably earnest, thoroughly convinced, and winning man, although he does not deliberately do or say anything to attract one. His very earnestness is provocative of argument.

Visit to Yásnaya Polyána and Praise for Sophia Tolstóy

On a winter's day in Moscow, the Countess Tolstóy said to me: "You must come and visit us at Yásnaya Polyána next summer. You should see Russian country life, and you will see it with us. Our house is not elegant, but you will find it plain, clean and comfortable." Such an invitation was not to be resisted.

Decidedly, the Countess Sophia Tolstóy is one of those truly feminine heroines who are cast into shadow by a brilliant light close to them, but a heroine none the less in more ways than need be mentioned. Her self-denial and courage gave to the world *War and Peace* and *Anna Karenina*; and she declares that were it to do over again she would not hesitate a moment. The public owes the count's wife a great deal of gratitude, and not of reproaches, for bravely opposing his fatal desire to live in every detail the life of a peasant laborer. Can any one blessed with the faintest particle of imagination fail to perceive how great a task it has been to withstand him thus for his own good; to rear nine healthy, handsome, well-bred children out of the much larger family which they have had; to bear the entire responsibility of the household and the business?

She remarked, one day, that there was no crying need for the Russian nobility to follow her husband's teachings and give away all their goods in order to be on a level with the peasants. Plenty of them would soon attain the blissful state of poverty in the natural course of things, since they were not only growing poorer every year, but the distribution of inheritance among the numerous children was completing the work, and very many would be reduced to laboring with their hands for a living. This is perfectly true. There is no law of primogeniture in Russia. The one established by Peter the Great having produced divers and grievous evils, besides being out of harmony with the Russian character, was withdrawn. All the male children share equally in the father's estate as in title. The female children receive by law only an extremely small portion of the inheritance, but their dowry is not limited.

After breakfast I sometimes sat under the trees with the countess, and helped her sew on baby Iván's clothes, for the pleasure of her conversation. Nothing could be more fascinating. This beautiful woman has not rusted during her long residence in the country. There are few better educated women than she, few better women of business, few women who are so clever and practical.

Tolstóy on Religion

In these excursions the count came to see how great a part religion plays in the life of the lower classes; and he argued that, in order to get in sympathy with them, one must share their ideas as to religion. Accordingly he plunged into it with his customary ardor, "he has a passionate nature"—and for several years he attended every church service, observed every rite, kept every fast, and so on. He thought it horrible if those about him did not do the same, if they neglected a single form. I think it quite probable that he initiated the trouble with his stomach by these fasts.

His religious ardor lasted until he went to church one day, during the Russo-Turkish war, when prayers were offered for the success of the Russian army. It suddenly struck him that it was inconsistent with "Love your enemies," "Love one another," "Do Not Kill," that prayers should be offered for the death of enemies. From that day forth he ceased to go to church, as he had also perceived that the practice of religious forms did not, in reality, bring him much nearer to the peasants, and that one must live among them, work among them, to appreciate their point of view.

The only surprising thing about this is that he should never have noticed that the army is prayed for, essentially in the same sense, at every church service.

But Count Tolstóy was logical, also, in another way. Once started on this train of thought, most worldly institutions of the present day, beginning with the army, appeared to him opposed to the teachings of Christ, on which point no rational man will differ from him. As to the possibility of living the life of Christ, or even the advisability of trying it, at this period of the world, that is quite another matter.

Tolstóy's Philosophy

The question naturally follows: If the countess holds the property, and the count continues to get the good of it, in a modest way; if the count does not do everything for himself, and earn his daily bread by manual toil, is not he mentally unbalanced to proclaim his theories to the world, and to change his mind so often on other points?

The answer is: No. Undoubtedly the count, when he attained to his convictions on the subject of poverty and labor, hoped to carry his family with him. The countess, like a brave woman, like a devoted wife and mother, refused to adopt his views. She is willing to shoulder the responsibility of her refusal, and her conduct is an honor to her. As for his changes of doctrine, we are all very much like him in the matter of inconsistency. Only, as very few of us enjoy the renown or the authority of Count Tolstóy, it rarely occurs to us to proclaim our progressive opinions to the world; at most, one or two experiences cure us of that weakness, even if any one thinks it worthwhile to notice them in the slightest degree.

The case is precisely the reverse with Count Tolstóy. He is so full of the missionary spirit, so persuaded of the truth and value of his beliefs, that he rushes into print with them instantly. There they are, all ready for those who do not sympathize with him to use as missiles when he gets a new inspiration.

The Holy City of Kiev

I know no town in Russia which makes so picturesque and characteristic an impression on the traveler as Kieff. From the boundless plain over which we were speeding, we gazed up at wooded heights crowned and dotted with churches. At the foot of the slope, where golden domes and crosses, snowy white monasteries and battlemented walls, gleamed among masses of foliage punctuated with poplars, swept the broad Dneyépr. It did not seem difficult then to enter into the feelings of Prince Oleg when he reached the infant town, on his expedition from infertile Nóvgorod the Great, of the north, against Byzantíum, and coveting its rich beauty, slew its rulers and entered into possession, saying, "This shall be the Mother of all Russian cities." We could understand the sentiments of the pilgrims who flock to the Holy City by the million.

It is easy to forgive St. Petersburg, in its giddy youth of one hundred and seventy-five winters, for its western features and comforts; but that Kieff, in its venerable maturity of a thousand summers, should be so spick and span with newness and reformation seemed at first utterly unpardonable. The inhabitants think otherwise, no doubt, and deplore the medieval hygienic conditions which render the town the most unhealthy in Europe, in the matter of the death-rate from infectious diseases.

But the chief charm, unfailing, inexhaustible as the sight of the ocean, is the view from the cliffs. Beyond the silver sweep of the river at their feet, animated with steamers and small boats, stretches the illimitable steppe, where the purple and emerald shadows of the sea depths and shallows are enriched with hues of golden or velvet brown and misty blue. The steppe is no longer an unbroken expanse of waving plume-grass and flowers, wherein riders and horses are lost to sight as in Gógol's celebrated tale, as were Taras Bulba and his sons, fresh from the famous Academy of Kieff, which lies at our feet, below the cliffs. Increasing population has converted this virgin soil into vast grainfields, less picturesque near at hand than the wild growth, but still deserving, from afar, Gógol's enraptured apostrophe: "Devil take you, steppe, how beautiful you are!"

The Petchérskaya Lávra

Naturally, our first pilgrimage was to the famous Kíevo-Petchérskaya Lávra, that is, the First-Class Monastery of the Kieff Catacombs, the chief monastery institution and the goal of pilgrims in all the country, of which we had caught a glimpse from the opposite shore of the river, as we approached the town. Buildings have not extended so densely in this direction but that a semblance of ascetic retirement is still preserved.

Monks Living Quarters

He informed me that from seven hundred to one thousand persons lived in the monastery. Not all of them were monks, some being only lay brethren. Each monk, however, had his own apartments, with a little garden attached, and the beautiful rugs which I had seen formed part of their cells. A man cannot enter the monastery without money, but fifty rubles (about twenty-five dollars) are sufficient to gain him admittance. Some men leave the monastery after a brief trial, without receiving the habit.

Breakfast in the Monastery

It occurred to us that it might prove an interesting experiment to try the monastery inn for breakfast, and even to sojourn there a day or two and abandon the open sewers and other traces of advanced civilization in the town. Our way thither led past the free lodgings for poor pilgrims, which were swarming with the devout of both sexes, although it was not the busiest season for shrine-visiting. But there was a sufficient contingent of the annual one million pilgrims present to give us a very fair idea of the reverence in which this, the chief of all Russian monasteries, is held and of the throngs it attracts. But, as usual in Russia, sight alone convinced us of their existence; they were chatting quietly, sitting and lying about with enviable calmness, or eating the sour black bread and boiled buckwheat groats provided by the monastery. I talked with several of them and found them quite unconscious that they were not comfortably, even luxuriously, housed and fed.

Monks at the Refectory

At last, a score of monks entered, chanted a prayer at a signal from a small bell, and seated themselves on benches affixed to the wall which ran round three sides of the room. The napkins on the table which stood before the benches consisted of long towels, each of which lay across four or five of the pewter platters from which they ate, as the table was set in preparation. If it had been a festal day, there would have been several courses, with beer, mead, and even wine to wash them down. As it was, the monks ate their black bread and boiled buckwheat groats, served in huge dishes, with their wooden spoons, and drank kvass, brewed from sour black bread, at a signal from the bell, after the first dish only, as the rule requires. While they ate, a monk, stationed at a desk nearby, read aloud the extracts from the Lives of the Saints appointed for the day. This was one of the "sights," but we found it curious and melancholy to see strong, healthy men turned into monks and content with that meagre fair. Frugality and dominion over the flesh are good, of course, but minds from west of the Atlantic Ocean never seem quite to get into sympathy with the monastic idea; and we always felt, when we met monks, as though they all ought to be at work somewhere—I will not say "earning money," for they do that as it is in such great monasteries as that of Kieff, but lightening the burden of the peasants, impossible as that is under present conditions, or making themselves of some commonplace, practical use in the world.

Russian Liturgical Music in the Cathedral
of Saint Sophia at the Lávra

I stood among the pillars, a little removed from the principal aisle, one afternoon near sunset, listening to the melodious intoning of the priest, and the soft chanting of the small week-day choir at vespers, and wondering, for the thousandth time, why Protestants who wish to intone do not take lessons from those incomparable masters in the art, the Russian deacons, and wherein lies the secret of the Russian ecclesiastical music. That simple music, so perfectly fitted for church music, will bring the most callous into a devotional mood long before the end of the service. Rendered as it is invariably by male voices, with superb basses in place of the non-existent organ, it spoils one's taste forever for the elaborate, operatic church music of the West performed by choirs which are usually engaged in vocal steeplechases with the organ for the enhancement of the evil effects.

Kazan

If Kazan is an article for the creed of all Russians, whether they have ever seen it or not, Mátushka Vólga (dear Volga) is a complete system of faith. Certainly her services in building up and binding the empire merit it, though the section thus usually referred to comprises only the stretch between Nízhni Nóvgorod and Astrakan, despite its historical and commercial importance above the former town.

But Kazan! A stay there of a day and a half served to dispel our illusions. We were deceived in our expectations as to the once mighty capital of the imperial Tartár Khans. The recommendations of our Russian friends, the glamour of history which had bewitched us, the hope of the Western for something Oriental—all these elements had combined to raise our expectations in a way against which our sober senses and previous experiences should have warned us. It seemed to us merely a flourishing and animated Russian provincial town, whose Kremlin was eclipsed by that of Moscow, and whose university had instructed, but not graduated, Count Tolstóy, the novelist. The bazaar under arcades, the popular market in the open square, the public gardens, the shops—all were but a repetition of similar features in other towns, somewhat magnified to the proportions befitting the dignity of the home port of the Urál Mountains and Siberia.

The Tartár quarter alone seemed to possess the requisite mystery and "local color." Here whole streets of tiny shops, ablaze with rainbow-colored leather goods, were presided over by taciturn, olive-skinned brothers of the Turks, who appeared almost handsome when seen thus in masses, with opportunities for comparison. Hitherto we had thought of the Tartárs only as old-clothes dealers, peddlers, horse-butchers, and waiters of St. Petersburg and Moscow. Here the dignity of the prosperous merchants, gravely recommending their really well-dressed, well-sewed leather wares, bespoke our admiration.

The Tartár women, less easily seen, glided along the uneven pavements now and then, smoothly, but still in a manner to permit a glimpse of short, square feet incased in boots flowered with gay hues upon a green or rose-colored ground, and reaching to the knee. They might have been houris of beauty, but it was difficult to classify them, veiled as they were, and screened as to head and shoulders by striped green *kaftáns* of silk, whose long sleeves depended from the region of their ears, and whose collar rested on the brow.

We found nothing especially striking among the churches, unless one might reckon the Tartár mosques in the list; and, casting a last glance at Sumbeka's curious and graceful tower, we hired a cabman to take us to the river, seven versts away.

We turned our back upon Kazán without regret, in the fervid heat of the midsummer morning. We did not shake its dust from our feet. When dust is ankle-deep that is not very feasible. It rose in clouds, as we met the long lines of Tartár carters, transporting flour and other merchandise to and from the wharves cross the "dam" which connects the town, in summer low water, with Mother Vólga. In spring floods Mátushka Vólga threatens to wash away the very walls of the Kremlin, and our present path is under water.

Haying Season on an Estate by the Vólga

Our life at Prince X's estate on the Vólga flowed on in a semi-monotonous, wholly delightful state of lotus-eating idleness, though it assuredly was not a case which came under the witty description once launched by a Turgeneff broadside at his countrymen: "The Russian country proprietor comes to revel and simmer in his ennui like a mushroom frying in sour cream." Ennui shunned that happy valley. We passed the hot mornings at work on the veranda or in the well-filled library, varying them by drives to neighboring estates and villages, or by trips to the fields to watch the progress of the harvest, now in full swing. Such a visit we paid when all the able-bodied men and women in the village were ranged across the landscape in interminable lines, armed with their reaping-hooks, and forming a brilliant picture in contrast with the yellow grain, in their blue and scarlet raiment. They were fulfilling the contract which bound them to three days labor for their landlord, in return for the pasturage furnished by him for their cattle. A gay kerchief and a single clinging garment, generally made of red and blue in equal portions, constituted the costume of the women. The scanty garments were faded and worn, for harvesting is terribly hard work, and they cannot use their good clothes, as at the haying, which is mere sport in comparison. Most of the men had their heads protected only by their long hair, whose sunburnt outer layer fell over their faces, as they stooped and reaped the grain artistically close to the ground. Their shirts were of faded red cotton; their full trousers, of blue- and red-striped home-made linen, were confined by a strip of coarse crash swathed around the feet and legs to the knee, and cross-gartered by rope. The feet of men and women alike were shod with low shoes of plaited linden bark over these cloths.

They smiled indulgently at our attempts to reap and make girdles for the sheaves—the sickles seemed to grown dull and back-handed at our touch—chatting with the dignified ease which characterizes the Russian peasant. The children had been left behind in the village, in charge of the grandams and the women unfit for field labor.

It was the season which the peasants call by the expressive title *stradá* (suffering). Nearly all the summer work must be done together, and, with their primitive appliances, suffering is the inevitable result. They will set out for the fields before sunrise, and return at indefinite hours, but never early. Sometimes they pass the night in the fields, under the shelter of a cart or the grain sheaves. Men and women work equally and unweariedly; and the women receive less pay than the men for the same work, which is, unhappily, not yet unknown in other lands and ranks of life. Eating and sleeping join the number of the lost arts. The poor, brave people have but little to eat in any case, not enough to induce thought or anxiety to return home. Last year's store has, in all probability, been nearly exhausted. They must wait until the grain they are reaping has been threshed and ground before they can have their fill.

Sundays were kept so far as the field work permitted, and the church was thronged. Even our choir of ill-trained village youths and boys could not spoil the exquisite music. Every one was quiet, clean, reverent.

Incendiaries and horse-thieves are the scourges of village life in Russia. Such men can be banished to Siberia, by a vote of the Commune of peasant house-holders. But as the Commune must bear the expense, and people are afraid that the evil-doer will revenge himself by setting the village on fire, if he discovers their plan, this privilege is exercised with comparative rarity. The man who steals the peasant's horse condemns him to starvation and ruin. Such a man there has been in our friends' village, and for long years they had borne with him patiently. He was crafty and had "influence" in some mysterious fashion, which made him a dangerous customer to deal with. But at last he was sent off. Now, during our visit, the village was trembling over a rumor that he was on his way back to wreak vengeance on his former neighbors. I presume they were obliged to have him banished again, by administrative order from the Minister of the Interior, the only remedy when one of this class of exiles has served out his term—before they could sleep tranquilly.

The Russian Orthodox Church

As I am very much attached to the Russian Church, anything connected with it always interested me deeply. One of the prominent features in Moscow is the number of monasteries and convents. The Russian idea of monastic life is prayer and contemplation, not activity in good works. The ideal of devout secular life is much the same. To meet the wants in that direction of people who do not care to join the community, many of the convents have small inclosures, which they let out to applicants, of whom there is always an abundance. The occupants of these houses are under no restrictions whatever, except as to observing the hours of entry and exit fixed by the opening and closing of the convent gates; but, naturally, it is expected of them that they will attend more church services than the busy people of "the world." The sight of these little houses always oppressed me with a sense of my inferiority in the matter of devoutness. I could not imagine myself living in one of those, until I came across a group of their occupants engaged in discussing some racy gossip with the nuns on one of the doorsteps. Gossip is not my besetting weakness, but I felt relieved. Convents are not the aristocratic institutions in Russia as they are in Roman Catholic countries, and very few ladies by birth and education enter them. Those who do are apt to rise to the position of abbess, influential connections not being superfluous in any calling in Russia any more than in other countries.

The Nízhni Nóvgorod Fair

The far-famed Fair of Nízhni Nóvgorod—"Makáry," the Russians call it, from the town and monastery of St. Makáry, sixty miles further down the Volga, where it was held from 1624 until the present location was adopted in 1824—was a disappointment to us. ... I think that our disappointment was partly our own fault. Had we, like most travelers who have written extravagantly about the Fair, come to it fresh from a stay of (at most) three weeks in St. Petersburg and Moscow only, we should have been much impressed by the variety of types and goods, I have no doubt. But we had spent nearly two years in the land, and were familiar with the types and goods of the capital and of other places, so that there was little that was new to us. Consequently, though we found the Fair very interesting, we were not able to excite ourselves to any extravagant degree of amazement or rapture.

The peculiarity of this Makáry Fair is that nothing is sold by sample, in modern fashion; the whole stock of goods is on hand, and is delivered at once to purchasers. The taciturn, easy-going merchants in those insignificant-looking shops of the Gostínny Dvor "rows," and, to a small extent, in the supplementary town which has sprung up outside the canal, set the prices for tea and goods of all sorts all over Russia and Siberia for the ensuing year. Contracts for the future are dated, and last year's bills fall due, at "Mákary." It is hard to realize.

All the firms with whose shops we had been familiar with in Petersburg and Moscow had establishments here, and, at first, it seemed not worth while to investigate their stocks, with which we felt perfectly acquainted. But we soon discovered that our previous familiarity enabled us to distinguish certain articles which are manufactured for the "Fair" trade exclusively, and which are never even shown in the capitals. For example, the great porcelain houses of St. Petersburg manufacture large pipe-bowls, ewers (with basins to match) of the Oriental shape familiar to the world in silver and brass, and other things all decorated with a deep crimson bordering on magenta, and with gold. The great silk houses of Moscow prepare very rich and very costly brocades of this same deep crimson hue, besprinkled with gold and with tiny bouquets of bright flowers, or in which the crimson is prominent. All these like the pipes and ewers, are made to suit the taste of customers in Bokhara and other Eastern countries, where a man's rank is, to a certain degree, to be recognized by the number and richness of the *khaláti* which he can afford to wear at one time. This is one of the points in which the civilization of the East coincides very nearly with the civilization of the West.

The part of the Fair which is most interesting to foreigners in general, I think, is the great glass gallery filled with retail booths, where Russians sell embroidery and laces and the handiwork of the peasants in general; where Caucasians deal in the beautiful gold and silver work of their native mountains; where swarthy Bokhariots sit cross-legged, with imperturbable dignity, among their gay wares, while the band plays, and the motley crowd bargains and gazes even in the evening when all the other shops are closed.

Yaroslávl

We left the steamer at Yaroslávl (it was bound for Rybinsk), two hundred and forty-one miles above Nízhni Nóvgorod, and got our first view of the town at daybreak. It stands on the high west bank of the river, but it is not so picturesque as Nízhni. Access to the town is had only through half a dozen cuts and ravines, as of Nízhni; and what a singular town it is! With only a little over thirty thousand inhabitants, it has seventy-seven churches, besides monasteries and other ecclesiastical buildings. There are streets which seem to be made up chiefly of churches, churches of all sizes and colors, crowned with beautiful and fantastic domes, which, in turn, are surmounted by crosses of the most charming and original designs.

Yaroslávl, founded in 1030, claims the honor of having had the first Russian theatre, and to have sheltered Biron, the favorite of the Empress Anna Ioannovna (a doubtful honor this), with his family, during nineteen years of exile. But its architectural hints and revelations of ancient fashions, forms, and customs, are its chief glory, not to be obscured even by its modern renown for linen woven by hand and by machinery. For a person who really understands Russian architecture—not the architecture of St. Petersburg, which is chiefly the innovation of foreigners—Yaroslávl and other places on the northern Vólga in this neighborhood, widely construed, are mines of information and delight.

With the exception of the churches, Yaroslávl has not much to show the visitor: but the bazaar was a delight to us, with its queer pottery, its baskets for moulding bread, its bread-trays for washtubs, and a dozen other things in demand by the peasants which we had to ask explanations.

A night's journey landed us in Moscow. But even the glories of Moscow cannot make us forget the city of Yarosláff the Great and Nízhni Nóvgorod.

$\sim$

Kate Marsden

An English Nurse in Siberia

Kate Marsden was born in 1859 in London and trained as a nurse, a career she began at the age of sixteen in a London Hospital. Years later she went to New Zealand with her mother to care for her sister who had tuberculosis (and who died shortly after they arrived). Kate worked briefly at Wellington Hospital, then returned to England. Florence Nightingale was her idol, and, following in her footsteps, she went to nurse Russian soldiers during the Russo-Turkish War of 1877. She was assigned to Bulgaria, where she met some lepers and was moved by their condition.

As a result of this encounter, Kate became interested in working with lepers and finding a cure for the disease. During her travels in the Middle East, she met an English doctor in Constantinople who told her of an herb found in Siberia that would cure leprosy. Inspired, she was determined to travel to Russia and make her way to Siberia to find the herb. Kate had an audience with Queen Victoria, who gave her blessing to the trip, and she wrote to the Empress of Russia to solicit her support for Kate's endeavor. In 1890, Kate left England to investigate the treatment of lepers in Jerusalem and Constantinople before going to Russia. She arrived in Moscow in November 1890 to prepare for the trip to the leper colonies in Yakutsk, Siberia.

For the next three months, Kate worked to obtain support and funding for the trip. She visited members of the nobility, both in St. Petersburg and Moscow, and was mentored by Alexandra Tolstoy, by Princess Gargarine, and by the Bishop of Ufa, who had worked with the lepers. Support also came from British citizens residing in Moscow.

On February 1, 1891, Kate Marsden and her translator, Ada Field, began their journey by train from Moscow to Zlatoust, where they met the sledge, their driver, and a soldier who accompanied them. Once they arrived in Krasnoyarsk, they changed conveyances to a tarantass, a low-slung wagon with four wheels. Arriving in Irkutsk, she asked the Governor-General to form a committee to alleviate the suffering of the lepers in the Viluisk region. At Viluisk, she found the herb alleged to cure leprosy but found it to be ineffective. From Viluisk, she traveled by tarantass to the Lena River, where she took a barge, then traveled on horseback to Yakutsk, arriving in May 1891. The Yakutsk region had a number of leper colonies, and she visited twelve areas and met sixty-six lepers. She found the conditions under which they lived deplorable. The lepers were left to fend for themselves. Despised by the local population, they were isolated, unfed, and unhealthy, and they lived in unsanitary conditions.

Kate also had an interest in visiting Russian prisons, where she gave prisoners tea and the gospel. She did the same with prisoners and their wives as they traveled into exile in Siberia.

Returning to Irkutsk, Kate asked the Governor-General for funds to provide warm clothing and shelters for the lepers. She arrived in Moscow in December 1891, after an eleven-month, two-thousand-mile trip to Siberia. Zealous to seek help for the lepers and their dire need for a hospital, she met with officials in St. Petersburg, including the Empress Maria Feodorovna, and Pobedenotsev, the Procurator of the Holy Synod, who gave a monetary contribution and had a pamphlet published about her journey that circulated all over Russia. Articles in the newspapers followed, and plans for the leper colony were drawn up. Back in Moscow, a ladies' charitable society provided clothing and furniture for the colony, and five nuns of the Sisters of Mercy volunteered to work with the lepers. The Czarevich contributed funds to cover the expenses of their trip.

Before returning to England in the spring of 1892, Kate made a final request to the Procurator of the Holy Synod that a collection for the lepers be taken throughout the empire on the Sunday of the Gospel reading of the Lepers, December 13, 1892. This final effort accomplished, she returned to England where she wrote about her trip to Siberia, dedicating the profits from *On Sledge and Horseback to the Outcast Siberian Lepers* to the alleviation of their suffering.

Kate Marsden was named a fellow of the Royal Geographical Society in 1892, was a member of the British Nurses Association and the Russian Imperial Red Cross Society, and was a founder of the Saint Francis Leprosy Guild in 1895. Several artifacts she brought back from Siberia are in the British

Museum. In 1897, she returned to Russia, where a hospital for lepers was opened in Vilyuysk.

She died in London on March 26, 1931, and was buried in Uxbridge. A monument to her is located in London.

Her book and the publicity it garnered led to criticisms of her story. She was accused of homosexuality (to which she admitted) and of exaggerating and embellishing her travels that were written in a pious tone. Despite the suspect motives for her journey, she is remembered today in Siberia: a fifty-five carat diamond was named after her and a statue erected in Sosnovka village in 2014. A scholarship in her name is given to the top English language student at North-Eastern Federal University in Yakutsk each year.

The following selections are from On Sledge and Horseback to the Outcast Siberian Lepers.

～

On Sledge and Horseback to the Outcast Siberian Lepers

Starting Out: Sledging along a Road

Our experiences of sledging along a road terribly broken up, owing to the immense traffic and almost endless string of sledges (a sleigh of planks) carrying heavy loads of goods to the annual Siberian fair, held in February, will be repeated in your case, dear reader, if you ever undertake a similar journey in Siberia at a corresponding period. Bump, jolt, bump, jolt—over huge frozen lumps of snow and into holes, and up and down these dreadful waves and furrows, made by the traffic—such is the stimulating motion you will have to submit to for a few thousand miles. Your head seems to belong to every part of the sledge; it is first bumped against the top; then the conveyance gives a lurch, and you get an unexpected knock against the sledge; and on gaining a footing, you feel more like a battered old log of mahogany than a gently nurtured Englishwoman.

And now, dear reader, let me introduce you to your somewhat primitive "hotel"… Have a pocket-handkerchief ready, if you can find it, and place it close to your nostrils the moment the door is opened. The hinges creak; and your first greeting is a gust of hot, fetid air, which almost sends you back; but you remember the cold outside and the cravings of hunger, and so you go in.

The menu is regulated entirely according to your own tastes; in fact, it consists chiefly of the viands which you have brought with you, and which do not happen to have bounced out of the sledge, or which you haven't flung to the wolves on your way. You will be badly off indeed if you cannot contrive to have a few dry biscuits and a glass of tea. There are no waiters to bother you at this hotel, and no fees of any kind; and that should relieve your mind.

The sheep-skin and rugs (none of the cleanest) are then laid in the middle of the floor. That is your bed; but don't suppose you will have sole possession of it. One glance around the walls at the numbers of moving specks upon them of different sizes and families will at once dispel the illusion, whilst the probable arrival of another tardy traveler will deprive you of even the comfort of a room to yourself.

The Prison at Ekaterinburg

The prison at Ekaterinburg is not one of the best of its kind. It appeared to me badly lighted, badly ventilated, and badly kept. This was my first prison experience; and a shiver went through my heart when, on entering the

Russian Prisoners
Library of Congress

prison, the grating noise of bolts and locks told of the many poor fellows doomed to be shut in from the world. Soldiers stood with their guns and bayonets ready to quell an outbreak. The rattling of the prisoners' chains, which extend from waist to ankles, is a sound one never forgets. In the yard were several prisoners, with the snow piled up around them, and wearing clothes too scanty to keep them warm, even on an autumn day in England. The frightened look on some, the despairing look on others, and the scowl on the faces of a few, produced a train of thought, calling up in imagination varied pictures in the past lives of these men.

The room where the prisoners took their meals was dirty, and badly ventilated. The food was contained in a large wooden bowl placed on the table; each man had a spoon, which he dipped into the bowl and passed to his mouth. The unwholesome condition of the room, the soup spilt on the table, and those dirty wooden ladles made me wonder whether any prison in my own country could show such a scene. The head warder informed me that, although the prison was built to hold only a specified number of prisoners, yet, in the summer, it often contained two or three times as many.

Post Stations

Another short spin and we arrived at the post-station at two o'clock in the morning. The hard dirty floor we hailed with delight, and slept heavily for five hours. At some of the post-stations other travelers may be found, of various ages and of both sexes, and they all have to find places on the one floor for the night. Sometimes we were disturbed in the midst of a peaceful slumber by the crying of an infant; but, as a rule, we were too ready for sleep to pay any attention to a disturbance of any kind. Now and then a clean post-station may be met with; but, generally speaking, they are places to be avoided.

Riding in a Tarantass

Now, this vehicle, which was never designed for comfort, is innocent of a single spring. It runs on wheels, and stands a long way from the ground, making it awkward for a woman to get in without assistance. The roads at this time of year are in a terrible condition; a ploughed field, containing a good many deep ruts, is the nearest description I can give of them. When a thaw commences the soft, pulpy state of affairs begins; then there comes a slight frost, and a thin layer of ice, frequently misleading the traveller. When he thinks he is going to glide along in tolerable ease, he suddenly bumps down through the ice into a great hole of sticky, pulpy mud, or if there has been a very severe frost during the night, all the roads are turned into solid blocks of frozen mud.

Now, when you are in a tarantass, loaded in the "hold" with all sorts of packages upon which you lie, you have to make up your mind before starting that during a journey of one thousand miles or so, you will have to be patient and resigned. At the very first move of the vehicle you will probably find yourself thrown onto its edge, with your poor feet dashed against the front part, which consists of sharp wood. Then, after scrambling back into position, the thing lurches, and you feel as if you were trying in vain to keep up with it; but, after an hour, you give up all effort, and leave your body to do just what is required. By that time, you have realized in what way the spirit of resignation must be testified.

Your limbs ache, your muscles ache, your head aches, and, worst of all, your inside aches terribly. "Tarantass rheumatism," internal and external, chronic, or, rather, perpetual, is the complaint from which you will have to suffer during the thousand miles.

The People of Yakutsk

The town of Yakutsk, with a population of about 7,000, is the chief administrative centre of the province, and stands on the River Lena. The town of Yakutsk is not a pretty place, and has a dreary, dead appearance. At eight o'clock the houses are shut up, and there are no amusements or recreations. The winter temperature is about 45 of cold, and the air is filled with mist and fog. Sometimes the cold is so frightful that strong people cannot go out of their houses for days together. It is not light till ten or half-past, and is dark about two; and this state of things continues for nearly eight months of the year.

The poverty of the people, in measure, arises from the ravages of leprosy amongst the able-bodied. The people play cards and smoke, sometimes six hours out of twelve. All the ladies smoke; and the first thing offered to a guest on his or her arrival is a cigarette. The samovar and tea follow, and whilst smoking, tea-drinking, and talking are going on, the men walk up and down the room the whole time. The stranger, of necessity, gets somewhat bewildered, until he makes up his mind to feel at home. ... On no account must the visitor enter the room in his outdoor costume; and if he declines the proffered tea he is guilty almost of a crime. The poorer people use sheets of ice three or four inches thick instead of glass windows, and how they keep themselves warm is almost incomprehensible. Stores come in once a year; and the people must buy for twelve months. There are doctors, but no chemists, and the doctors only buy drugs from Irkutsk once a year.

Visit to the Bishop Regarding the Herb

On my referring to the herb he said, much to my surprise and delight, that he had a few specimens and before I left he placed some in my hands. He could give no definite information as to its curative or alleviating properties. It was, however, a source of some satisfaction that the reports I had heard were not altogether groundless.

Not only from the Bishop, but also from a doctor in the town, I heard fearful accounts of the lepers in the forests and on the marshes, which were almost inaccessible. The doctor begged me to take tea and tobacco, luxuries unknown to them.

Notwithstanding my credentials, a suspicion existed that I was nothing better than a political spy; and it is not always pleasant to find that there is "a chiel among us takin' notes," which "notes" may be used against one at some future time. It seems to be one of the primary duties of some of the officials in Yakutsk to look out for suspects, and carry a note-book and pencil in their pockets for jotting down any matters which may appear to them of a compromising nature.

Preparing for the Journey to Visit the Lepers

After some delay, I began buying stores for the journey. Dried bread (almost as hard as stone, and which had to be soaked in tea before being eaten) packed in fishskins and boxes, covered with fishskin, and, for this reason, smelling and tasting for ever after of bad fish; tea, sugar, tobacco, tinned meat and fruits, biscuits, and an assortment of drugs and an *en-route* basket from Drew & Sons, Piccadilly.

The Cossack, Jean Procopieff, knowing of my small pecuniary means, and being touched deeply by the suffering of the lepers, offered, with expressions of sympathy, to lend me all the horses required for the journey as far as Viluisk. He further offered his services as leader of the cavalcade. It was therefore absolutely necessary to make the journey on horseback, and also necessary to employ a number of men not only for carrying stores, but also as a means of protection against the dangers to be encountered, not the least, amongst them being the bears, with which the woods are infested. Our cavalcade was a curious one. It consisted of fifteen men and thirty horses. I carried a revolver, a whip, and a little traveling bag, slung over the shoulder. I was obliged to ride as a man for several reasons—first because the Yakutsk horses were so wild that it was impossible to ride safely sideways.

I have not sufficient space to enumerate all the difficulties and troubles of this first part of the journey as far as Viluisk. Pushing through forests, plunging into bogs, camping at night, plagued with mosquitoes, sleeping at time in disgustingly filthy yourtas, which swarmed with vermin of many kinds, myself more than once so wearied and aching that I could not dismount, having to be dragged off the horse, my clothes sometimes wet through with rain, with no possibility of taking them off to be dried; after such experiences, I arrived at Viluisk.

We were met at Viluisk by Father John Vinokouroff, who is an earnest Christian man, and devoted to the lepers. He frequently goes amongst them, fearless of contagion, simply to minister to them, and to speak of the Saviour's love. From him and from other persons I learned additional details – worse than those contained in the Medical Inspector's report of the frightful condition of the lepers in the province.

Traveling to the Site of the Hospital for the Lepers

After meeting several of the leading Yakut people of the town, and consulting about plans and prospects, we visited the site which had been proposed for the much-needed and longed-for hospital. On account of the intense heat, we deferred starting until evening. ... We had about twenty miles of ride, chiefly through forests, and found on arriving that the place proposed would not do at all for the hospital.

The poor lepers are so looked down upon as the very dregs of the community that even those wishing to befriend them have fallen into the way of thinking that the worst is good enough for them. Thus, when the question rose about materials and workmen, it was very hard for me to impress upon the people the necessity of having the very best in both cases, not only on account of it paying the end, but because I wanted to make these poor sufferers realise that it was our Lord who was sending help.

Finding the Lepers

At last I thought I could discern ahead a large lake, and beyond two yourtas. My instinct was true to me; and the peculiar thrill which passed through my whole frame meant that, at last, after all those months of travelling, I had found, thank God! The poor creatures I had come to help. A little more zigzag riding along the tedious path, and then I suddenly looked up and saw before me the two yourtas and a little crowd of people. Some of the people were limping and some leaning on sticks, to catch the first glimpse of us, their faces and limbs distorted by the dreadful ravages of the disease. One poor creature could only crawl by the help of a stool, and all had the same indescribably hopeless expression of the eyes which indicated the disease. I scrambled off the horse, and went quickly amongst the little crowd of the lame, the halt and the blind. Some were standing, some were kneeling, and some crouching on the ground, and all with eager faces turned towards me. They told me afterwards that they believed that God had sent me.

I at once ordered the things to be unpacked, and had them collected on the grass. A prayer was then offered by the priest, and, next, a prayer for Her Imperial Majesty the Empress, in which the poor heartily joined. As we distributed the gifts, some of the distorted faces half beamed with delight; whilst others changed from a look of fear to one of confidence and trust.

The condition of the yourtas is best described by my quoting the documents of two officials, who were sent there by the Government.

The medical inspector, Mr. Smirnoff, says, in his report to the Governor: "One is struck at the sight of the smallness of these nomad huts, in which they dwell. Light hardly penetrates, and the atmosphere is so infected by the conglomeration of the lepers, and the exhalations of rotten fish, that one is quite suffocated on entering them. These unfortunates have neither beds nor linen; their clothing consists only of sheep and cow skins, all in rags, and it is under these conditions without any change, that they are obliged to live tens of years, till at last death releases them from their sufferings."

The lepers have no beds. Round the inside of the yourtas were placed trunks of trees, upon which were fixed pieces or planks of wood. On these the lepers slept, closely packed as near to each other as possible, the feet of one to the head of the next. Men, women, and children were all mixed together; calves were also kept there in the summer, and cows during the winter. There was no kind of sanitary arrangement; and, sometimes, in the depth of the winter, none of the inmates venture outside for days together.

In this place, the lepers eat, cook, sleep, live, and die. If one of them dies, the body is kept in the hovel for three days. The smoke fills the place—stifling both the lepers and the cattle. Not long ago they had smallpox amongst them and four of their number died, and the dead bodies were kept in the same yourta for three days. The dead are buried only a few yards from the dreadful abode, so that the lepers cannot pass their threshold without being reminded of the end daily drawing near.

The Settlement of Hatignach

We pushed our way through the usual dense forest, along the track which had been cleared for me by the kind natives … and which otherwise would have been impassible. Halting at the leper settlement of Hatignach, a scene met my eyes too horrible to describe fully. Twelve men, women, and children, scantily and filthily clothed were huddled together in two small yourtas, covered with vermin. The stench was dreadful; one man was dying, two men had lost their toes and half of them their feet; they had tied boards from their knees to the ground so that by this help they could contrive to drag themselves along. One man had no fingers; and the poor stumps, raised to make the sign of the cross, were enough to bring tears to the eyes of the most callous.

During the eight or nine months of winter, these people huddle together with the cattle as closely as possible in their dreadful hovels, in order to keep warm. They, too, had been attacked by typhus fever and smallpox. I said farewell, and, mounting my horse, heard angry words behind me. Turning round I found that some of the lepers wanted to come near to speak to me, and the Yakuta were driving them away in horror, fearful lest they might catch the disease. Of course, I quickly went to them. They pleaded hard that the hospitals might be built speedily, and that they might be supplied with bread, because the food brought to them was generally putrid.

After a ride of some twenty miles, we came across a lonely leper, who had lived in the forest, for six years, with no companion but his faithful dog. This dog, like the other mentioned, was his master's guardian against the bears. He seemed to smell the bears in the distance, and then dashed off to tease and tantalise them, leading them away and away, and then returning to his master voiceless and half dead. No word of murmur came from this man's lips; he only appealed that the hospital might be quickly built.

Farewell to Escorts

And now, with many regrets, I had to part with my escort. I need scarcely speak of my great indebtedness to all the worthy men, from the Tchinovnick down to the Yakut guide, who went with me, on that long journey. Their steadfastness and readiness to do all that I required are sufficiently obvious throughout my account of the 2000 mile ride and need little praise from me now. They were chivalrous and devoted, without exception. I was always at their mercy; but never for one instant did they betray the confidence reposed in them. Two things kept them staunch and true—that a woman was entrusted to their care, and that they were bound on a mission of mercy to their outcast brethren. May God ever bless them for all the help they gave me!

Returning to Irkutsk

My journey up the Lena towards Irkutsk was accompanied by just as many inconveniences and difficulties as I experienced on my outward journey. I was exhausted and ill on the voyage, and had to lie in my berth, half dazed, all day. During the evening I sometimes crawled on deck, looking at passing boats and the scenes on the banks. To add to the discomforts, about 150 men from the gold mines, with wives and children, joined us. Babies crying, and men and women quarreling, were bad enough; but the fearful smells were worse to endure. When the river became shallow, we had to change into small post-boats, which, though covered at the top, are exposed to rain, wind, and fog at both ends. We were short of provisions, and for five days we lived on eggs, potatoes, and tea. Sometimes we grounded on the mud, or on stones, and then, as the men hauled us off clumsily, and we tumbled about I began to wonder how long it would be before we were all at the bottom.

On landing, I had to finish the journey by tarantass, so there was more bumping and jolting.

On arriving in Irkutsk, I went to a quiet, clean hotel, which, though an unpretentious place, was, to me, a luxurious palace after all I had gone through.

Help for the Lepers

On the morning after arriving at Irkutsk, I had to call on the General-Governor, who at my request, summoned the committee to hear an account of my visits to the lepers. The committee consisted of His Excellency the General-Governor, the two Archbishops, an aged priest, Mr. Sievers, the doctor, the inspector, Captain Lvoff, and myself.

I read a *résumé* of my travels, and begged hard for help for the lepers; I asked, first, for warm clothing and, thank God! About 150 [pounds] were at once contributed for that object. When the question of building a hospital arose, a great deal of discussion ensued, principally on the account of the necessary funds.

However, when I informed them of my intention to plead with all the leading people of Moscow and St. Petersburg on behalf of the lepers and, if possible, lay the sad state of their existence before Her Imperial Majesty the Empress—but that I hoped the Siberians would come forward and help their own outcast people first—the General-Governor then said that he would do all in his power to get sufficient money to build four large temporary huts, where the lepers could be sheltered, to provide them with cows, and to endeavor to obtain contributions toward the hospital.

Shortly after, a sum of 1000 [pounds] was contributed, which was left in charge of the governor.

Fully realizing that had I known the Russian language much more could have been collected, nevertheless, I was deeply grateful to our Lord for this good beginning, and rejoiced to think that the poor unhappy people would, at last, have a decent place to live in, proper clothes, and good milk to nourish them.

The General-Governor, who was most kind, gave me an order to visit the vast central penal servitude prison at Alexandrovsky, where there are 3500 prisoners, thus some of my time was again taken up in visiting prisoners, distributing tea and sugar, and giving copies of the Gospels.

Looking back upon the results of the few days I had spent in Irkutsk, I praised God for the help He had enabled me to get for His lepers; and prayed for further guidance at every step.

Now that the first contributions had been given, God would send others, and my next special prayer was for earnest Christian women to be found, who would be willing to go and nurse the lepers, as well as others to do menial work.

Leaving for Tomsk

I left Irkutsk in October for Tomsk, a distance of over a thousand miles.

We travelled in a tarantass, which, at an early stage of this journey broke down, the front wheels giving way. ... We managed to get another vehicle and off we went galloping again.

Siberia is doubtless one of the richest countries in the world; but its untold wealth lies in the earth almost untouched. If only English or American enterprise could be imported there, Siberia would be turned literally, upside down, and the veins of rich ore be brought to light. Then would come the flourishing days of gold and silver, as well as of milk and honey.

A great change had taken place in many respects since my outward journey towards Yakutsk. The Grand Duke had been making his tour, and, to prepare for his coming, old bridges had been repaired, telegraph poles repainted, and post-stations scraped, scrubbed, cleaned, and white washed. But all the white-washing in the world would fail to rid the stations of vermin.

My diminutive Russian vocabulary was insufficient now and then to save me from extortion at the hands of keen-witted drivers. Once, when the interpreter had left me in order to attend to some work at a distant place, I found I had paid for seven horses instead of four, the number harnessed to the vehicle. I did not wake up to the fact that a swindle had been perpetrated until I had gone through a series of arithmetical calculations between the one station and the next. And when the next station was reached, those Jehu fellows actually tried the same trick! But I was too sharp for them this time. I sat down, wrote "four" on a scrap of paper, then held up four fingers, and shook my head when I saw them exchanging knowing looks, which meant a conspiracy to extort the price of seven steeds. Then they shouted and yelled, but I kept cool and waited; and it is astonishing the effect that English coolness has on the Russian temper.

Tomsk

My return visit to Tomsk was a very memorable one. I arrived in November 1891, and after much deliberation and prayer, visited the convent. The Abbess received me very kindly; and when I described the condition and wants of the lepers, both she and all the sisters were deeply affected. Self-sacrificing women were needed to go to the lepers—would some of these sisters volunteer? So I went again to the convent, and begged the mother in Christ's name, and for Christ's sake, to undertake the mission. When I ceased speaking, she calmly and deliberately said, "Yes, in his name, and for his sake, I will do it."

In Tjumen

At last I arrived in Tjumen in a rather lamentable condition. What with exposure to bitter cold and tropical heat, and all the fatigues of the previous months—with the jolting, broken rest, and little food—I was now, vulgarly speaking, "done up." I was sore in every joint, frightfully exhausted, and, even with a comfortable bed and surrounded by kind friends, I could get no sleep. My dear friend Miss Field came to meet me at Tjumen. I was glad to get under her care again; but, notwithstanding my friend's remonstrances, I started to Ekaterinburg the next day, feeling very anxious to move on toward St. Petersburg where so much work awaited me.

Back in Moscow

I arrived once more in Moscow in December, nearly eleven months since setting out on that fateful day, February 1, 1891. I kept quiet and rested for three days, seeing none of my Russian friends but Madame Costanda, and then set off for St. Petersburg, where I hoped to establish the headquarters of a scientific society for investigating the state of lepers, and controlling measures for their relief wherever lepers existed throughout the Russian Empire.

St. Petersburg

Her Imperial Majesty the Empress was indisposed on my arrival in St. Petersburg; and my audience with Her Majesty was therefore delayed for some time. At last I was honoured with a long audience, which was a private one; but I may be allowed to say that Her Majesty took the most lively and tender interest in the lepers, and promised to exert all Her Imperial influence to help forward the work. Her Imperial Majesty also headed the list of donors to the fund which was shortly started.

Countess Tolstoi

Here I must speak of the Countess Tolstoi. Next to Miss Florence Nightingale, the woman I love and reverence the most of is the Countess Alexandrine Tolstoi. Holding a position of immense power and influence, remarkable for her wisdom and discretion, a clever linguist, a perfect lady and a true Christian, one who knows not how to stoop to any littleness in life, who possesses the very soul of honour, the Countess Tolstoi is unique amongst women who are placed by God in circumstances of serious responsibility and wide-extending influence.

Meeting with the Head Procurator of the Holy Synod

My interviews with His Excellency the Head Procurator of the Synod brought about results which exceeded my highest expectations. I gave him the written account, signed by the Russian official who accompanied me, of my visits to the lepers. This account was published, by the Procurator's instructions, in the *Church Intelligence*, a weekly paper circulated all over Russia. Not content with this notice, which would probably come under the eye of nearly every reader in the Empire, the Procurator had the article reprinted in pamphlet form, with the title, "The Journey of an English Sister of Mercy into the Yakutsk Government to Help the Lepers." He ordered 40,000 copies to be printed and to be spread throughout Russia, in order that the interest of all classes of people might be secured. The proceeds were to be devoted to the Leper Fund, to which the Procurator had contributed 300 [pounds]. I should also mention that the pamphlet contained a note to the effect that contributions might be sent for the lepers to the Synod.

The newspapers then took up the subject, and discussed it from various stand-points, thus giving further publicity to the wants of the lepers, and the measures proposed to relieve them.

Plans for the Leper Colony

The Medical Department kindly appointed Professor Peterson, a known student in leprosy, to assist me in the preparation of my work. With his help a plan was drawn up for the projected colony, and a small meeting convened of doctors who had been to Yakutsk, and were well acquainted with the conditions and customs of both country and people. The general arrangement of buildings was settled as follows:

Ten separate houses for the lepers, each constructed for the accommodation of ten inmates; two hospitals (one for each sex) for patients in an advanced stage of the disease; a house for the doctor and his two assistants; a house for the sisters; a church and house for the priest; a building for workshops, also a bath-house, a bakehouse, and a mortuary. The sexes are to be kept apart, except in the case of a leper family; each house is to be provided with a garden, and space is left for a large kitchen garden to supply the wants of the whole of the colony. Each household is to have two cows, for which a proper stable will be provided. In designing this plan one object was steadfastly kept in view, the happiness of the lepers.

Material and workmanship are to be of the very best quality procurable; and no pains will be spared to give the most miserable of God's creatures the best things that can in any way add to their comfort and happiness. I want this colony to be in every sense, a model one.

But what I may call the crowning result of my efforts remains yet to be named. I understood that on the Sunday when the Gospel of the Blind was appointed to be read, a collection was made in the churches throughout Russia on behalf of the blind, and that this collection amounted annually to over 20000 [pounds]. I went to the Head procurator, and in the name of Christ, I begged that a collection might be made for the lepers on the Sunday when the Gospel of the Leper is appointed to be read, and, to my joy, the request was granted; and on the 13th of next December the first collection, I hope, will be made in aid of lepers throughout the Empire. I cannot adequately express my gratitude to the Head Procurator for so willingly granting this boon and all the requests with regard to the lepers which were presented to him.

CHAPTER TEN

~

Annette M. B. Meakin

A Passenger on the Trans-Siberian Railroad

Annette M. B. Meakin was an Englishwoman who grew up in India, where her father, Edward E. Meakin, was a tea planter. Born on August 12, 1867, she was educated in England at the Royal College of Music and studied Classics at the University College in London. Though she had some work experience during World War I, writing was her occupation and travel her passion.

Independently wealthy, Annette traveled in Europe and developed an interest in Russia, which she visited several times before embarking on the Trans-Siberian Railway from Moscow to Vladivostok in June 1900. She wanted to be the first woman to travel this route to Japan, and she was—accompanied by her sixty-year-old mother. Warned that going to Siberia would be difficult and dangerous, both mother and daughter were intrepid; they went without hotel reservations and were always helped by strangers. Knowing no Russian—only German, French, and English—they managed to make acquaintance with aristocrats, Russian military officers, and the governors and mayors in the towns they visited.

Once they reached Vladivostok, they hoped to return to Moscow by the same railroad route, going in reverse; however, the Boxer Rebellion prevented them from doing so. They went to Japan, then sailed to Canada, and arrived in New York City, where they departed by ship on August 22, 1900, for London, arriving on August 31. Annette had many years and other travels ahead of her before she died at age ninety-two in 1959. Her personal papers are in the Bodleian Library at Oxford University.

Annette M. B. Meakin's books include A *Ribbon of Iron*, *Women in Transition*, *Galicia: The Switzerland of Spain*, *Hannah More*, and *What America Is Doing: Letters from the New World*.

The following selections are from A *Ribbon of Iron*.

~

A Ribbon of Iron

The Siberian Express

The Siberian Express, or *Train de Luxe* as it is called, leaves Moscow for Irkutsk every Saturday evening, whilst the ordinary post train leaves daily at 3 pm. There is no difference in the speed of the two trains, but by stopping less time at the stations the express gains two days on the entire journey.

We took up our abode in the express on Saturday, May 12, and did not emerge from it till the following Wednesday evening, when we alighted at Omsk station after a journey of four days and four nights. We shared a luxurious *coupé* with two other ladies. I retired at one to my comfortable bed and remained there for three days, after which time I was well enough to get up.

The Siberian express is a kind of "Liberty Hall," where you can shut your door and sleep all day if you prefer it, or eat and drink, smoke and play cards if you like that better. An electric bell on one side of your door summons a waiter from the buffet. Besides the ordinary electric lights you are provided-

Trans-Siberian Railway
Library of Congress

with an electric reading lamp by which you may read all night if you choose. Time passes very pleasantly on such a train and it is quite possible to enjoy the scenery, for there is none of that fearful hurry that makes railway travelling so risky for body and nerves in Europe and America. Our average speed was about sixteen miles an hour.

At one end of the cheerful dining car was a Bechstein piano, and opposite to it a bookcase stacked with Russian novels; doubtless it will contain plenty of French and English books in time. On the fourth day we had an agreeable concert. Amongst the performers were a gentleman with a good tenor voice and two lady pianists of no ordinary merit. Three portraits adorned the dining car walls—those of the Emperor and Empress and that of Prince Hilkof—while ferns and flowers gathered by the way gave a homelike appearance on the whole.

We stopped at a great many stations; indeed on some parts of the route we seemed to get into a chronic state of stopping. At large stations there was often a halt of twenty minutes or half an hour. Passengers anxious for a change of fare seized such opportunities to dine at the station buffet. Card playing went on all the time and small sums of money were played for. If a Russian sets down to a game of cards, nothing but a matter of life and death will induce him to stir from it until it is finished.

The train was quite full. One lady about thirty years of age, who spoke French, told me she hated Siberia, and was only going to Irkutsk to sell some property. She intended to return to St. Petersburg by the next train but one; that is, in less than a fortnight, which meant twenty days of railway travelling and a journey of some 8000 miles within a month. Distance, like time, counts for nothing in Siberia. This lady thought us bold, if not rash, to travel without a revolver. "I always carry two," she said. Later on the Mayor of Vladivostok, who shared the next *coupé* with the manager of the Amur Steam Company, took out his little pocket pistol and handled it fondly. "It saved my life once," he said. "You had better get one in Omsk if you haven't brought one with you."

The conductor was a good-looking man in uniform. His position on the train seemed to be something like that of a purser on a steamer. We tried to find out from him whether there was any hotel at Omsk, and what sort of a place it was, but the only information we could extract was that it was warmer at Irkutsk than at Moscow. He knew nothing of Omsk, and could not even tell us when we might expect to arrive till we were within a few hours of the place.

After a day and two nights of steady traveling we came in sight of the Volga. All were eager to see something of the famous bridge over which we were to cross. Some, who feared they might not wake at 4 a.m., got up before daylight. I myself saw nothing of it then, but on another occasion when we passed at four on a lovely autumn afternoon I had a splendid view standing while we crossed the water on the platform between two carriages.

The Volga too was most picturesque at this point, and the passengers got a fine view both up and down the river, as the train slowly crossed the bridge.

Samara, the first town of interest after Moscow, has a population of ninety-one thousand. I once spent a few days there, and was much impressed by the frightful dust storms in the streets, the worst I have met with outside Siberia. The best caviar in the world comes from the Volga; it can be had in boxes at the Samara station, but is very expensive when bought in that way.

The next place of interest is Ufa. This was formerly the central town of the Bashkirs, a dark Mohammedan race, who, in their days of independence, were renowned for their skill in shooting arrows. One still finds them in their old haunts, peaceful enough now, though for many years after they had sought the protection of Russia against the persecution of other neighbors they continued to give the Russians a good deal of trouble.

Zlatoust in the Ural Mountains is the last Russian town through which the train passes. The situation is most picturesque, with fir-clad mountains as a background. This is the point at which travelers should break their journey if they wish to spend a few days in the Urals. Pleasant excursions can be made in the neighborhood, and there are interesting mines to be visited, mines whence came so many of our precious stones.

Gradually the landscape becomes more and more insignificant till there is at last nothing for the eye to rest on but a wide stretch of grassy plain. This is the steppe.

The appearance of the steppe varies very much according to the time of year. With the exception of solitary groups of birch trees few and far between, nothing will grow there but grasses and herbaceous plants of a hardy nature; there is too much salt in the soil.

You can hardly look out of the windows without seeing water somewhere, for lakes, large and small, are numerous. This part of the steppe alone is said to contain more than a thousand; in most of them the water is salt.

The City of Omsk

It was quite dark long before we reached Omsk, and feeling rather timid we made anxious inquiries as to whether any one else was stopping there. The conductor took pity on us as we were nearing our destination. "There is one lady in the second class," he said, "who is bound for Omsk."

In the meantime our other fellow passengers did their best to persuade us to abandon the idea of seeing Omsk, and go on with them to Irkutsk. Horrible things had happened, they said. "Remember you are now in Siberia," said the conductor warningly.

The lady going to Omsk was met by several friends at the station. They very kindly suggested that a gentleman of their party should drive us to town, and we were only too glad to avail ourselves of the offer. He helped us both to climb into his little Siberian droshky, and telling an *isvoschek* to follow with our baggage took his seat in front. We were soon jolting along in the moonlight over very uneven, but stoneless, ground. The only buildings in sight looked like barns and cattle sheds. I learnt afterward that many of these were temporary shelters for emigrants who were obliged to halt there on their way further east.

Omsk is about four miles from the station, and the drive seemed an endless one that cold, dark night. We were very glad to find ourselves at last in the sheltering inn.

The chief street of Omsk is lined on one side with thriving shops, and on the other with a succession of tea gardens. Each shop has large pictures of its wares painted outside in true Russian fashion, a most convenient one for foreigners ignorant of the language, as well as the peasant population who cannot read, there being no display of the goods themselves.

Before our first morning was over, we had been kindly welcomed to more than one hospitable house. Invitations to dinner quickly followed, and we soon felt quite at home amongst so many kind friends.

The wife of the German pastor introduced us to a gentleman who had lived there for thirteen years. He was curious to know why we had come so far.

"We have come to see something of Siberian life," I said, "for we know very little about it in England."

"Quite so," he replied quickly, "and what you do know is wrong."

Omsk was once a fortress town and bits of the old fortifications are still to be seen. They date back to the year 1765. We are told that Lieut-General Springer, who in 1763 was appointed chief of those who guarded the Siberian frontier, had the fortress built to instill awe into the hearts of the neighbouring Kirgiz and all other Asiatics who might prove troublesome.

Lieut-General Sannikof has done a great deal for the place by persuading private individuals to plant trees and to have an eye for external appearance. In short, it is clear that Omsk, with its rivers, its railway and its growing population, has a grand future in store in spite of the fact that it lies in the centre of so vast a steppe.

The Empress is not forgotten in Omsk. Her name day was the occasion of a great holiday. Church bells woke us in the early morning with their peals. We found all the government buildings decorated with flags. Madame Sannikof gave a dinner at which we were present. Conversation was carried on briskly in Russian, French, German, and English.

Everyone laughed heartily over the warning we received about coming to Omsk; and the Governor himself, to whom every evil deed has been reported by the chief of police for the last ten years, assured us that we could not have come to a safer place, or a more peaceful one.

Visit to a Kirgiz Village

The Kirgiz, who are Mohammedans, also, come to the mosque. They, like the tartars, belong to the Turki race, and speak a Turkish dialect. According to the latest statistics they number about a million souls.

Our Hebrew friend kindly offered to drive us out to a farm of his that was close to a Kirgiz village. We accepted gladly, for this gave us a chance of making a closer acquaintance with the steppe and the Kirgiz at the same time.

After tea, or rather after a picnic in the lovely fresh air of the steppe—we started on foot for the Kirgiz village.

The Kirgiz live in a kind of hut, much the shape of our beehives, with a round hole in the centre, which serves both as a chimney and air hole. The yurta, as these dwellings are called, are made partly of wood and a kind of trellis work covered with hides and felt, and can be taken to pieces at short notice. When their nomadic possessors wish to follow their herds to fresh pasture they pack up their huts and transport them with the greatest ease. Each yurta is placed so that its entrance faces the east.

The Kirgiz are acknowledged by all who come in contact with them to be the best-natured people on the face of the earth. The only sin of which I have heard them accused is horse stealing; they have a great weakness for other people's horses.

Kirgiz horses fly like the wind, and are restrained with difficulty. They can journey for ten hours without food; they bear every severity of climate, and have been known to cover a distance of twenty versts at the rate of half a mile a minute.

They make a great deal of Kumya from mares' milk and keep it in goatskin bottles. Russians buy it from them and drink it as a tonic in spring time. They spend their lives in cattle breeding, and their herds are their one interest in life. When a man meets a friend, he inquires first not after the health of his wife and family, but after that of his cattle!

Returning to our hotel in the evening, we were struck with the picturesque appearance of the town, especially by the river Irtish, whose banks
were lit up with a thousand twinkling lights.

The Post Train

We left Omsk by the post train which ought to have started at 9:30 p.m.,
according to the time table. It was only four hours late, a mere nothing in
Siberia, where time is not money. As we sat waiting at the station the good
news was brought us that Mafeking had been relieved. The bearer of these
tidings was the Finnish Pastor, who had only an hour before received word
by telegram from Finland. The Finns have all along shown great sympathy
with the English with regard to the Transvaal war.

The train seemed to carry music with it as it glided into the station, and
the crowded platform was a whirl of gaiety and excitement. All this in the
middle of the night! We found our *coupé* on the post train not less comfortable than the one we occupied on the express. The cushions were covered
with neat washing covers, and looked tolerably clean. Under the window was
a little folding table which was most useful for reading and writing. I speak
of *the* window because there was only a window at one end of the carriage.
Like the express, the post is also a corridor train. The door opening into the
corridor had a mirror in place of a window; it opened outwards and could be
fastened back against the outer wall when we wished to travel with it open.

On wet days we could get a walk here of about twenty-five paces; seats could
be opened out from the walls between the windows as in the express, and passengers used to congregate here in the evenings when it was too dark to read.

The post train has no dining car, and we were obliged to keep a sharp look
out for stations where there was something to eat. The first day after leaving
Omsk we passed a buffet station about 11 a.m., but, being asleep, did not take
advantage of it.

"You must be hungry," said a fellow passenger pityingly about seven in the
evening, "but we shall reach Kainsk in about an hour, and there is a good
buffet there." Just then the train began to pull up. It soon came to a dead
stop. There was no human habitation in sight.

"The engine has smashed up," said a jolly Russian sailor in broken English
(he was bound for Port Arthur). "She is sixty years old," he continued. "She
was made in Glasgow. She is no use any more."

The conductor had got out. He came along the line and confirmed what
the sailor had said. The other passengers did not seem to mind; they were
soon exploring the neighborhood. The children from the fourth class began

to paddle barefoot in a muddy stream not far from the line. The poor old engine was now "towed to her last berth."

After a delay of two hours a fresh engine arrived from Kainsk and we reached the buffet at last. Never again, we vowed would we be subject to such pangs of hunger as we suffered that day; in future we took care to have some food always with us, if it was only a loaf of bread. The serving man was willing for a few kopecks to fetch us hot water at the stations, so that with the help of bread and tea there was no use to starve.

After a journey of fifty hours we alighted at Taiga, from which station runs the branch line to Tomsk. Here we were told we should have nine hours to wait. Entering the waiting-room we found it filled with weary travelers who had been waiting twenty-four hours for a train! We whiled away part of the time with drinking coffee and writing. Then, just as we had got out our pillows and were preparing to have a sleep, the Tomsk train was announced. It was now 9 p.m. At 1 a.m. we reached Tomsk.

We thought Taiga one of the prettiest stations in Siberia. It is only a few years old, built something after the style of a Swiss chalet. The country round is covered with forest, from which ("taiga") the place derives its name.

Tomsk

Before the days of the railway, Tomsk conveniently situated on the river Tom, was the greatest centre of all Siberian trade. Immense quantities of corn still pass through the markets every year and the wealthiest merchants reside there. After a long drive from the station we reached Hotel Europe about 2 a.m., very cold and very tired. Our train being expected, the waiters had not gone to bed. There were plenty of them, but a more untidy set I never saw. The room they gave us was large but very dirty. During the night a mouse ran about the floor; it was nibbling something under the table while we were sitting by it, and there was an unpleasant sound of gnawing.

In spite of the discomfort of our hotel we stayed several days in Tomsk, for there was much to see.

We saw several buildings of red brick in the course of construction. There were many women among the bricklayers; they were working as busily as any of their male companions. None of the streets were paved. Indeed I never saw a paved street in Siberia. Every *droshky* raises a cloud of smoke-like dust. If you are within fifty yards of it you get smothered. As soon as it began to rain there was mud, and after a wet night it was not unusual to find a pond several feet deep in the centre of one of the chief streets. Your driver never flinches, but takes his *droshky* through the shallows at a headlong gallop.

The best streets in Tomsk have side walks made of boarding, but the wood is roughly nailed together that there are plenty of gaps to twist an unwary foot. If in an absent fit you happened to step from the side walk into the road without waiting till you came to a stepping place, the drop of half a yard would not be agreeable, even if you missed breaking your ankle.

In the poorer streets men and women sat lazily smoking at their doorways. The poor of Siberia are the laziest in the world. For six months of the year whole families shut themselves into their hovels and go to sleep on top of the kitchen stove. Too idle to work they prefer sleeping to the expensive luxury of eating.

No Fruit in Siberia

Fruit does not thrive in Siberia; in fact, with the exception of wild strawberries and one or two kinds of berries, there may be said to be none. From the 9th of May till the 3rd of July we neither tasted nor saw any fruit except oranges and lemons. These had been brought by train from Sicily. The price of an orange was sixpence, of a lemon threepence. A lady whose home is on the Amur told me she had not seen a cherry or any such fruit for thirty years. In winter there is very little rain, always snow, snow, snow; and as the long winter merges suddenly into a hot summer, fruits have no chance. The only month that is entirely free from frost is July.

Visit to the Prison at Tomsk

We walked in upon the prisoners just as they were. Everything was in the most beautiful order, and the deal boards of the floors were spotlessly clean. Each man had his own bedding, with the board which served him as a bedstead chained neatly back to the wall, and every one had his own stool to sit on.

The men in each compartment, hearing footsteps arranged themselves, quickly into two lines, and saluted the Procuror with a unanimous *good-day, sir.*

The weight of the chains worn by the prisoners differs considerably: the ordinary weight is from six to ten pounds. Every prisoner is allowed to bring baggage with him to the weight of thirty pounds, but it all has to be disinfected—a rule which must meet with the heartiest approval from all who know anything of the state in which the Russian peasants live. The cleanliness of the prisons must seem strange to them at first.

Krasnoiarsk—the Yenisei

Returning to Taiga, we proceeded by the main line to Krasnoiarsk. The scenery had quite changed, and our route lay through many miles of thick forest. We passed patches of ground where hundreds of trees had been destroyed by fire, and occasionally saw the lurid glare of what looked like huge bonfires through the trees. Smoke darkened the atmosphere just like a London fog. Such fires have been particularly frequent in 1900 owing to the fact that an insufficient amount of snow fell during the winter.

The town is nine hundred and thirteen feet above sea level. It was originally a fortress built to protect the Russians in Yenisei from the neighboring Tatár tribes, and dates from 1429. We noticed many well dressed people in the streets as we drove to our hotel, and, altogether the place struck us as being more Russian than Siberian. The *Russia* was a fairly comfortable hotel, the best we had seen since we left Moscow, and the cooking was good.

The Vice-Governor kindly took us to see the printing office where a local paper is printed three times a week. Eighty persons, six of whom are women, are employed there. They also undertake the printing and binding of books. We next visited the museum. Here, as at Tomsk, were some wonderful mammoth bones, found in the immediate neighborhood.

Krasnoiarsk is proud of its public gardens, they are the best in Siberia, for in most towns it has been difficult to make the trees grow.

On to Minusinsk

On May 31 we embarked on the comfortably fitted up house boat that was to take us up the Yenisei to Minusinsk. There was a nice deck for passengers, and the dining saloon, where meals were ordered *a la carte*, had windows down both sides and at the further end, so that in bad weather we could sit there and enjoy the view all round us as we glided along.

Travellers have compared the scenery of the Yenisei to that of some parts of Switzerland. For myself I think it has a beauty of its own, and find it hard to draw any comparison, especially as the scenery changes so frequently, though it reminds one somewhat of the Italian lakes.

On and on we glided, curving in and out with every bend of the river, and drawing nearer every hour to the borders of China. The second day the scenery became less rugged. ... Then the river grew wider and wider till we could hardly distinguish its further bank from the many islands covered with tall grass. We now seemed to be no longer on a river, but continually passing from one lake into another surrounded all the time by a glorious changing panorama of mountain scenery.

Minusinsk

It was our original intention to break our journey to Minusinsk at a spot on the left bank of the Yenisei from which, by the aid of horses, we should proceed to Lake Tschuro. This lake is famed for the medicinal qualities of its water, and the village on its shore is fast becoming a popular health resort.

"Yes, you must see Lake Tschuro," said a high official to whom we applied for further information, "and I will give you an introduction to the manager of a large gold mine a few miles further on than the lake."

Emigrants

Emigrants meet you at every turn on the Siberian railway and on the river steamers. Indeed I might almost say that we saw them with us wherever we went. Russians are emigrating at the rate of 200,000 a year, and Minusinsk is one of the districts to which they are being sent in shoals. In cold weather we used to see them lying in heaps at the railway stations sleeping away the time and keeping one another warm.

Yet these poor creatures are by no means uncared for. To begin with, when, of their own free will, they make up their minds to emigrate the Government allows them to send delegates ahead to inspect the land that is to be their home. When these men return a final decision is made. On the frontier, at Cheliabinsk, all their passports are carefully examined before they are allowed to proceed.

Returning from Minusinsk to Krasnoiarsk we had for our companion on the steamer a young medical lady who had just accompanied a batch of emigrants from Moscow to Minusinsk. She had with her a large wicker basket in which she carried medicines, bandages and other articles that might be wanted. Her duties consisted in going a round of inspection every day. On the steamer she had to see that the babies got proper food, taste their milk, and see that they were fed white bread, the ordinary black bread being too coarse for very young children. She expected to spend the following summer months attending various batches on their journeys from Krasnoiarsk to Minusinsk.

The Government allows each man a certain amount of land, and this he is free to cultivate for ten years free of taxes. If he is very poor to start with, he may borrow thirty roubles, or some such sum, from the local official who has charge of Government money for that purpose.

As for the souls of the emigrants, their welfare is also looked after by the Government. A church-railway carriage is hooked on the end of the train when required, and a long-haired priest officiates. The church being very small the air soon becomes vitiated from the presence of such dirty people; none but an emigrant could stand it.

Back to Krasnoiarsk

The following evening, at five o'clock, our steamer came at last. We went on board at once, but she did not start till five the following morning, thirty-six hours after the appointed time.

What a nice change it was to get back to Krasnoiarsk and have eatable food once more! At Minusinsk there had been so little one could eat. The eggs were peculiar, bread, milk, and cream were sour, while a strange taste in the water spoiled the flavor of the tea we had brought from England.

Arrival at Irkutsk

Irkutsk was enjoying a lovely April day when we saw its streets for the first time. Taking a stroll through the town we gazed with delight on the Siberian crab trees, whose branches were covered with snowy blossoms. These trees seemed to be in every garden and at every street corner.

The hotel in which we stayed was called the *Métropole*. We had been advised to go there rather than to any other "because it is the cleanest." We noticed throughout the tour that people comparing the respective merits of Siberian hotels invariably designated the different establishments as "clean," "cleaner," "cleanest," unless indeed they were obliged to use the words, "dirty," "dirtier," "dirtiest."

There were some fair-sized rooms in the *Métropole* and sheets and pillows could be had for the beds by paying extra for them but the service better be passed by in silence. There was a "commissioner" attached to the hotel who understood German; but he was invariably out, or asleep in bed when we wanted him to interpret. When surrounded by six gaping waiters I asked for a spoon they brought me a glass of vodka!

Irkutsk, as we find it today, is one of the most Russianized towns of Siberia, and therefore one of the least interesting to the superficial traveler. He who looks more deeply sees that the town is passing through a crucial point in its existence and that it must be considered with regard both to what it was a short time ago and what it will be in the near future. Today, with all its handsome stone churches, its public buildings, its schools and its shops, it has not a single paved street; it has neither water works nor electric light. Yet these blessings of civilization are not far off. A scheme for their introduction involving an outlay of some three and a half million roubles, has already been set on foot.

The Great Siberian Railway has done wonders for Irkutsk. Its inhabitants no longer feel themselves isolated from the rest of the world. A pleasant journey of nine days now brings them to Moscow without the ordinary fatigue of travelling. They have simply to get in and out of their moving hotel.

The chief gold melting establishment in Siberia is here. Gold is received straight from the mines, melted and weighed. According to its weight cash is paid down in roubles to those who have brought it. The surrounding neighborhood is rich in silver and copper ore, which only awaits capital and enterprise. Coal mines are already being worked, and their owners have lately made a contract with the Government to supply so many tons of coal regularly for the railway. At present a great deal of wood is used.

More than two hundred thousand roubles were spent in building the theatre. It is a handsome edifice entirely of stone. Some years ago, when the churches were almost the only stone buildings in existence, a terrible fire broke out and destroyed half the town. Such a disaster now could not occur in Irkutsk, as the chief streets contain only a small proportion of wooden houses, and a law has been passed that no more are to be built there.

A few capitalists have so far had everything their own way, for in a new country, poor men, however energetic they may be, can do nothing without capital. "Millionaires," as they are called, of forty thousand roubles or thereabouts, live in the utmost simplicity far out in the country. They have traveled and seem something of the world, and now an occasional visit to Irkutsk is all the change they require. Anyone who has not heard of their comparative wealth would take them for well-to-do farmers.

Prices are very high; ground rent is simply enormous considering it is Siberia. The oats used to feed the horses are very dear; consequently a drive in a *droshkey* costs double the amount one is accustomed to pay in St. Petersburg. Hotels, too, are expensive considering the lack of comfort.

The schools are large and well managed; their teachers are from Russia. French and German are taught, but English has not yet penetrated so far. Those who have learned it elsewhere have forgotten the little they knew for want of opportunity to practice it. Many Siberians bring their children to town for the winter and return to their country houses when the summer holidays begin.

Here, as elsewhere, a strict line is drawn between those who are and those who are not "in society," but there is, notwithstanding, a kindly feeling between the classes, and a *Gemüthlichkeit* that other spots on earth might do well to imitate. Taking all in all, Irkutsk has its favorable points; and there is certainly "a good time coming."

Traveling Fourth Class

"One thing I must tell you," said a gentleman of Irkutsk as we sat at the hospitable board. "Your difficulties are only just beginning."

"We heard that in Moscow," I replied, laughing, "and it has been repeated to us in every town on our way."

"It is all very well thus far," continued our friend, shaking his head, "but now you will have to travel fourth class. There are no other carriages on the line; you will have to spend four nights and three days in the company of filthy emigrants, in very close company, alas! for the train will be crowded."

At the post office I met a Dutchman who was going the same way.

"It will be very rough travelling," he said. "I hope you have brought a letter from St. Petersburg?"

"Yes, we have a letter," I replied, "but how can that help us?"

"You had better take it at once to the stationmaster," was the reply, "he may be able to prevent your compartment from being overcrowded."

I at once took a *droshkey* and drove to the station, a distance of two miles, for we were to leave at twelve that night for Lake Baikal, and there was no time to lose. Not a soul at the station understood anything but Russian. However the station-master read the letter and reassured me with bows and smiles.

When the evening came we had kind friends to see us off, and just before starting had the good fortune to be introduced to some agreeable German-speaking tourists. These gentlemen were going no farther than to the other side of the lake. Like every one else they did their utmost to discourage us, "There will be no porters to carry your luggage," they said. "You will have to carry it yourselves."

"We are taking no heavy baggage," I replied.

We passed the night in pleasant conversation, forgetting the hard seats in thankfulness that there were no emigrants in our division. At 5 a.m. we saw the Baikal. Then, in their own efforts to help us, the tourists seized our baggage and lifted it out as soon as the train stopped, declaring that we might look in vain for porters. At that very moment several of those useful personages hurried up and relieved our "Job's comforters" of their self-imposed tasks.

There lay the far-fetched ice-breaker, puffing dark smoke from its three huge funnels, and standing so high above the water level that we shuddered to think how it would roll if caught in a storm. Of the storms that are to be met with on the Baikal we had heard enough.

Lake Baikal

Like the model we had seen at the Paris Exhibition, the ice-breaker had a great door in its stern with rails laid down to receive goods in their trucks direct without unloading. As this part was not yet in working order ... passengers who had hurried ahead to secure the best berths were returning with downcast faces; they had been told they would not get admitted for an hour or so.

Just as we were preparing to sit down on our baggage and wait with the rest, a ship's officer came out inquiring for the English ladies. He told us that a first-class cabin had been reserved for us and proceeded at once to conduct us thither. Here was a luxurious saloon fitted up with every comfort and a buffet at the inner end. A passage round the outside of it—reached by descending a few steps to the right or left—opened into first class cabins on the right and second on the left. Ours was delightfully airy, with a nice square window instead of a porthole, and two comfortable velvet-covered couches. We crossed the lake in about four and a half hours. The ice-breaker might have been on rails so steadily did it move along.

The neighborhood round Lake Baikal is of a volcanic nature. In winter the ice on the lake has the peculiarity that it closes together after having been cut through. This is the result of the continual pressure of water from the sides and of the many currents.

The greatest depth that has been measured as yet is three thousand one hundred and eighty-five feet; its height above the sea level is one thousand five hundred and sixty-one feet; hence its bottom is much below the sea level. Some of the mountains in the neighbourhood are very beautiful, but they do not rise more than four thousand five hundred feet above the water. The surrounding scenery is compared by some to that of certain parts of Scotland.

In June and July one may generally count on having a calm passage. It is during these months that a quantity of wrack is thrown up from the bottom of the lake, and the natives call this "its flowering time."

In winter, when the lake is crossed by sleighs, the ice becomes three and a half feet thick; but, owing to the continual and violent movement of the water, it freezes slowly and the surface is not completely covered with ice till the end of December.

The railway round the end of the lake will hardly be completed before 1905, on account of the numerous tunnels required.

When we had landed, and were waiting for our train, we suddenly heard a great clanking of chains, and turning our heads to that direction saw a handful of criminals march out of the great doorway, and deposit, one after another in a large heap, the regulation sacks in which they carry their worldly goods.

Transbaikalia

A train composed of fourth-class carriages stood waiting for the passengers as they came off the ice-breaker. We got into a compartment and tried to keep it to ourselves, but there was no sign of starting, and more and more people kept coming in. Those who got there first took the lower places, and the rest clambered up to the shelves above, which were three deep. At last those above us became an object of desire to two men of so dirty and unkempt appearance that we became desperate. I put up my hands to ward them off, and cried "Conductor" in the most threatening tones I could muster. It was no use: they had gone into the next division but only to climb quietly over into our shelves when they thought we were not looking. The sight of a wretched pair of feet hanging out over my head was too much for me. I rushed on to the platform, and addressed the first man in uniform I came across. This happened to be an engineer who had charge of that part of the line. As he spoke French I was able to explain what was the matter. He came with me at once to our compartment. The two men seeing him approach slid stealthily back the way they had come in.

"This is not a fit place for ladies," said our new friend, looking round at our grimy companions—"and English ladies too! Oh, this will never do. I will arrange something better for you." Then he hurried off. In a few minutes he came back to say that he had ordered an engineer's private carriage to be put on the train for us. "You will have sleeping berths and a little room with a samovar, where you can make tea," he added, "but it will not be ready for two hours. I fear you must wait here till then."

The two hours seemed as though they would never pass, and the dirty men had climbed above us once more. At last, when it was getting quite dark, the engineer came again.

"I am very sorry," he said, "but a telegram has come ordering us to keep the carriage I promised you for an official from St. Petersburg, who is expected shortly. His Excellency, M. Iswolsky and his family, who passed through last week, took all the other carriages. What I can do for you I will. A captain and six soldiers have got a luggage van to themselves. If you don't mind sharing it with them as far as Stretinsk, I will have part of it curtained off for you."

"Anything, anything but this," we cried.

Once more he left us and we waited on. The night was getting chilly and rain began to come down in torrents. At length two men appeared with a lantern. They were the engineer and the conductor. The engineer gave my mother his arm, and they escorted us out into the rain and along the line to the last carriage on the train. The step was very high, but we clambered in.

How we blessed that kind engineer! With curtains from his own house he had partitioned off one corner of the carriage van for our use. The deal boards that had been put there for the soldiers were all we had to sleep on by night, or to sit on by day. But that was nothing so long as we had it to ourselves. The size of the *coupé* was ten feet by eight. In the centre of the van was a stove with a chimney going through the roof.

With heartfelt thanks we bade our deliverer good night, and the train started. It was just midnight.

Of course there was no going to bed for us that night, or for the three that followed. We lay down just as we were on our rugs, which we had folded as thickly as possible to take off the hardness of the eighteen inch boards. Oh, how our bones ached after ten minutes in one position!

My mother had the side nearest the curtain; a soldier slept on a similar board to ours on the other side of it, and she occasionally felt his elbow. We had a tiny window in the corner, so high up that to look out we had to stand on the seat.

Three days and four nights we spent in that luggage van. The soldiers and their captain were kindness itself. They fetched us hot water and milk at the stations, and when we came short of bread gave us some of their own, which was brown, with sour lumps of uncooked dough here and there.

As the line was not yet open to the general public there were no buffets ready. We lived on bread, milk, and tea. We washed our faces every morning with some of the water brought for tea. Happily we had neither dust nor extreme heat to contend with; for there was a gentle and continuous rain nearly all the time.

The next two vans to ours were prison vans. The windows were strongly barred, and instead of ordinary doors they had a sliding one in the side with a special lock.

We had introductions to people in Chitá, and we fully intended to spend a few days there, but the thought of leaving our cosy corner and having to travel the rest of the way with emigrants was too appalling. We decide to go on in the luggage van, to which we had become quite attached, and not to break our journey again till we got to Stretinsk.

We were now travelling through the region known as Transbaikalia, which covers more square miles than the whole of the German Empire. Lying between Lake Baikal and the Upper Amur, it is bounded on the north by Yakutsk, a country of reindeer, frozen marshes, and unfriendly climate, and on the south and south-east by China.

The temperature of Transbaikalia is peculiar. Sudden changes from great heat to intense cold are frequent, and July is the only month of the year that is entirely free from frost. It is here that the earth is in many places frozen all the year round to the depth of several feet beneath the surface. Yet in spite of this phenomenon the country is in the main wonderfully fertile, and well adapted to the several branches of agriculture. Healthful rains in springtime, cloudless sky in summer, and a transparent atmosphere coupled with the strength of the sun's rays, all work marvels, and within an almost incredibly short space of time the wintry scene is transformed to one of verdant beauty.

In July 1900, that section of the great Siberian railway, which runs through Transbaikalia as far as Stretinsk, was declared open. It has in all thirty-four stations. The first, Myssova, is situated close to the eastern landing stage of Lake Baikal, and takes its name from the neighboring town, or rather village, whose population is composed of exiled criminals of the worst type. Robbery, theft, and even murder are here the order of the day. Every respectable Russian must be able to produce his passport when required, and escaped convicts having no papers of their own are anxious to possess themselves of those belonging to their neighbors. Many a foul murder is the result.

From Myssova our train passed through Verkne-Oudinsk, Chitá, and Nertchinsk to Stretinsk, which is at present the terminus of the railway.

Verkne-Oudinsk, on the Sélenga, is one of the oldest Russian towns in Transbaikalia. Its chief church, which goes by the name of a cathedral, dates as far back as the year 1745. There are three other churches, a number of chapels, a Jewish synagogue, and flourishing schools for boys and girls respectively. An annual fair held in the month of January has an important effect on the trade of the country, and numerous factories of soap and candles, with a brewery and seventeen tanneries, keep the lower classes of the population well employed.

The town of Chitá, to-day the most important in Transbaikalia, is reached, starting from Lake Baikal, after a journey of three days and three nights, the train moving at the rate of ten to seventeen miles an hour. With the exception of Verkne-Oudinsk no towns of interest are passed on the way. The stations all along the line at regular intervals are hardly worthy of the name; a tiny log cottage and a water tower are often the lonely signs of life visible when the train pulls up, and it is well for the comfort of travelers that they have a buffet on board.

Three days and three nights had passed since we crossed the Baikal, and we were half through our fourth night in the van when the captain woke us with the words "Stretinsk, Stretinsk!"

The train had stopped, but there was no need for haste, for we had reached the terminus of the railway, and could go no farther. We strapped up our rugs by the light of a candle which the captain provided us, and were just wondering where we should find a hotel, when a man of the Hebrew race in ship's uniform appeared on the scene. He told us in broken German that he was the captain of a steamboat bound for Blagovestchensk, and would take us there for I forgot how many roubles each.

"That sounded very tempting," but I replied, "We are going by the post steamer."

Waiting in Stretinsk

I was just trying German on the little girls, who looked greatly bewildered, when a lady came up. I turned to her in desperation and asked if she spoke French.

"Of course I speak French," she replied, and she tossed her head with a look of astonishment, as much as to say, "Pray what comes next?"

"They have put us to sleep in a cowshed," I cried. "Oh, when will the post steamer arrive? This is beyond endurance."

"We have just come by the post steamer," replied the lady, gradually thawing. "It will remain here two days, after which it will start for Blagovestchensk. You can go on board at once. It is not a steamer, but a barge drawn by a rope. You will have to change into a steamer at Pokrovskaya, where the Shilka joins the Amur. I will come with you to the agent and interpret."

During the two days and a half that we were obliged to wait in Stretinsk we made a home of the cabin and went to the Station Hotel for our meals. When entering it for the first time we turned back on the threshold, thinking we had got into the kitchen quarters by mistake. Such was the best hotel in Stretinsk.

Stretinsk is a Cossack town extending for nearly three quarters of a mile along the east bank of the river Shilka. Houses are rapidly springing up on the other side of the river; but behind them also there are hills, so that by the very nature of the place it must always increase lengthways along the river.

On the Shilka

On Monday, June 18, we began our river travelling in good earnest. A lady, whose husband was director of a boys' gymnasium at Blagovestchensk, had come on board the previous night. She had a little boy three years of age with her. These two shared the third berth in our cabin. Opposite our door was that of the dining saloon. Here was had lunch, dinner and afternoon tea.

The scenery on the Shilka was very beautiful. Almost immediately after leaving Stretinsk we had high granite rocks on both sides of us, some rising bare and jagged, others covered with short thick fir trees. Once in a ravine we saw a large patch of unmelted snow.

It was considered dangerous to proceed in the dark, so the little steamer that tugged us along used to bring us to a convenient resting place about ten each night, and then, dropping the rope, by which we were drawn, into the water, wheel quickly round and attach itself to the shore for the night. At 5 a.m. we used to be off again.

This was our third day on the Shilka, and we hailed its close with delight, for we were heartily tired of our shadeless barge.

The Amur

Early on Thursday morning, June 19, we reached Pokrovskaya, a village on the banks of the Amur, just where the Shilka joins it. The word *Pokrovskaya* is one that I shall never forget, for it was on everybody's lips from the moment they stepped on to the barge till the moment they left.

"At Pokrovskaya we shall change into a steamer."

"After Pokrovskaya we shall get food that we can eat," and so on.

The water in the Shilka was so shallow that there was a delay of several hours before we could come alongside of the steamer for Blagovestchensk.

It was 11 a.m. when we changed into the steamer. The sun's rays were cruel as we crossed the bridge of planks that had been laid down for our benefit. There was plenty of room for all who wished to travel first class. There was a pleasant saloon across the prow, and a passage running down the centre of the ship opened into the middle of it. Cabins, each containing two wide berths, opened into the passage on both sides.

The Amur is not a wide river as compared to the Yenisei or the Angara, and there is not much that is remarkable about its scenery after the first few miles. For hours together we saw nothing but undulating hills covered thickly with fir-trees. These would often change after a time to green pasture land without a sign of human life to relieve the monotony.

Here, as on the railway, we experienced great changes of weather and of temperature. The intense heat of the first day was followed by autumnal cold and heavy rain. The very sailors we had seen at their posts in cotton blouses were now going about in fur-lined ulsters.

During the day there was always a sailor at the prow with a measuring pole. He called out the depth in a sing-song tone as he dropped the pole into the water and drew it out again. There were so many sand-banks and small islands that it would have been impossible to proceed at night. Happily for us we continued to have plenty of water.

Here and there we passed a scattered Cossack village and stopped to take the letters of the priest, the schoolmaster, or the doctor, if there was one.

There were few signs of life on the Chinese frontier. Sometimes, however, we passed close enough to a village to distinguish the peculiar shape of the Manchurian houses, or the junk-like canoes tied up on the bank.

At certain points the river curves round in a most remarkable manner. There are times when you see no opening in front of you at all. In one place our steamer twisted in and out between the rocks almost forming the figure 8; and it seemed that in another minute we should run ashore. We stood watching in silence for some minutes. All at once the steamer made an abrupt turn to the right.

Blagovestchensk

We did not reach Blagovestchensk till Sunday morning. Blagovestchensk, or "The town with the swear name" as I have since heard it called, unrolled itself with tantalizing slowness to our impatient eyes. We were all on deck, and there was a mustering of field glasses. Six whole days had passed since we left Stretinsk. We might have crossed the Atlantic in that time. No wonder we were all impatient.

First came a few straggling *isbas* or peasants' huts, then some pleasant-looking villas, far apart, with their front windows looking out upon the river; then an avenue of trees, and finally several solid-looking business houses of red brick, and a hotel.

"You have missed the post steamer," was the first piece of news that greeted our ears, "you will have to wait four days for the next." One of the passengers who had landed new came back very kindly to tell us that we had no time to lose. "The captain has received orders to return at once to Pokrovskaya," he said.

Not wishing to see Pokrovskaya again so soon I hurried on land to find a porter. Having been advised to stay at the *Grand Hotel* we drove there at once, and were glad to find more comfortable quarters than we had dared to expect. I have heard since that this hotel is famed all over Siberia as the best throughout the length and breadth of the land.

It was now three weeks since we had left Irkutsk. As we had been travel-ling with the post all the time no letters or newspapers had caught us up, and we literally thirsted for European news.

I took a walk in the town, and made one or two purchases. Most of the people I met in the shops and in the streets were Chinamen—that is, Man-chus. Many of them carried poles balanced across their shoulders with swing-ing baskets of vegetables or fruits. I had never seen so many of the yellow race in my life, and was much interested in studying their faces as they passed. They struck me as being very ugly indeed. I tried to feel kindly towards them, and even went so far as to picture myself a missionary in a Chinese town. I returned to the hotel with a feeling of thankfulness that I was not a mission-ary, at least not to so unattractive a people. Alas! at that very hour hundreds of poor missionaries in China were escaping for their lives, while many others were being cruelly murdered; and, what is more, the days of many a Manchu into whose face I looked that morning, were numbered.

On Wednesday I was utterly incapacitated owing to the heat and the food. I remained in my room till about 3 p.m., when the manager appeared at the door. "War has broken out, and all the steamers except the 'post' have been chartered to carry soldiers to the seat of action. If you do go under the present state of affairs you will run the risk of being shot at, if not stopped altogether. It will all be finished in a month, and then you can go on in safety."

As soon as the manager had left us I drank a glass of strong tea to settle my nerves. It was quite clear that Russian troops were being mobilized. We could see that with our own eyes from the window.

The situation of Blagovestchensk, so close to two navigable rivers, has been most favourable to its growth. Manchus came across in great numbers and helped to people the place, while emigrants and Cossacks formed the bulk of the Russian population. Gold mines in the neighbourhood were exploited, and another class of men was attracted. There is no beauty about the town.

Sakhalin and Aigun

It was too hot to be on deck, but we would not go in till we were fairly off, as we were anxious to get a good view of Sakhalin, a Manchurian village situated exactly opposite Blagovestchensk, on the river bank. From this vil-lage begins the Chinese road that passes through the valley of Aigun and … branches off into the interior of Manchuria.

Twenty versts farther on we passed Aigun. The river was much wider at this point, and our steamer kept well to mid-stream to avoid dangerous sand-banks, so that our view of the place was a distant one. There was not a sign of life stirring as we passed, and we laughed to think of all the rumours we had heard, and felt very glad we had not allowed ourselves to be frightened into staying at Blagovestchensk.

Khabarovsk

We were three days and three nights travelling from Blagovestchensk to Khabarovsk. On the third day we passed the village Blagoslavenny; it is not Russian, but a Corean village. In the year 1871 some Corean emigrants settled there; they had come from the Ussuri district, and, while they became members of the Orthodox Church, retained their own language, their own way of life, and their own system of agriculture.

We had been told that there were no hotels in Khabarovsk, so we obtained permission from the agents to spend the night on the steamer that had brought us.

Khabarovsk is now a rapidly growing town perched on undulating hills that sloped down to the water's edge just where the Amur is joined to the Ussuri. It is now an administrative centre of the Maritime Province, and the Governor-General resides there. The town is essentially military in its character that it can hardly be called anything else but a garrison.

To Vladivostok

Our train was to start for Vladivostok at 7 a.m., and it was a long drive to the station. I shall never forget the state of the roads; it was like driving over ploughed fields after rain.

As we walked up and down the platform we were struck with the great number of nationalities represented on it. Coreans dressed all in white with strange white headdresses, that made a striking contrast to their jet-black hair and dark yellow skins, were squatting on the ground in rows. Servian gipsies were walking amongst the crowd and telling fortunes; Chinese and Japs were everywhere.

The express train by which we travelled to Vladivostok was not so luxurious as the "*train de luxe*" by which we had travelled to Omsk. It was like an ordinary post train with a rough kind of dining car attached. At one end of the dining car was a buffet behind which stood two Jap boys always alert for orders.

I observed that the train seemed to be managed by soldiers rather than by the usual railway men, and that the stations were, many of them, quite military in appearance; whereupon I was told that this was because in time of war the Ussuri railway would become a military one, and that the soldiers should have some practice in the management of it.

The country through which we now passed was very beautiful. There were hills and valleys and meadows all following one another in quick succession.

Our train was due at Vladivostok at 1 p.m. on the day following that on which we had left Khabarovsk, and at 12:30 we caught sight of the waters of the Amur Gulf, an arm of the Bay of Peter the Great. The train ran close to the water's edge and a delicious sea breeze blew in upon us. Then came the last station we had to pass—Khilkovo. I need hardly say that it had a special interest for us as having received its name in honour of our kind friend Prince Hilkoff, the Minister of Ways and Communications.

We found ourselves speeding through the very centre of Vladivostok. Our first view of the town was pleasing. Its semi-European houses seemed to spring up in the most unexpected places, while the bay of the Golden Horn curled itself round the undulating hills, and pretty boats on the water added life to the scene. This "Paris of Siberia," as it has been called, we found in a state of unusual stir and excitement, owing to the mobilization of its troops for the quieting of a rebellion which the Chinese government was itself unable to quell.

In Vladivostok

Hotel Moscow was full of people waiting like ourselves for a steamer to Nagasaki, the Japanese port to which, in times of peace, there is regular and frequent service.

In the evening Colonel D—looked in. "I have come to say good-bye," he said. "I shall probably start either for Taku with soldiers before daybreak, or cross to Otaru in the north of Japan by a cargo boat leaving at 9:30 a.m."

"If you go to Japan take us with you," we both cried in a breath.

"I fear there will be no accommodation for ladies," he replied.

"Please take these," said my mother handing him some rouble notes, "and secure our passages on the cargo boat."

At the appointed hour the following morning the Colonel appeared. "I have taken your passages," he said. "The captain is going to let you have his own cabin, so you'll not have to sleep on deck."

We found ourselves the occupants of a comfortable cabin with two berths. There was truly nothing more to be desired but a calm passage.

We had left on Friday, Vladivostok, July 6, and it was 7 p.m. on Sunday evening when we arrived at Otaru.

At Nikko, Japan, a telegram from the Governor of Vladivostok read: "All passenger traffic on the Amur suspended." At the same time it was stated in the Japanese newspapers that all the foreigners in Pekin had been massacred, and that four Russian steamboats had been sunk by Boxers on the Amur.

Not wishing to run needless risks we decided, with much regret, to give up all thought of returning through Siberia, and took our passages in the first steamer leaving for America. We sailed from Yokohama on July 27 in the *Empress of Japan*.

CHAPTER ELEVEN

~

Julia Cantacuzene, Countess Speransky, née Grant

Life in Russia as a Princess

Born Julia Dent Grant in 1876 in the White House, she was the grand-daughter of President Ulysses Grant. Her father, Brigadier General Frederick Dent Grant, was the son of the president and had a long career in the United States Army. Her mother was Ida Honoré. Julia and her mother followed General Grant to his various posts, and when he was appointed Minister Pleni-Potentiary to the Austro-Hungarian Empire, they lived in Vienna from 1889 to 1892. There, Julia learned German, made her debut, was presented to Emperor Franz Joseph, and enjoyed the balls and parties among the elite of the court. She also made her debut in Newport, Rhode Island, where her Aunt Bertha Honoré Palmer summered.

In 1898, Julia and her Aunt Bertha, a wealthy Chicago matron, toured Europe, visiting London, Paris, Rome, Cannes, and Cairo. In Rome, she met Prince Michael Cantacuzene, an army officer, who was assigned briefly to the Russian Embassy. Once they went to Cannes, the prince appeared again at their hotel, and in the next two days the couple were engaged. Later, he went with Julia and her aunt to Paris, where they made plans for their wedding.

Prince Michael was a graduate of the Imperial Alexandrine Lycee in St. Petersburg and a career cavalry office in the Russian Army. His pedigree was impressive as his ancestors included the fourteenth-century Byzantine Emperor John Cantacuzene, and he was the grandson of statesman Count Michael Speransky. The Cantacuzenes had estates in Yalta, the Crimea, in Poltava, the Ukraine, and a home in St. Petersburg. Julia, upon her marriage, would live a life that she had been exposed to in Vienna and she adapted to easily.

Wedding of Julia Grant
My Life Here and There (Public domain)

The couple were married at Beaulieu, a Newport mansion, on September 25, 1899, in both a Russian Orthodox and Episcopal ceremony. They immediately departed for Europe and the Russian Empire. By the standards of the day, Julia had a whirlwind courtship and entered upon her marriage knowing little about the country or its customs where she was to live for the next eighteen years. No doubt, her title as princess and the glamour of an aristocratic lifestyle had its appeal, and she expressed no regret about her choice of husband. She had a sense of adventure and was open to new experiences.

Julia lived in St. Petersburg and at Bouromka, the family estate in the Ukraine, and their villa in the Crimea, with trips to the United States and Europe during her years in Russia. Her parents visited Russia several times. The couple had three children: Michael (1900–1972), Barbara (1904–1991), and Zinaida (1908–1984), all born in St. Petersburg and educated there. When the revolution of 1917 began, the children were sent, via the Trans-Siberian Railroad, to their grandparents in the United States.

Julia was caught up in the social life of the capital and was presented to the Empress Alexandra and was well acquainted with the Grand Duchess Marie. She also entertained a salon of prominent men and women who visited her home regularly. They included members of the aristocracy and politicians, as she followed the ever-changing events in Russia closely, including the Russo-Japanese War (1904–1905), the revolt of 1905, and the Russian Revolution of 1917.

The Russian Revolution changed the lives of the aristocracy forever. Prince Michael, as an officer in the army, faced possible execution by the

Bolsheviks; hence the couple made plans to leave the country with the few belongings they could take, sewing Julia's jewels carefully into her garments and hats. Their preparations for their departure and their train journey out of St. Petersburg to Sweden were successful but harrowing, as they feared being discovered. Once safe in Europe, they made their way to the United States.

In the United States, the couple followed news of the revolution closely. Being an aristocrat, Prince Michael supported the Whites, who fought against the Bolsheviks (Reds). In 1919, he went to Omsk, Siberia, to see what he could do to support Admiral Alexander Kolchak's forces. Later that year, he returned to the United States to gather support for Kolchak, but the opposition was defeated, and Kolchak was executed.

Once in the United States, Julia wrote articles about Russia for weekly magazines. She also wrote two books of her life experiences: *My Life Here and There, 1876 1917* and *Revolutionary Days: Recollections of Romanoffs and Bolsheviki, 1914–1917*. The Cantacuzenes had lost their land, homes, and finances once they left Russia, so her efforts may have provided some needed income.

Ultimately, the Cantacuzenes settled in Sarasota, Florida, where Michael worked for the Palmer enterprises there. In 1934, the couple divorced and Julia moved to Washington, D.C., where she no longer used her title, but she befriended and helped Russian emigres. She became blind at seventy and regained partial sight later on. Julia died at age ninety-nine in 1975 and is buried at the Washington National Cathedral.

In 1935, Michael married Jeanette Draper, an employee of the Palmer Bank, of which he was vice president. He died in 1955 and is buried in Manasota Memorial Park in Sarasota.

Julia's life, as related in *Revolutionary Days*, is a firsthand account of the stirring events leading up to the Russian Revolution of 1917. She was an astute observer and, being a Russian citizen and married into the aristocracy, she had definite prejudices, although she was not entirely against change in Russia, as were others of her class. In fact, she welcomed a more liberal Russia and supported the Dumas that were established.

Julia closely followed the events of the Russo-Japanese War, 1904–1905, and she knew about the poor condition of the fleet. She supported the war effort by preparing bandages and was patroness of two hospitals. On Bloody Sunday, in January 1905, when protestors demanded bread, she believed that the seeds of revolution had been planted.

Princess Julia took an interest in the victories and defeats of the Russian forces during World War I. She knew the circumstances of the resignation of the Emperor Nicholas II and the arrest of Empress Alexandra, as well as the machinations and intrigues surrounding the court influenced by Rasputin.

She supported the provisional government that was headed by Alexander Kerensky, but the Bolshevik takeover in November 1917 made it impossible for the wealthy and aristocratic Cantacuzenes to remain in Russia; hence they left as soon as they could.

The following selections are from *Revolutionary Days*.

～

Arrival at Bouromka in Poltava, the Ukraine, the Cantacuzene Estate

The superintendents of the estate met us with the traditional bread and salt on silver dishes, covered with towels embroidered by the women of the estate. They kissed my hands, while my husband embraced each of the old servitors heartily. They had seen him grow up and were his devoted friends, it seemed.

The Estate's Ballroom and Welcome

On a table stood a collection of icons that were to be ours and with which we were to be blessed. Some of them were ancient and rare, offered by the family or friends; others in modern enamel or beaten bronze were donated by the house servants and the superintendents of the estates. Incense burned, voices rose in beautiful strains, and the whole scene was most touching, with a charm different from any I had ever experienced. It was a far cry from Newport, New York, and Paris to this new life just opening, and somehow, in spite of its strangeness, it attracted me more than I could express. I began at that moment to feel a drop of sympathy with the nation that created such a frame and lived in it, filling it so well.

The Estate

There was much I liked and much that was amusing at Bouromka. The average American housekeeper would have gone quite mad from the inconvenient arrangements. The pumping by hand of all the water for the enormous establishment; the fetching and carrying necessary; the mere fact that two men spent their entire days cleaning, filling and lighting kerosene lamps; that we all lived with doors and windows unbolted, even open ... that all one's treasures lay about in complete safety for years, generations even; all this seemed amazing!

The Peasant Village

The village outside our gates were very picturesque, but it gave me a heartache to see the wretchedness that reigned there. And the unhealthy looks of many of the people. ... Cattle and people both drank and bathed in the crystal water. Their homes, smothered in trees and gay flowers, were of a charming effect from a distance. Close by it was different, for the thatched roofs all needed mending, were blown about terribly, and let in rain and snow. The houses themselves usually had crooked walls with tiny windows fixed in the plaster. One saw evidences of poverty, misery, filth, shiftlessness, crowding, and discomfort. To me it was deeply distressing.

Arrival in St. Petersburg

It was a drizzling morning with dirty snow covering the streets thinly. Scarcely light as yet, the place looked dull, and a very raw, icy wind swept across one's face. The carriage, through mistake or neglect, was not there, so perforce we drove across the city in a queer vehicle called a *droshsky*, with a driver as odd as his turnout, conducting a horse which had a night's work already in his weary legs, I'm sure, from the slow way he moved.

That drive was my only bad experience in the magnificent city, which I was to love so dearly as my home through the years, but it was horrid, and it seemed miles from the Warsaw station to Fontanka, where the princess lived.

Society in St. Petersburg

Getting to know people in St. Petersburg was an interesting experience. It was not like meeting a society when passing through some foreign city, with the idea that one would be moving on soon and that mutual impressions made were only of casual importance. Some of these Russians were now my relatives; all of them potentially were my friends, and I knew I must live among them through the remainder of my days. They were different from any companions of my past. I had the feeling they were much simpler and more natural. Etiquette existed, but its hand was less heavy in St. Petersburg than in Vienna.

Meeting the Empress Alexandra and the Grand Duchess Marie

First, at a small ball at the palace of the Grand Duke Vladimir, the Grand Duchess Marie, our hostess, came and took me by the hand, saying: "Come,

Joy, I have been talking to the Empress of you, and she says I may personally present you to her"; so I was taken up to where the young empress stood, and the grand duchess said a few kindly words and pushed me forward into the empty space kept clear about the sovereign. The latter was exceedingly quiet and timid. After two or three perfunctory questions, which I answered, she fell into her usual attitude of silent distraction so I curtsied and wandered off. However, I had actually talked with Her Majesty, which made everyone say that I must ask for a formal audience at once, not only of the empresses but of all the grand duchesses as well. Once one had bowed before Her Majesty, to neglect these latter would be wrong, apparently.

My first years in St. Petersburg, until the outbreak of the Japanese War, were the most brilliant socially I saw there. The Empress Mother did not appear often, but when she did so, she took first place at court. Her conversation was as gay and agreeable as she herself was. Putting each one at his ease, she seemed most human and womanly, an inspiration to do one's best. Her manner was exactly that of her sister the Duchess of Cumberland, and I felt somehow I had always known her.

Russia in 1903

During these early years, I spent my time exclusively between the duties of our attractive home, with its nursery, and the gay functions that made up my round of society life, intimate or official. I began to feel I was making many friends, both men and women, and I was growing Russian in my ways. I loved all I was doing and was anxious to make those whom I admired realize my sympathy and enthusiasm. They answered my expressions and understandings as if sure of my sincerity and adopted me completely within a short time.

My youth and high spirits did not prevent me seeing much that was sad in Russia. Both in the country and the city, there was a yearning spirit among the people that promised trouble in time. This was especially so toward the end of 1903.

Princess Julia's Salon

It became the pleasantest hour of the day—one for quiet talk and restful discussions, from which I learned more of Russia and my new compatriots than in any other way. With freezing weather outside, inside, the open blaze, singing kettle, and cozy armchairs helped any caller who dropped in to thaw his ideas. Pleasant regimental comrades, a few agreeable foreign diplomats, gradually, also some older men whom I met at dinners came and began the intimate circle that later through the years was to grow considerably. I scarcely had to study or even to ask questions. My education progressed rapidly.

In listening to my visitors each day, I began to catch their attitude and atmosphere, to realize what remarkable culture they had. The literature, art, and music of the country, its history and great past, made them, as well as the peasantry, what they were. It was absorbingly interesting, and I grew to love my Russians more and more.

Problems Ahead

Strangely enough, in the apparent quiet that reigned, these men showed signs of anxiety as to what was ahead of us. Often they spoke of the peasant, of his backwardness in education, yet of his cleverness—and they spoke of their own efforts to develop these dark millions. They would almost always talk of the bureaucracy with impatience and annoyance, sometimes criticizing Peter the Great for installing it, with all the general clumsiness of our government machinery. They complained of the difficulty each man had in obtaining action in cases when it would be an advantage all around. Of the injustice and favoritism being practiced or allowed, there was also much said. The party that wished reforms or improvements was large, and their blame of the empress's policy in isolating herself—of the undesirability of the shut-in and exclusively family life of the sovereigns, of the protection given to cover various scandalous exploitations by a group in our Far Eastern Siberian country—was extremely marked.

The Russo-Japanese War, 1904–1905

One felt great changes with each succeeding season. The Japanese war came unexpectedly. Shortly before the great Ito passed through St. Petersburg, hoping for a friendly reception and to make a loan. He was badly received by our government and pushed on to England, where he affected both a loan and soon afterward a treaty, I think.

The *Varig* was sunk, and the declaration of war followed almost instantly. My husband's regiment was not ordered to Manchuria, so I knew little of the war only by hearsay. I could not yet read enough Russian to follow in the newspapers our progress at the front.

As time progressed, however, I became more and more absorbed by events in the East—Port Arthur's siege and splendid defense; the heroic fighting of our troops, always insufficiently supplied by a single-track and newly built railroad; the noble efforts of Prince Khilkov, minister of transport, to keep the provision and troop trains moving.

For many months no one in St. Petersburg talked of anything but the Manchurian news, but little by little changes occurred in the tenor of our conversations. There were tales of disappointments and disillusions. There also was bitterness, pity, the desire for rest and peace, and an ever-increasing anxiety; tales of battles and ships lost; tales of incompetency of the commander-in-chief and some of the other favorites; tales of confusion and sufferings among our troops; tales of officers and men under fire during heroic work.

Contributions of Women

We women worked with one or another of the sewing groups, preparing bandages and underclothes or warm woolen garments for the soldiers. A lot of my women friends went out to Siberia with various hospital trains or Red Cross units.

Results of the Russo-Japanese War in Russia

The war had an excellent effect on our people. The era of war and the miserable management of everything brought out a new spirit in many classes of Russians. The liberals—and most of the nobility I saw were in this group—felt it was high time the country should be put in order and helped forward, with education given and land reforms made. The army officers were keen to see a saner policy pursued by the government and wished the sovereign would make reforms of his own accord. These might be gifts now. We were beginning to feel that otherwise they would become concessions torn from him in the near future.

1905

Politically, through the ebb and flow of opinion, we felt Russia was moving forward and that in a few short years, the emperor would give a constitution, for it would be demanded of him by healthy elements in the nation. They sanely waited, worked for progress, and were not mere degenerates or hasty visionaries. Parties were forming of some substance in the second and third Duma, and were learning to handle themselves. Russia was growing fast.

Rasputin and Madame Anna Vyrubova

There was no doubt in anyone's mind regarding Madame Vyrubova's relations with Rasputin, or of the fact that she had invented him and declared him to be a miracle-worker, thus installing him as a sort of backstairs prophet. His prayers were said to do the empress good, and also the young heir to the throne, who was an invalid. Madame Vyrubova had persuaded Her Majesty that she herself could not survive being separated a day from the mistress she adored. Also, she was convincing about Rasputin. He was a simple peasant; it would please the people of Russia to know a representative of theirs stood high at court.

As for Rasputin, I never met or saw him. Coarse, vicious, hideous he was known to be, yet he exerted an unholy fascination on any number of women who had crowded about him and composed his clientele. He drank and in general lived brutally, though without other plans than to be materially enriched or to have warmth and finery and food.

Both Madame Vyrubova and her occult partner Rasputin were growing arrogant in 1914 toward the members of the court, whenever their Imperial protectress was not watching; but in her presence they always played modest roles and represented themselves to be a pair of humble saints who spent their time in prayer. Officials were approached by them for favors, however, and in their petitions covert threats were felt.

July 1914, Prelude to War

For July 25, 1914, Saturday evening, a gala performance of the Imperial ballet was "commanded" in the quaint theater of our military camp at Krasnoe Selo. Since the time of the great Peter, the guard regiments of Russian autocrats have summered here; and this night, for the last event of the season, the pretty playhouse and garden were illuminated and decorated with flags, our own and the French. The latter were a remaining tribute to our allies, who had left us a few days previously after a lengthy visit. Satisfaction in the past, hope for the future showed on all faces, now that Poincaré and the brilliant René Viviani were on their homeward route across the northern sea; and we breathed easily in the sense of relaxation from ceremonious functions.

A few friends dined at our camp-cottage; and in the party some diplomats came down from town, brought us the unexpected news—which we called "sensational and exaggerated"—of an agitated stock exchange, an anxious foreign office, complications with Vienna, and a possible crisis that might mean war. This set us all speculating, though we treated the subject with only passive interest.

I shall never forget the stress and strain of those few days, from the twenty-sixth until the twenty-ninth of July. Disturbances and strikes were feared and predicted in the capital where German agents were arrested, and German money was found and confiscated among our factory workmen! All St. Petersburg lived in a state of indescribable nervous tension, and gossip said the pressure brought on the emperor by certain court influences against war was so heavy that perhaps His Majesty would still be persuaded not to uphold our fine Slav policy of defending Serbia.

Women and War Work in St. Petersburgh

When the war came, a number of women felt with me that nothing counted but our patriotic duties; and in a desire to make a demonstration of loyalty, we all called on Mme Vyrubova, asking for any work in the various Red Cross organizations that would be organized by Her Majesty's orders. We were told by her that "Her Majesty was suffering from one of her frequent attacks of nervous pains"; and all those wishing to help were begged to join in the work at the Winter Palace, where the doors would be thrown open as they had been at the time of the Japanese War. Wives of government and court officials, wives of officers, wives of simple soldiers, and work girls from shops and dressmaking establishments were there, rubbing shoulders, all filled with zeal.

I found myself drawn into the stream, making and packing bandages like all my friends, while we talked of the daily news. The latter was most encouraging and gratifying to our national vanity. The campaign in East Prussia progressed rapidly, and we captured town after town until our armies had advanced far on German soil.

I loved St. Petersburgh in those fine first weeks of war and admired my compatriots as never before. In the streets everyone hurried, everyone was busy, and autos, houses, and women wore the sign of the Red Cross. The humbler elements especially were touching, and each poor shop readily sold things for the soldiers at a discount, just as each poor work girl gave of her strength in the good cause. The rich were vastly generous; not only their money, but their time and thought, palaces and motors, filled out and completed the omissions in the government's care for its sons.

The Winter of 1915

During the first winter of the war, courage was kept up by the news of our fine military record; and though there were no large parties for society, small dinners abounded in hospitable homes.

Toward spring I felt a change in the capital's mentality. Michael's letters from the Grand Duke's staff, day by day, also reflected the impressions made there by the terrible retreat. In Petrograd the national and individual sorrow was very great, and the cheerfulness that marked gatherings through the winter departed, once and for all. There was a quantity of gossip about the "Occult" or German forces beginning to influence events, and a general foreboding as to the future created an atmosphere difficult to live in. Parties were forming; and it was a growing complication to steer a straight course among the eddies of suspicion.

The Duma Meets on August 1, 1915

As the always impressive president of the Duma, Rodzianko went to his place and rapped upon his desk, there was immediate silence. His speech was short and patriotic, much applauded and appreciated. Enthusiasm was the order of the day.

When we left the Duma, it was with a feeling that whatever our troubles and the terrible mistakes that had caused them, they were being corrected now. The crown was well supported by a fine cabinet, and the future could not fail to be good. The days passed, and this impression began to wear away. The retreat all along the line continued. Warsaw surrendered; and many other great cities, rich with our small reserves of ammunition or supplies, were ceded one after another, inevitably, to the enemy.

Rasputin's Assassination, December 1916

When I arrived in the Crimea, I found at first the quiet country life delightful in comparison with the capital's mental atmosphere. But soon I discovered that all letters from the north were severely censored; and the papers were allowed to contain little concerning politics.

I saw much of her [the Grand Duchess Xenia] these dark weeks, and she roused all my sympathy by the weight of care she bravely carried and by her anxiety for the safety of her brother and his family. She fully realized the dangers ahead, yet could do nothing to save those she loved. In fact, it was her son-in-law, young Prince Yusupov, who opened the dramatic action of the revolution by killing Rasputin with his own hand at a supper party given for that purpose in his Petrograd palace. This hideous business which was planned and carried out in cold blood, made a sensation impossible to describe all over the country. Everyone breathed with relief at Rasputin's disappearance. Some openly hoped it would lead to a series of murders, including

Mme. Vyrubova's, Protopopov's and even their august protectress's, as these crimes would finally rid the nation of tyranny, they said, and save us from a bloody revolution, inevitable.

Some few optimists hoped that once their "prophet" was gone, the clan of evil-doers might fall to pieces and the empress's eyes be opened at last to their sins. But just the opposite happened. Rasputin had never been the brains of his party, only a mask behind which the real conspirators hid themselves, and his sudden death turned him into a martyr, as well as a saint in Her Majesty's eyes. The ex-"followers" made much of his remains, which were brought with great honor to lie in the chapel of the Tsarskoe Palace, where night and day the women of his group watched and prayed by them. Then he was buried in the Imperial Park, and a daily visit was paid the spot by the empress.

The Revolution

I returned to Petrograd after the New Year, remaining there four weeks on business. I was perfectly shocked at the changes I found. No one had any confidence in the future of the government. General depression was extreme and very contagious, since one heard the most sober and reliable people stating facts that did not seem believable but were nevertheless true. The silence and the anxious faces of members of our court and government, who were the most loyal, were perhaps those marks of coming downfall that struck me most.

We believed the Grand Duke Nicholas's prophecy was coming true, and that our soldiers and people could no longer be forced to defend a government of which so much evil was commonly known. Long lines of poor stood waiting hours to receive insufficient rations of bread and other necessities; the weather was exceptionally cold—twenty or thirty degrees below zero—and fuel was scarce; everyone was suffering, and there were continuous strikes and great discontent.

It got about that a palace revolution was being planned, where assassination would clear the way for a new era. Everything else had been tried to no avail, and this was the only remaining remedy.

Emperor Nicholas Resigns and the Aftermath

Sunday, the eleventh [of March] appeared in the papers an Imperial proclamation over the emperor's signature, but not that which was expected. This one dissolved the Duma.

The day was one of heavy, angry silence. In the streets, no tram-cars, almost no sleighs or autos were in circulation, and few people walked about. In various directions shooting was heard, and sinister rumors floated about threatening law and order; yet nothing could be done.

Monday morning, the twelfth, it had come. The town was in an uproar. Public buildings were burning. There were encounters in the streets in almost every direction between the loyal troops and revolutionaries. Wild shooting on both sides.

The Emperor Abdicates in Favor of His Brother Michael

He [the emperor] said he would abdicate his rights, along with those of the tsarevich, in favor of his brother Michael. The deputies consented to this and gave him a paper to sign, which had been prepared beforehand on these lines. With no show of emotion, the emperor took the paper and moved into the office next to his salon, leaving all the company behind him. In a few moments he returned, with a typewritten sheet in his hand, presenting it to the deputies to read. He asked if it was what they had wished. Upon hearing their affirmation, the sovereign put his signature immediately to the document.

Amazing calm had been the emperor's attitude. Helpless in the hands of conspirators until now, the emperor was apparently equally unable to resist these new domineering spirits; and he neither protested or complained of his fate nor showed the slightest desire to defend his inheritance. On the contrary, he gave in at once, without argument, and did as he was instructed. He seemed to be entirely content to feel he might now lead a quiet life and was to be free from his burden of state affairs. It never occurred to him to order these deputies arrested or to make any other order of self-defense.

The Provisional Government

It was immediately decided to form a provisional government to carry on the war and the administration of the country. That same Thursday a ministry was named. It included all the best liberal thinkers and theorists available. Nearly all the men in this cabinet were honest and inspired with a fine ambition to set the country on its feet.

The revolution had lasted but a week. When the old ministers had been arrested, none of them had been seriously ill-treated, though a few had suffered from exposure to the cold or from the hardships of poor lodging and inconvenience.

Many times the lives of all occupants of the palace hung by a thread, and always the situation was solved by Kerensky's eloquence and his clever handling of his clients.

Hundreds of prisoners were set free immediately after their arrest while others lingered many days. None was actually ever executed, as one of Kerensky's first measures was the suppression of capital punishment.

Over the whole country the news of the revolution was received with a thankfulness almost religious; and order reigned everywhere; though the police were at once gathered in by mobilizations and sent to the front to fight, leaving our prison doors open, and streets and highways unguarded. Unfortunately, even the frontiers were free to all for six days, so anyone might pass in without question or papers. By the time the provisional government sent soldiers to replace the ordinary frontier guardians, thousands of German spies and agents had passed our gates unmolested and had settled down to their deadly work of organizing and forming the Bolshevik party, which in the beginning had been but a rabble.

Arrest of the Empress

In some strange way, no news of the abdication reached Her Majesty until a deputation was announced to her during the day of Thursday. She immediately replied she would receive its members in audience in one of the palace halls. As she entered the room, she found that she was facing a group of unpretentious looking men whose spokesman, a young colonel, announced to her that he had the painful duty of "arresting Her Majesty." She indignantly asked how and why, and was given a short history of events in the capital, of which she had been totally ignorant.

The Imperial Proclamation was handed to her to read. In spite of all the bitterness and despair she must have felt, she drew herself up proudly and faced the deputies. "I have nothing more to say."

But in the whole great empire, where they had reigned for more than twenty years, there seemed no word of praise or pity for the miserable pair who had been all powerful sovereigns only a few days previously, and not one person raised a hand to defend their banner. This seemed to me one of the most eloquent details of the whole revolution.

Aftermath of the Revolution

Provision reserves carefully made by the old government were being rapidly squandered now, while nothing was done to gather new stores, and our transportation was as disorganized as ever. The police had been destroyed, and the vague civilian militia that replaced them could be of no service in case of real necessity.

The factories were not working. The workmen were all members of committees, and they were busy "governing" or were merely doing nothing, and finding life too agreeable to return to their duties. The "soviets of workmen and soldiers" still in residence at the Tauride Palace, composed the real government and were becoming a force with which the ministry were obliged to reckon.

Kiev

Kiev's attitude was much more optimistic than had been Petrograd's. The hotels and restaurants were crowded. There were musicals, plays, and festivities, with enormous numbers of new arrivals and new settlers. All the Polish aristocrats, who were refugees from the war-devastated provinces, had settled here in 1915.

Back in Petrograd

There were disorders everywhere, and shops, banks, and offices were closed.

I found out by telephone the government offices were also closed. We remained where we were that day and the next—Tuesday and Wednesday—as if besieged, in our big rooms with windows closed and curtains drawn to prevent any stray shots from coming in.

The shooting increased and decreased periodically, for no apparent reason. I learned that the question in the cabinet was a difficult one to settle. It would probably and disastrously bring about the resignation of the last conservative elements still in power, thus giving the Socialists another forward push.

Thursday the whole town resumed its normal aspect. The trains were running, and we went about our business, as if nothing occurred to disturb life. The anarchists had gained a step in their advance toward power. Prince Lvov had resigned, and Kerensky was made prime minister, with various other socialist elements put into the cabinet. All patriots, not only those of conservative ideas, were growing anxious at the lost ground each day showed, and the increasing power of the mob and their German leaders. It was decidedly marked that Lenin's propaganda was growing more aggressive; and Trotsky, the anarchist (whose real name was Leo Bronstein), had arrived, or was arriving, to inflame the unbalanced brains and help Lenin to do his utmost.

The government apparently was too weak to assume anything but a propitiating attitude toward those avowed anarchists, or else there was no feeling in administrative circles of danger to the nation from the Lenin and Trotsky theories. It all seemed fatal in its menace for the future of the country to those of our class, who had no desires politically and who thought only of winning the war and of preserving Russia. But our military and conservative groups had lost the power to even speak.

Fear of the Future for Russia

Now influenced by the poisonous German propaganda, which was being daily injected, these same creatures of the plains and woods were working themselves into a passionate folly and were suffering from hideous moral indigestion, following too much liberty, which might well bring about their ruin, together with that of the whole country. And seemingly, no one could help us now, while it was still time! Everyone, at home and abroad, was either too busy, or was blind. Some said we had primitive strength enough as a nation to live through our trials, and after knowing these people for so many years, I was of those who kept faith in their final resurrection. I only wept for the sufferings and destruction that the immediate future must bring, and for the reaction of our troubles on the war. It took all my courage to face the months ahead, and I wondered whether I should leave Kiev alive and with my husband or whether we should find our end there.

Life in Kiev

Kiev was full of acquaintances, and there were even several old friends settled there or passing through. I found my husband was the center of an agreeable group whose motto was openly to "Eat, drink, and be merry in the insecurity of tomorrow." Life was expensive, but people had plenty of ready money and were trying to spend it on their immediate enjoyment, since rumors floated southward that there might be later a confiscation of ready funds for the government needs. Parties on the river, auto-picnics to the chateaux in the neighborhood, dinners and suppers with gypsy-bands and chorus, bridge and even tangos, poker and romances were the order of the day. It seemed even gayer than in the spring, perhaps a bit feverishly so.

Committees became an epidemic everywhere. Committees of workmen at Count Bobrinsky's sugar factories decided when they would work, also at what prices, and when to enjoy a holiday; and they over-ran the Bobrinsky home, camping in the rooms, and using furniture and valuables. It was the same at other factories, and production was practically at a standstill. Likewise, committees of peasants on all estates fixed their own wages and labor, and said what should be done with the master's harvests after the year's grain was brought in. The village cows were grazing on proprietors' lawns, the village people walked in gardens and parks, ate fruits and vegetables found there, requisitioned machinery and stock, and though the chateaux were still respected, there was already talk of taking them for places of amusement or for school buildings.

As yet, our country place Bouromka was quiet, which was a great blessing. We gratefully attributed this to our intendant's personal talents. In September there came to Bouromka village, however, a committee from outside. Ukrainians and Bolsheviki, the intendant reported they were, and these preached the most inflammatory doctrines.

The peasants were still resisting, explaining they were content with us and that their work had always been well paid for and themselves well treated. The agitators then said the land was by right the peasants', and they declared the house, buildings, and stock should be appropriated by them now, as everything according to the law of our new republic belonged to the people. Still the peasantry were quiet, but we knew our hour would soon come, and this anxiety for the old family home was added to other troubles.

Bouromka

We had horrid news from Bouromka, and none at all from the other estates, and we were seriously concerned. We ordered the intendants and certain faithful house servants to bring to Kiev what smaller objects they could from the more valuable collections at Bouromka—ancient silver, the old snuffboxes, the jewelry worn by various ancestresses, as well as a very rare and a beautiful collection of old cameos and the jewels of my mother-in-law and sister-in-law, which had been left in their safes at Bouromka.

The bronzes, pictures, furniture, and collections of china could not be handled or transported without attracting attention and, above all, it seemed important to avoid arousing suspicion among the village committeemen. So these and some 20,000 volumes in the library, some of them of infinite value (intrinsic and sentimental), all the family archives, and a cellar of rare vintages—many of which were more than a century old—remained to their fate.

The worst of these forebodings were soon realized. First, our cattle and horses were confiscated. A few days later the distillery was broken into and burned, and the drunken crowd invaded our farm buildings, taking possession of the chateau stables. Then our house cellar was rifled, and the faithful servants were driven out back to the village, while the crowd cap-tured the parks and gardens, the orchards and espaliers, and rifled the mill and storehouses, destroying machinery, workshops, and so on. The chateau was spared, though the strangers advised its burning.

Daily Life

We had reduced our meals to coffee and black bread with a little butter in the mornings; at lunch, two dishes, generally a stew of some kind and the second course of potatoes, cabbage, or tomatoes; while our supper consisted of one dish only, which was generally cold and was prepared from the remains of lunch, with coffee, bread, and a little honey as dessert.

There was lack of fuel, too. We had put in our supply of wood in the summer, and we hoarded it with care, heating baths and stoves with utmost economy.

The Revolution of November 7, 1917

And thus we reached 25, October, Russian style—7 November—when we received the first news of the great Bolshevik uprising in the capital, the attack on the Winter Palace, Kerensky's flight, and the complete eclipse or arrest of the remainder of the provisional government! Chaos evidently in Petrograd; and complete silence, with the telegraphic, postal, and press communications all cut off.

Train to the Crimea

It was hot, stuffy, and frightfully uncomfortable, and the stench from the corridor was unbearable. I was persuaded by my companions it would be better if, in spite of the November cold, we left our windows open, and only this kept us alive.

At night we slept, sitting up on the hard, unmade berth. There were neither cushions nor bedclothes, which had long ago been stolen. It was impossible to move or change places either, and equally impossible to stretch out.

It was now three nights and two long days we had traveled, without once lying down or being really comfortable for a moment, and as we drew near Simferopol I felt I should be able to stand no more. My husband was ghastly, and I began to wonder if he would not break down before we reached our destination. I counted we could get hot food at the station which I remembered as clean and gay in the summer.

The station I looked forward to with such anticipation was a terrible disappointment; and because I had hoped for good air, seats, and breakfast, it seemed to me this was the worst experience of all. My tired eyes saw millions of men, in worn and dirty khaki, all pushing us or lying under our feet; and the stench was so dreadful that one could hardly breathe.

Eating was out of the question, and chairs we seized through luck, after more than an hour's waiting. Rest was impossible in such noise, and I proposed moving out to the platform for our long wait. But after inspection my husband refused, saying the crowd was greater there and even rougher than inside.

Men, women, children lay about us on the floors, asleep or half awake, unpacking, eating, dressing there without scruple. We had to watch our bags constantly and two or three times we turned suspicious-looking people, whom we judged to be thieves, away from them.

Train to Petrograd

It was infinitely difficult, we found, to get places and tickets to go north to Petrograd; but fortune served us as usual, and a kind friend who was giving up her trip ceded us two compartments, which she had retained long ago.

My husband and I discussed with some hesitation what we should do, but we finally decided circumstances would not be improving for a long time and that if we wanted to go abroad, we must try to do so now. Going seemed a necessity because of Cantacuzene's health. From every point of view, we found it better to put our luck to the test, while we still had sufficient strength of nerve and money in plenty, and while communications seemed possible.

By way of beginning, my jewels were sewn into our traveling clothes, where they would attract less attention and be less encumbering than in the jewel case. We then divided our money, so each should carry half in case one or the other of us should be searched and robbed, or we became separated. We reduced our baggage, leaving two trunks with my mother-in-law.

Arrival in Petrograd

Petrograd looked frightfully run down. The streets were lost in deep snow, frozen hard on them, but worn in ruts and holes, and the going was dreadful. The crowds were greater and more disorderly than ever. Hardly anyone ventured out at night without accident, which consisted generally in one's being stopped and relived of money, furs, woolen clothes, and boots, then left to go one's way, almost naked in the cold. Misery stared out of every decent face. It was the dreadful soldiers who had now taken to selling every kind of stolen merchandise, and we bought on the street pavements several valuable editions of rare books for absurdly small prices. Evidently these came from some of the palaces that were constantly being looted.

Half the shops were closed, and many had been sacked, with their windows left broken, or they were boarded up against the street. Criminals infested the town; well-to-do people were feeling the pinch of actual hunger, while the honest poor were starving.

Each day some part of the city was in darkness, and the water supply was constantly expected to break down. All other public service was erratic, and telephones and cabs were accidental luxuries. Even in our well organized hotel, where we had gone into my same old apartment, with almost a feeling of home-coming and of being protected, everything was more or less up in the air. We could not complain, however, as compared to those about us we lived in the lap of quiet luxury.

Leaving Russia

When finally we were sure we should go by the Swedish route, I was greatly relieved. At the last moment the problem of what to do with my jewels became the worst of all, and I grew almost to hate the pretty things I had worn with such delight formerly.

Finally, Cantacuzene left the disposition and hiding of my jewelry to me. I sewed it into my furs and heavier clothes, scattering the latter about in different trunks, with a silent prayer that I was choosing places wisely, where rough soldier hands would not encounter weights or hard surfaces.

For the trip we wore the clothes that had served until now for hunting and winter sports in the country which looked unpretentious, shapeless, and comfortable. We decided we would thus be quite inconspicuous in the crowd of travelers, and hoped for the best.

I felt triumphant over our very successful passage through the custom house in spite of its dragons. I had always prided myself that no guilt of smuggling on any frontier was mine, but now I had no scruple with reference to the Bolshevik government, and enough was to my credit in that direction during past years to balance the debts of tonight. Besides, we were carrying nothing away of all Cantacuzene's fortune which lay behind us and smoking, an absolute loss.

We were in Sweden, and I turned back to look my last at the home-land we were leaving. Three or four hours before we had left our train at Torneo, the sky had been dark and threatening. Now there was a complete transformation. It was hung with millions of stars, while on the horizon rose high into the heavens the most splendid halo of a magnificent aurora-borealis. Perhaps it was a promise for the future of our unhappy country.

Mysterious as always, Russia stretched out her great plains toward the light, and that was all we could see of her.

Then I faced around again, and I saw the gay lamps of Haparanda station, which we were approaching; and I realized we were out of danger now, and free, though we were refugees in a strange kingdom.

CHAPTER TWELVE

◠

Bessie Beatty

A Reporter in Petrograd

Elizabeth Mary Beatty was born on January 27, 1886, in Los Angeles, California, one of four children of Thomas and Jane Beatty, who were Irish immigrants. She attended Occidental College but did not graduate. During her college years, she worked for the *Los Angeles Herald*. Thereafter, a large part of her career was that of an independent journalist, writer, editor, and host of her own radio program.

Bessie Beatty was a reporter for *The San Francisco Chronicle* when she was sent to Russia in 1917 to report on the political, economic, and social aspects of the Russian Revolution. She arrived in June after a twelve-day trip on the Trans-Siberian Railroad. Not knowing Russian, she was assigned a translator who accompanied her on trips in Petrograd, where she was based, as well as to Moscow and the wartime Russian front.

Russia was still fighting on the side of the Allies during the First World War when she arrived, and she knew that revolution and war were incompatible bedfellows. The enormous casualties that the Russian Army suffered, the battles lost, and the disillusionment of the troops with the war, the inept government, and a war-weary population led to the Treaty of Brest-Litovsk in March 1918. But before that Bessie wanted to see conditions on the front herself.

An intrepid reporter, she traveled to the southwestern front twice, went to the trenches, and was so close to the German lines that she barely escaped a shelling. There she met soldiers who were revolutionaries and others who spoke freely about the lack of weapons and ammunition and the conflict between officers and recruits that weakened discipline in the ranks. She visited a woman's army training camp where recruits were being prepared for war-time service; they formed the Women's Battalion that suffered casualties on the front lines. The patriotism of the women and their desire to serve their country made a profound impression on her.

The Russian Revolution brought great political, economic, and social changes to the country. By the time Bessie arrived, Tsar Nicholas II had been overthrown in the 1917 February Revolution; however, she was witness to the events leading up to the October Revolution that brought the Bolsheviks to power and resulted in a changed and, at first, a conflicted country.

The political events leading up to the October Revolution, including the Korniloff Affair, an attempt to overturn the provisional government, Kerensky's departure, the attack on the Winter Palace, and the success of the Bolsheviks, are described as she saw them. She had a special pass to visit the Winter Palace and the Peter and Paul Fortress, where former government officials were imprisoned.

The revolution issued decrees on land, labor, education, the Russian Orthodox Church, and personal lives. However, the immediate consequences of the Bolshevik takeover for citizens were shortages of food and goods, the impact of which Bessie experienced herself. Somewhat of a feminist for her times and a suffragette, Bessie heralded the fair and equal treatment of women by the Bolsheviks. In fact, in 1919, she spoke favorably of the Bolsheviks before a Senate Committee led by Senator Lee Slater Overman, Democrat of North Carolina.

Once Bessie returned home from Russia, she wrote *The Red Heart of Russia* and worked as a journalist for several years. She traveled again to Russia in 1921, where she interviewed Lenin and Trotsky. In 1926, she married actor William Sauter and lived in Los Angeles, where she wrote for Metro-Goldwyn-Mayer Studios. In 1932, she co-wrote a play entitled *Jamboree* that was on Broadway. During World War II, she hosted a popular women's radio show in New York City, raising $300,000 in war bonds.

Bessie died of a heart attack in 1947.

The following selections are from *The Red Heart of Russia*.

⌒

The Red Heart of Russia

What the People Think of the Revolution

While official Russia was getting ready to welcome my countrymen, I had been trying to find out what unofficial Russia was thinking about. With the help of an interpreter, I had been listening to the babble of voices that sounded through the golden days and white nights. Already I had learned that revolution is a term as variable as truth, and newly mined by every man who speaks it.

I discovered that the Revolution that overthrew the Tsar and absolutism was a simple thing, beautifully logical, gloriously unanimous. Everyone wanted it; everyone was glad when it came. The monarchy that had brought such desperate misery to the millions crumbled to dust with the first vigorous blow of the rising peoples like a thing long since dead. The heavy heart of Russia lifted in a mighty shout of joy: "Svoboda! (Freedom.) We are free!"

For the moment this was enough. That single word with its age-old power of placing man on the mountain tops, made Russia happy.

Soon her people began to be specific.

"Freedom for the peasant," they said. "Freedom for the worker." "Freedom for the soldier." "Freedom for the Jew." "Freedom for women."

Russia still rejoiced, but with vague mental reservations faintly disturbed by this diversity. Then came definition. Each man translated revolution into the terms of his own life.

Nicolai Voronoff, whom I met at dinner one night, voiced the conservative intellectuals' idea of freedom.

"Things could not go on as they were," he said. "We had to have freedom. Freedom of speech, freedom of press, freedom of assembly, inviolability of person—Freedom as you American and English know it."

Old Chekmar, the peasant delegate from a remote south Russian village, spoke of freedom in terms of land.

"Freedom for the peasant," he said. "Yes, yes, land—we shall have land. The Tsar Alexander gave it to us when he freed the serfs but the landlords have kept it away. Mother earth—it is ours at last!—God's and the people's."

The same light was in the eyes of Andrey Krugloff from the great Putiloff works, when he said: "Freedom for the worker. The day of the proletariat has come. The men who use the tools shall control them, the fruits of labor shall belong to labor. We will put an end to capitalistic exploitation; we will do away with poverty; the workers of the world shall unite."

Ivan Borovsky, who had come to the front to attend the all-Russian convention of Workmens' and Soldiers' Deputies, saw freedom in terms of the soldiers. "Peace, peace," he said. "We dig our graves and call them trenches. What is the use of freedom to a man in his grave? We will stop this bloody slaughter. This is not our war. This is the Tsar's war. The soldiers of all the world shall rise as we have done. There shall be no more court-martial, no more capital punishment. We will have honest, democratic peace. Then we can go back to our farms and our factories and put an end to all wars."

So it went. Revolution was to every man the sum of his desires.

The honeymoon of Revolution was already waning on that day when the American commission came to Petrograd; but the consciousness of "the people" as an entity still remained. Slowly the years of political and economic slavery, land hunger and hideous physical poverty imposed upon the many by the few had brought about a mass consciousness that was the most vital force in revolutionary Russia.

I discovered with surprise that the Tsar's name was seldom mentioned. He ceased to count for anything. A month after the first revolutionary attack, he was as completely forgotten as if he had never lived.

With the tragic failure of the first Revolution of 1905 and 1906, when the Workers tried to take control and lost everything, still fresh in their memory, they were trying desperately to cooperate, to give and take, to use the powers of the intellectuals and at the same time direct revolution into the channels through which they wanted it. They were theorists who had always been denied the right of action. Never having been allowed to try to put any of their theories into practice, they had never learned to compromise. Each group was willing to die for its own particular definition of revolution, but no group was able to yield to the theory of another. Consequently, Cabinet crises followed Cabinet crises.

The demand of the people for a republic was insistent. The republican idea satisfied some but not enough. A social democracy—a socialist state—became the loudest cry of the articulate proletariat.

I heard it on the street corners and in the crowded trams, along the wide paths of the parks, and in the assembly rooms of palaces whose ancient walls might well have shuddered at the strangeness of such sentiments.

Much of the time they talked of war, and I heard unkempt soldiers in dilapidated uniforms and workmen in shoddy suits demanding "an interbelligerent conference," "statement of Allied war aims," "publication of the secret treaties," as glibly as workingmen at home discuss hours and wages.

The great driving force—fear—was gone. That greater driving force of war—a cause—Ivan had never known.

Suddenly the facts were changed. The old gods were swept away in a single hour. Tsar and church and country crumbled together. Revolution took their place. Russia had a cause. "Save the Revolution!" became the rallying cry. To save the Revolution, and what it meant to each, became the common faith. However men differed in their definition of terms they were all agreed as to the slogan. Russia would follow no other flag.

To the Front and the Trenches

After dinner, Johanna Ivanovna, head nurse for the military hospital next door, took me for a walk through the woods. Johanna Ivanovna was young, fresh, and softly, sadly pretty in her Sister's garb. She was lonesome out there on the edge of the forest. She spoke a little English, rusty from long disuse. She was the only person in all those fields and forests who understood even a stray word of my native language.

As we turned toward the lazaret, a Russian rocket flashed into the western sky. It was followed by another, and another.

"A German scouting party had been sighted outside the barbed-wire entanglements," Johanna Ivanovna explained from long experience at the front. "The rockets are torches to help trace their movements."

I slept that night on a narrow army cot in a typical camp room the only unfamiliar feature of which was a strange contraption like a knapsack hanging on the wall. It proved to be a gas mask, and bore the warning: "Keep your gas mask always with you—it will save your life."

I put the mask back on its nail, and turned down the gray army blankets, to find white sheets. My clothes had not been off for two nights, and these sheets were alluring. My last recollection was the sound of the low grumble of artillery on the firing line to the west.

Division Staff Headquarters was our immediate objective next morning. A *breechka*, with one horse in the shafts and another to run alongside in the strange Russian fashion, was at the door of the lazaret when we finished our coffee. The road led over a hillside and through a typical Russian village: a cluster of wooden houses huddled together in the center of fields of grain and flax. They were pitiful little homes, weather grayed, straw-thatched, and dilapidated. The main street was thronged with soldiers who had come to buy picture post-cards, cigarettes, and candy from the meager store. Beyond the village we headed into the forest, bumping our way over a military corduroy road of rough logs laid together like the boards in a floor.

The wagon path bristled on both sides with barbed-wire entanglements, and the woods were honeycombed with trenches. They were timbered with logs, and the roofs were covered with moss and delicate wild flowers.

The sentries glanced curiously at me. Women, even Red Cross nurses, seldom penetrated this far into their domain. But they allowed me to pass unchallenged. We stopped in front of an old-fashioned farm-house with a passion-vine growing over the veranda, and rustic summer-house build around an aged tree in the front yard.

The General's aide came out to meet us. He took us to the commanding officer, and we drank tea while plans and permits were being made and horses saddled. Once permission was granted to visit the Russian front the military host left nothing to be desired.

The General offered me his aide as a guide; and he, Lieutenant Gustaroff, mounted me on his beautiful black "Arabka." The pony and I covered eighteen miles through the dark forests that day, and before I left we were thoroughly familiar with that sector of the forest. Every mile of the way was bounded by trenches running off into the depths of the woods. Here and there we passed a pine snapped in the middle as if it had been a match, and great cavities in the earth marked the havoc of enemy artillery fire.

We lunched with the Colonel and a group of young officers in a log-lined dugout, with flower upon the table and an elaborate hanging lamp made from pine cones suspended above it. In one corner of the living-room was a tiny wire pen in which three baby chickens were being carefully reared.

Table conversation turned to the question of the offensive on the southwestern front. Most of the men were hopeful that it might once more mean active participation of all the Russian troops. Some were dubious. It was evident that none of them liked the new committee system of managing the army. It was hardly to be expected that they would, for it meant a complete overturn of all their training.

Many were sympathetic with the Revolution; a few were revolutionists; but most of them wanted revolution to behave according to their own well-ordered plan and not according to the nature of revolution.

The quiet of the morning departed. The rumble of the guns seemed quite close now. When luncheon was over, we all mounted horses and rode off in the direction they called. We came to a halt on the shores of another and much larger lake, a great inland sea nearly fifteen miles long. ... Here we dismounted, and they led me to an observation station cleverly screened by trees. Young Gustaroff adjusted his glasses and turned them over to me; then—"Bvistra, Miss Beatty, bvistra!" he shouted.

I looked, and at the opposite side of the lake a great cloud of sand rose suddenly into the air. A section of a German trench blew up in a puff of smoke.

Stretched out before me, beyond that powerful lens, were the Russian and German trenches. Above the ground the barbed-wired entanglements zigzagged across the gray hillsides. Under the surface, facing each other with watchful eyes and ears and ready trigger-fingers, were two long lines of silent men.

In the reserve trenches beyond were more men—thousands of them talking, sleeping, playing cards, brewing tea, living their lives like so many ants—who were of the earth and knew no other world.

Back at staff headquarters again, we sat down at a table with military maps spread before us. Gustaroff was an engineer and loved every line of the complicated maps.

"If we had had enough ammunition in 1915, you would not have to be fighting to-day," he said.

"Here"—pointing to a spot in Poland now in the possession of the Germans—"sixteen thousand of us went into battle in 1915, and only five hundred of us returned. The artillery retreated, not because it did not want to go on fighting—not because it was beaten—but because it had only two rounds of ammunition left."

"Yes," said another officer; "if we had had the ammunition in 1915, I would be back with Mother Moscow, practising law, and all this business would be over. What will happen now—I don't know. It is very bad."

"War and revolution do not get on well together, yet we younger men realize that revolution had to come. Things could not go on as they were."

For two days I stayed away from the trenches. The rain oozed through the cracks in the rough pine boards in my room and spread in puddles over the floor. It showed no signs of ceasing. One morning, regardless of Peter's protest, we set out to cover the three miles to the staff. A very much astonished young Russian met us at the door.

I explained that we had come with much ease and some exhilaration on our own feet, and were none the worse for the walk.

"But surely you don't want to go to the trenches on a day like this! You will be up to your knees in mud. You can't imagine what it is like," he said.

"I have a very strong desire to find out at first hand," I answered.

He consulted two brother officers, who in turn consulted the telephone. Finally they decided: "It is possible, but foolish."

Still smiling, but frowning indulgently upon me, they put me in the General's big gray motor-car, and we started for the forest.

Twice the heavy car stuck in the mud, and Lieutenant Gustaroff told me to tell my government to send some American Fords parcel post.

The officers were waiting for us, curious to see these strange Americans who didn't stay indoors when it rained. We made our way through sandy trench roads, untimbered ditches bordered with shaggy lavender poppies, green oats, and blue cornflowers clinging close to their sloping sides. Then we went into the trenches. There were miles and miles of them zigzagging back and forth like the Greek border on a guest towel. At intervals big metal plates were placed near the top, flanked on each side by sand-bags. Through the observation holes I peeped out on No Man's Land with the barbed-wire entanglements of the Germans beyond. Once they told me we were within a hundred and sixty feet of the enemy's first-line trench.

Our friends at the staff had not exaggerated the mud. Soon puddles disappeared—the trench became a continuous river of red mud. I plunged in up to the top of my high boots.

Twice we lost our way in communication trenches and had to retrace our steps. Intermittent artillery fire punctuated the journey.

At one point we discovered that a "suit-case" had preceded us and caved in the timbers. Once, where the lay of the land was permitted, I was allowed to put my head over the trench to see the remains of a Russian village. All that was left were the skeletons of two Russian brick stores and their chimneys.

Electric lights and kindred comforts such as they have in the enemy trenches were utterly lacking here. Mud! Mud! Here was nothing but mud! In one small trench house—a burrow in the ground in the back-wall of the trench—three soldiers were playing cards; another was washing his shirt. Here and there we found men polishing their guns, and others brewing tea in aluminum pails over tin fires. More of them were snatching a little sleep in order to be vigilant for the night.

Though none of them saluted the officers, there seemed little to indicate disorganization here; but the commanding Colonel told me that some of the men had deserted, and more were sick. Scurvy was making frightful inroads in the Russian ranks on every front, and to the north, in the vicinity of Riga, the men were in pathetic condition as a result of poor food.

The dirt, the flies, the vermin, the monotonous round, the endless soup, and *kasha*, the waiting—these are the things that take the last ounce of a man's courage and faith. The Russian, like the Frenchman, the Englishman, and the Belgian had had three years of it. Each had a cause; each had a country standing behind him and trying to send some fragment of comfort into his meagre life. The Russian went to the front and stayed there simply because he was told to. It was tragic that he was leaving the trenches, but it was understandable.

One of the officers hurried back and said something in Russian to his commanding officer. He turned to me. "You got out just in time," he said. "They are bombarding the trenches—down where you were."

And this was war! I had seen the trenches—walked through them with men whose chief concern was that I, a woman, should not get my feet wet. Hardly an hour later, the guns of the enemy were crashing them to pieces.

The hereditary distrust between the officer class and the private was growing continually. Old and ancient grievances were unforgotten, and, as always, many of the innocent paid the price of the guilty. ... The soldiers generally looked upon their officers as the natural enemies of the revolution, and regarded orders with suspicion. Tragedy followed tragedy on the Russian front, and enemy treachery and pitiful misunderstanding on all sides were chiefly to blame.

Militarism was a product of autocracy, and the Russian front, at a terrible cost, demonstrated that the larger freedom and the militaristic ideal can not live in the same world. The Russian revolutionist knew this. ... He knew that the sword of militarism must be broken beneath the feet of the peace-hungry multitudes of the world before even the most limited of the freedoms are safe.

Marie Bochkarevska
Library of Congress

The Women's Battalion

Later, on a dreary, rainy night, I dropped off a troop train at the military station of Malodetchna, and prepared to wait for dawn to show me the way to the headquarters of the Women's Battalion. I had that day plowed through miles of trenches, with the red mud oozing over my shoe-tops, and I was taking into barracks with me some recently acquired and very definite impressions of the horrors of war.

Here were women—two hundred and fifty of them—on their way to battle, and just a fraction of the women's army soon to be.

Destiny, dawn and an occasional inquiry led me at six o'clock in the morning to their door. They were housed in pine-board sheds, sandwiched between a dug-out of Austrian prisoners and the barracks of a battalion of Cossack cavalry.

I found myself in a building a hundred or more feet long, with steep roofs sloping to the floor, and just enough width to allow for two shelves eight feet deep and an aisle between. The shelves at the moment were covered with brown bundles, and as I followed the sentry a hundred close-cropped heads emerged from them.

Above my head, hanging from the rafters was a jungle of gas-masks and wet laundry, boots, water-bottles, and kit-bags. Beside each girl lay her rifle. At the far end of the barracks we stopped before one of the brown bundles, and the sentry announced, "Gaspandin Nachalnik." The man's head and man's shoulders of Bachkarova arose from the blanket. Next to her, another bundle stirred and Marya Skridlova, aide-de-camp, moved over and invited me to come up.

In that spot, between the social poles of Russia, Rheta Childe Dorr and I spent all the nights and most of the days in the week that followed.

Without delay I changed my too feminine dress for "overettes," and established myself as unobtrusively as possible in the life of the barracks.

We ate our breakfast sitting on the edge of a bunk, slicing off hunks of black bread, and washing it down with tea from tin cups.

The routine of the day began with the reading of the army regulations. The women soldiers had chosen to submit to the stern discipline of the Russian army in the days before the Revolution. The ceaseless rain made drilling in the field impossible but within the narrow limits of the barracks they marched back and forth, counting "Ras, dva, tri, chetiri; ras, dva, tri, chetiri" for several hours a day.

Very soon one soldier girl after another detached herself from the mass and became to me an individual. Bit by bit I gathered their stories. Little by little I discovered some of the forces that had pushed them out of their individual ruts into the mad maelstrom of war.

There were stenographers and dressmakers among them, servants and factory hands, university students and peasants, and a few who in the days before the war had been merely parasites. Several were Red Cross nurses and one, the oldest member of the regiment, a woman of forty-eight had exchanged a lucrative medical practice for a soldier's uniform.

Many had joined the regiment because they sincerely believed that the honor and even the existence of Russia were at stake, and nothing but a great human sacrifice could save her. Personal sorrow had driven some of them out of their homes and on to the battle-line.

They had come for many reasons, these women soldiers, but all of them were walking out to meet death with grim confidence that it awaited them in the dark forests a few miles distant.

Day and night the rain pounded upon the low roof, and all that week our feet and boots were soaked beyond all drying. It was bitterly cold in the barracks, and the odors of cheese and sausage purchased at the soldiers' store mingled with the smell of wet clothes and greased boots.

Every night Bachkarova announced that tomorrow they would leave for the trenches, and every night the announcement brought a cheer. In the morning they packed their kit-bags and rolled up their blanket-coats; at night they were still in the same place.

Always there was something lacking. First it was the boots. ... When the boots arrived, the medical supplies were missing. When the big metal soup kitchen on wheels had come, there were no horses to pull it. A week went by, but gradually the entire camp equipment was collected.

Late on Sunday afternoon Bachkarova and Skridlova were summoned to staff headquarters. When they returned, they brought the news for which every girl in the barracks was longing. The Battalion was ordered to march at three o'clock next morning.

Neither hardness of the plank beds nor the cold kept anyone awake that night. There was far too much excitement to think of sleep.

Before the dawn had come everything was in place, and they trudged away through the rain and mud of Malodetchana, singing a Cossack marching song to lighten their packs and their spirits.

All the world knows how they went into battle shouting a challenge to the deserting Russian troops. All the world knows that six of them stayed behind in the forest, with wooden crosses to mark their soldier graves. Ten were decorated for bravery in action with the Order of St. George, and twenty others received medals. Twenty-one were seriously wounded, and many more than that received contusions. Only fifty remained to take their places with men in the trenches when the battle was over.

There were nearly five thousand women soldiers in Russia at the beginning of the fall of 1917. All over the country—in Moscow, in Kieff, in Odessa—they were learning to load, aim, and fire.

September 1917

In the hours I had spent at the Soviet, in the Peasants' Convention, and talking with soldiers and workmen everywhere, I had become convinced there was no power in Russia that Kerensky or any other man could use; that the masses would regard any attempt to install a dictator as an attack on their Revolution and would desert the man responsible for it.

The Korniloff Affair

The anniversary of the sixth month of Russian freedom was at hand. Petrograd, ready at all times to expect the worst, believed there would be some tragic celebration of the day. Part of it trembled in its boots for fear of a Bolshevik uprising; more of it predicted a German air raid; some of it longingly scanned the horizon for a Russian Napoleon. Nobody was prepared for what happened and everybody was amazed by what did not happen. When the official announcement was made, "The Korniloff adventure has been liquidated," the populace was still gasping.

Kerensky declared Korniloff counter-revolutionist and traitor. The Workmen and Soldiers in Petrograd, convinced that their Revolution and their throats were both in danger worked day and night in munition plants, and prepared to throw a trench around the great city. Another part of the population looked upon Korniloff as a deliverer, and waited impatiently for his coming.

While we were still in the dark as to what was happening I went one morning to the Winter Palace and climbed the stairs to Katherine Breshkovskaya's little room. Through all the troubled days of the last six months, she had been the right-hand lieutenant of Kerensky.

"What do you think of Kerensky?"

"Very well I think of him. He is a square man, and, what is better, he is not selfish. He works only for the welfare of the people, and not only his people but for all the Allies, too. He is all around a good man. It is not strange to have a good man; but to have a man who is good and brave and clever is unusual. I esteem him from the profound of my soul."

During the Korniloff rebellion she amply proved her faith; for day and night she went from barracks to barracks, urging the soldiers to stand by Kerensky.

Korniloff was captured and placed under arrest, and the government announced that the Korniloff adventure had been liquidated.

The first attempt to install a man on horseback resulted in driving the radical forces further and further to the left and creating a mass solidarity that was ultimately to prove fatal to the existing order.

The Korniloff adventure paved the way for the Bolsheviki Revolution.

Aboard the *Polar Star* of the Baltic Fleet

The business before the Baltic Fleet concerned soldiers on the Riga front. News of the distress of the northern army had reached them, and they were collecting money and buying warm clothing to send to the men who were hungry and cold in the trenches.

In that committee meeting were eight Mensheviki, three Anarchist Communists, nine Social Revolutionists, and forty-five Bolsheviki. Those figures were the most significant I found in all of Russia. Before the Korniloff Rebellion there had been only eighteen Bolsheviki in the committee, and no anarchists. The men were chosen by the vote of the entire fleet, and they reflected the complete swing to the left that was taking place in Russia from Vladivostok to the Black Sea.

The sailors, almost to a man, believe in the principles of international-ism, in the socialization of land and the control of industry by the workers. To them the Revolution meant the ultimate realization of all these dreams.

A *Komplectatsea*, or "make-up committee," decided all problems related to the crews. A "selection committee" studied the men to find promising material to make officers. The judiciary committee was the new disciplinar-ian. Disputes between officers and men were submitted to it and when the offenses were serious civil lawyers were employed to defend the men.

Fortunately for the sailors, the average humanity is fairly decent, whether it be Russian or anything else, and there were men in the Russian navy who did not abuse their power. But there were enough of the other kind to stir a deep and intense bitterness in the breast of the Russian sailor, and this ha-tred found tragic utterance where the Revolution came. Many of the crews simply arrested their officers, and some asked them to sign a paper declaring they would support the Revolution.

The bourgeois feared and hated the sailor most of all the revolutionists; but he was the cleanest, staunchest, finest-looking man I found in revolutionary Russia. He knew what he wanted, and was determined to get it. War-weariness played little part in his psychology. He was willing to fight Germans, if he believed Germans were the enemies of the revolution. Six hundred of them formed a volunteer battalion of death and went to the Riga front to fight with the soldiers in the trenches, and the battalion was practically annihilated.

The Proletariat Take Over

There was nothing in the situation that night that augured well for Kerensky's government. "All power to the Soviets!" grew louder and more insistent with every passing hour. The Russian workers, the youngest proletarian group in the world, were the most class-conscious and determined, and—they had guns.

The fleet was Bolshevist—I had no doubt of that. The Petrograd garrison was Bolshevist. Every report from the front indicated that the men in the trenches had swung farther and farther to the left. The land and peace hunger clamored for immediate satisfaction.

Winter Palace
Library of Congress

Kerensky, trying like the true democrat he was to please everyone, succeeded in pleasing no one. He had lost touch with the masses. Attacked from above and below, from within and without there seemed little hope for him.

The Bolsheviki promised peace and land. They promised more: they promised that the workers of the world should "arise and put a stop to war and capitalistic exploitation forever."

Overthrow of the Provisional Government and the Fall of the Winter Palace

We picked our way across the glass-strewn square, climbed the barricade erected that afternoon by the defenders of the Winter Palace, and followed the conquering sailors and Red Guardsmen into the mammoth building of dingy red stucco. On the strength of our blue-sealed passes, they permitted us to enter unquestioned. A squad of sailors mounted the stairs to the council chamber and placed the Provisional Government under arrest.

With the surrender of the Winter Palace, the victory of the Bolsheviki was complete. The dictatorship of the proletariat had become a fact. The only power in Petrograd at dawn that morning was the power of the People's Commissaries, headed by Nikolai Lenin and Leon Trotzky, and backed by the Russian Fleet, the bayonets of the Petrograd garrison, and the Red Guard rifles.

Petrograd was stunned. That morning the storm center shifted to the city Duma, which refused to acknowledge the victory of the Bolsheviki or accede to their demands. A Committee for the Salvation of the country and the Revolution was quickly formed, and all the anti-Bolshevik groups gathered around it.

The Bolsheviki had achieved a degree of success greater than they suspected. The leaders, exhausted by lack of sleep, depressed by the rejection of the *Intelligentzia*, and conscious of their inadequacy for the mere physical task of bringing bread to keep Petrograd alive, failed utterly to realize their strength. A heavy pall of discouragement settled on Smolney.

Visit to the Fortress of Peter and Paul

At the request of the Duma and the American Mission, I became one of a committee of four to visit the prison and interview the inmates. Two of us—Daddy R. and M. Mikhailoff of the London *Telegraph* were Russians.

We walked in awed silence through the arched gate in the massive outer wall, each busy with his own thoughts. Both of them had been old revolutionists, and Mikhailoff had been a prisoner in this very fortress not many years before.

In another part of the bastion we found the members of the Kerensky Cabinet. Tereshchenko, the late Foreign Minister, sat cross-legged on his cot, a cigarette in his mouth. He greeted us pleasantly, and in the softest, most musical English I ever heard inquired for news of the French front and of Moscow.

In similar cells we found Kiskkin, Borurtzeff, Rutenberg, Paltchinsky, and other men arrested after the fall of the Winter Palace.

It was quite plain that their position was a precarious one, because they were in a sense hostages, and any violence done to the Bolshevik leaders would very quickly have met with retaliation from the Bolshevik followers in the prison garrison.

We came away, agreed upon one thing: whatever might come of chaos and disorder in this new regime, the Peter and Paul of to-day would never be a match for that Peter and Paul of the old days when violence and cruelty was an organized and deliberate policy.

New Soviet Policy: Abolition of the Old Order

The first decree passed after the creation of the government was the decree of peace. By this decree the government proposed at once to begin negotiations for a "just and democratic peace."

The Soviet government knew that the peasant would not tolerate further delay in the settlement of the land question.

The land decree was passed, not by the People's Commissaries, but by the whole Russian Soviet. It abolished the landlord's property in land and confiscated all landed estates with their moveable and immovable property excepting the small holdings of peasants and Cossacks.

What the land decree was to the peasant, the labor control decree was to the worker. It applied to all industries employing labor, and provided for control by committees, representing laborers and employers, called "organs of labor control."

The workers in government-owned industries, such as posts, telegraphs, and railroads were given the same right of control as the workers in privately owned industries.

The decree on education, drawn by Lunarcharsky, a writer and scholar, set forth the Soviet's ideas of instruction. Local self-government in education was the fundamental principle of the program.

All decrees regulating the individual lives of people inclined toward wide freedom. The (marriage) decree declared church marriages to be personal and private matters, and prescribed that the government recognize only civil marriages.

Social insurance against injuries, sickness, and non-employment was also provided in an elaborately worked out decree.

When the Soviet had completed decree thirty-one, the five classes in civil life had been abolished, and only one title was left in Russia—"Citizen of the Russian Republic."

Revolutionary Justice

There was no longer a secret police in Russia. The *Okhranka* had gone with the Tsars into oblivion. But the people themselves were on the watch for evidence of anything that might threaten the power of the Commissaries. There was little that did not soon reach the ears of Jacob Peter's Commission.

Wherever the death penalty was inflicted, it was done by mobs having no official sanction—by mobs aroused to an uncontrolled fury, and momentarily conscious of no other passion than that of reprisal.

Life after the Revolution

The Russian seems to be always equal to the emergency of the moment. It is in organizing the daily round of living that he seems to fail.

It was impossible at any time during the year to buy any of the necessities of life without standing in a queue. There were queues for bread, sugar, kerosene, tobacco, galoshes, and sweets. The families who could afford it kept what they called "queue maids," who had no other occupation than to wait in line for provisions. In one of the "want ads" I found a request for a servant, stating, "For queue work only." It became a regular source of livelihood for many people.

I frequently stopped to listen to the people in the queues, and to get a better idea of their attitude toward the various governments. I sent Marya, my interpreter, to stand in the lines. She told me that the character of the queues changed with the goods the people were buying; but the people themselves were always in opposition to the government and the women say: "It is no good for the government to be Socialist if the queues grow longer every day."

The trunk queues were the strangest of all. Marya described them as "respectable people whom fear has obliged to forget their respectableness." She said it was universal, direct equal, and open fear. They had completely lost their wits. They were afraid of Germans, of Socialists, of peasants, of soldiers. They feared to lose their peace, their comforts, and their lives. They feared to stay in Petrograd, and they feared equally to leave.

Even the foreign colony, whose members were far better off than the Russians, heard the gray wolf howling. We were a hungry lot from morning until night. Most of us developed an appetite such as we had never known. We scraped the plates clean. The first time I dined with a man who put the leftover sugar in his pocket, I gasped. It was not until I had drunk many glasses of sugarless tea and eaten many breadless meals that I was able to overcome sufficiently the inhibitions of my early training to permit me to follow his example. Even to the end, I had a guilty sense of committing a horrible crime every time I whisked the last piece of black bread repetitiously into my hand bag. Usually, by dint of much scheming, I managed to keep a small quantity of food on hand for the hungry mortals who drifted through my little blue room each day.

Life was naked in Russia—bare as the arms of the silver birches before winter came to cover them up. All that was real, all that was vital—the best and the worst of men—lay close to the surface. Heroes have never appealed to me; but the amazing number of simple, unobtrusive virtues that the ordinary mortal can carry about his human person is a miracle that never ceases to thrill me. There is a bond between those of us who searched for values beneath the turmoil of the revolutionary year that would be hard to break. A broader base of friendship, a deeper comradeship, is building for men and women the world over in the stress of these days of living under the shadow of death and disaster.

The Peasants

To the peasant, revolution meant land, freedom means land. He knows land. He wants land. He thinks in terms of land. Land means food for his children, warmer *shubas* for himself, and education for the next generation. Land means life.

No revolutionary party that did not make land to the peasants the first plank in its platform could hope to survive in Russia.

After the serfs were freed, the situation changed. The peasants, instead of receiving the land from which they were used to making their living, frequently received inferior land and a smaller quantity.

As soon as the peasants were convinced that a real revolution had taken place in Petrograd, they began demanding their land; and, since its distribution was delayed, they began to take it.

I went to three peasants' conventions in Petrograd, another in Moscow. They started peacefully enough, but before they were over, the bearded men from the faraway places were shaking their fists in one another's faces, and generally it ended with the majority going over to the left, and the minority starting another convention all its own.

The dream of the Soviets was communally owned modern farm machinery that would lift Russian agriculture out of its primitive state and lessen the dreary drudgery of the peasant's struggle for life.

No one who has not seen those peasant homes can know the sordidness of that struggle. Often the live stock, which was the peasants' entire fortune, shared the same roof with the family. In one peasant hut I found the cow occupying the most comfortable corner of the room. I picked my way to the door through a barn-yard full of oozing black mud and refuse. A flock of chickens ran in and out, leaving the marks of their feet on the floor; Plumbing, there was none.

The samovar was frequently the one luxury. In the days before the vodka prohibition, the white liquor was the peasant's only escape from the sordidness of life. It was a poor escape, because it meant that his wife and children paid with greater misery for his momentary relief.

Women in the Revolution

There was no feminist movement in Russia. In the old days in Russia the rights of women were slightly fewer than those of men but the difference was so small as to be negligible. Russia's struggle was the struggle of human beings as human beings, rather than human beings as males or females.

When freedom came to Russia, no one questioned the right of women to share it.

Revolution did not lessen the burden that war had placed upon the back of the mass of Russian women. Increased disorganization of the country necessitated effort on the part of women to keep their families from starvation. They tilled the fields and tended the cattle; they swept the streets and mended the railway tracks, and stood for endless hours in front of the food shops to get bread and milk for their babies.

The Russian Church

When the Tsar crashed down from his throne in March, he carried more with him than the rest of the world dreamed at that moment. His picture shared a place on the wall beside the sacred ikon. He represented on earth what God represented in heaven. It was a dangerous partnership; for when the state fell, the Church tottered also.

The Russian Church of the past was on the side of the established order. It was as much a tool of absolutism as the secret police. The priests were used to help intrench the Tsar, enforce the will of the bureaucracy, and carry out the orders of the gendarme. The deep religious craving of the Russian nature was perverted to keep the people in subjection. The Church was not of the people, nor for the people. When the great crisis came, they repudiated it. Despite all attempts at democratization, the people drifted further and further away. ... The great power of the Russian Church, around [which] so much of the life of the past clustered, was gone. No one could predict what the future would hold.

In the meantime, the candlesticks before the ikons are empty.

Lenin Speaks and the End of the Constituent Assembly

"The February Revolution was a political bourgeois revolution overthrowing Tsarism. In November a social revolution occurred, and the working masses became the sovereign authority. The Workmen's and Soldiers' delegates are not bound by any rules or traditions to the old bourgeois society. Their government has taken all the power and rights into its own hands. The Constituent Assembly is the highest expression of the political ideals of bourgeois society which are no longer necessary in a Socialist state. The Constituent Assembly will be dissolved."

"If the Constituent Assembly represented the will of the people, we would shout: 'Long live the Constituent Assembly!' Instead we shout; 'Down with the Constituent Assembly!' he finished.

Conditions in Petrograd after the Dissolution of the Constituent Assembly

Petrograd in the closing days of January (1918), became more and more bleak. The hotel had been taken over by the People's Commissaries. In the dining-room I sat down to frugal meals with peasants, workmen, soldiers, agitators, and poets.

Food was daily less plentiful. Cabbage soup, black bread, and *rabchik*, a wild bird for which we all acquired a deathless hatred, made up the daily menu. Only the glasses of steaming tea saved us from gastronomic despair. The supply of knives, forks, and spoons, dwindling ever since the beginning of the war, was now almost exhausted. Frequently a single knife served instead of a teaspoon for an entire table. Often we waited for tea until the people across the room finished with their glasses.

Most of the time we were in total darkness. There were no lamps or candles in the halls, and we groped our way up the dark staircases, bumping blindly into one another's arms. There was an unhappy affinity between the electric light, the elevator, and the water system. Frequently my face remained unwashed until the late afternoon, when I went to the Hotel Europe for tea.

The waiters in the War Hotel complained that there was no money to buy food. A few of them, used to the generous tips of pre-revolutionary days, bemoaned the fall of the monarchy and prayed for the coming of the Germans. They were not the only ones who awaited Prussian deliverance. Most of the upper-class Russians no longer made any attempt to hide their willingness to have the Germans come to Petrograd.

They were demonstrating the Marxian theory that one's conduct is dictated by one's economic desires. They were being forced by the new order to give up their privileges, and to ask them to like it was to expect the impossible. For some of them the situation was tragic. They were products of the system, just as were the uneducated Russian peasant and the class-conscious revolutionary worker.

Final Thoughts

The train that carried me away from Petrograd was almost the last to pass in safety through war-torn Finland. Troubled days were still upon her, but the frozen face of her was as calm and peaceful as a sleeping child.

The City of Peter lay behind me, wrapped in the gray morning mist. Tragedy was in the air. The vague, frightful thing—the Terror—was on every man's tongue. Apprehension was in every man's eye. Lurking there in the black shadows of every human brain were the words: "The Germans." To a few they were a secret hope—restored titles, estates returned. To the mass— death and destruction and shattered dreams.

Time will give to the world war, the political revolution, and the social revolution their true values. We cannot do it. We are too close to the facts to see the truth.

Mingled with my sorrow, the morning I left Petrograd, was a certain exultant, tragic joy. I had been alive at a great moment, and knew that it was great.

CHAPTER THIRTEEN

◟◞

Pauline Stewart Crosley

A Navy Wife in Petrograd

Pauline Stewart was born in 1871 in Columbus, Georgia, and graduated from Mary Baldwin College in Staunton, Virginia, in 1885. She was a member of the Daughters of the American Revolution, as the Stewarts had settled in the South in the eighteenth century and served in the Revolutionary War. Pauline married Ensign Walter Selwyn Crosley, USN, in Annapolis, Maryland, in 1895 and was a Navy wife for forty-four years. They had two sons, Floyd Stewart (1897–1979) and Paul Cunningham (1902–1997), both of whom graduated from the United States Naval Academy, as did their father.

The Crosleys had an exciting life together, culminating in Captain Crosley's assignment to Petrograd as a Naval Attaché in February 1917. Their time together in Petrograd comes alive in a series of letters that Pauline wrote to her children and family members during the 1917 Russian Revolution when the Bolsheviks took over the government. This correspondence forms the content of the book *Intimate Letters from Petrograd* published in 1920. In it, Pauline describes the political events: the provisional government under Alexander Kerensky, the Korniloff Affair, the breakdown of governmental authority, the violence and chaos, World War I, the October Revolution, and, finally, their harrowing escape from Petrograd through Finland to Stockholm, Sweden, in March 1918.

Mrs. Crosley also gives a picture of daily life: the lack of food and fuel, the cultural life in the midst of chaos, the evenings at the opera and ballet, tea parties and dinners with the diplomatic corps and military both U.S. and foreign, her Russian friends, learning the Russian language, walking the dangerous streets, the crimes committed by the Russian sailors and army against the population, the German influence on the Bolsheviks, and her opinion of the Russian people and the Communist government. As a firsthand observer of events, she presents an American woman's astute and fair assessment of Russian politics and a sympathetic and friendly feeling for the Russian people during a world-changing historical period.

In 1920, Captain Crosley was awarded the Navy Cross for his diplomatic service in Russia and for his leadership in successfully escorting Americans out of Russia in 1918. In 1927, he was promoted to rear admiral. His last naval assignment was as commandant of the Fifteenth Naval District and commanding officer of the Naval Station, Balboa, Canal Zone. He retired on November 1, 1935. From 1937 to 1938, he was director of the International Hydrographic Bureau in Monaco. Presumably, Pauline was with him on those assignments, and they shared in more foreign adventures together. Rear Admiral Crosley died on January 6, 1939, and is buried in Arlington Cemetery.

Pauline Crosley was a sponsor for the U.S.S. *Crosley* (DE-226) that was launched on January 1, 1944. Before commissioning in 1944, the ship was converted to a high-speed transport and designated U.S.S. *Crosley* (APD 87).

Mrs. Crosley died in 1955 and is buried in Arlington Cemetery.

The following selections are from *Intimate Letters from Petrograd.*

~

Intimate Letters from Petrograd

On the Siberian Railway

Saturday, April 28, 1917.

My dear—

At last we are in the sleeping car that is supposed to take us to Petrograd and we are away from Harbin. I use the word "supposed" after some thought, for while I believe we will reach Petrograd in this car, there is no certainty about that.

Something is the matter in Russia!

Of course we have read of the Russian Revolution, but we have not read of the things which make us wonder. While in Pekin, Walter was advised by those who have made this trip to wear his uniform after leaving the region of Japanese influence. Yesterday morning, in the sleeper from Mukden, he put it on, but while it is a new uniform it does not seem popular with the Russian soldiers.

Moreover, there are some Russian generals and officers of less rank on this train who are not treated with courtesy by the soldiers.

There is a look on the faces of the soldiers that almost frightens me at times, while again they seem to be well-disposed grown-up children.

At Harbin yesterday the "heavy mental atmosphere" was apparent. It is becoming heavier!

I was worn out when we finally got to our berths last night at Harbin. It was most difficult to get our baggage attended to and it annoyed me to have two of our trunks broken by the surly porters we eventually succeeded in getting to handle them.

This morning, with the train in rapid motion, a gorgeous sunshine, snow on the nearby mountain, snow and ice in the streams, a wonderful landscape and something to eat, I felt more refreshed, but I cannot convince myself, when the train stops at a station, that all is well in Russia.

April 30th

Seemingly it will not be worth while to mail this letter while en route. We are told mails are unreliable; we believe it. I now expect to add to this letter as opportunity offers and mail it when there is a possibility it will reach you.

The weather and the landscape remain impressively beautiful; this morning we passed Lake Baikal and began to realize the engineering difficulties that had been overcome in building this road. We crossed more bridges and were guarded as before.

There is an interesting mixture of races and nationalities on board this train. At a table of four in the dining car I observed a well maintained conversation being carried on in three languages.

Our train stopped nearly two hours at Irkutsk and we would have welcomed an opportunity for exercise and sight-seeing, but, owing to the now very evident disorganization we realize that the railroad officials do not know when the train may proceed, so we may not know either. No one wandered far from his own car; it would have been a real calamity to get left behind.

We have seen many red banners and have heard groups of Russians singing the Marseillaise. There are many revolutionary placards which we cannot read but which astonish our American friends who translate them for us. They find difficulty in realizing that this is Russia; they note the great changes that are not evident to us.

When we left Irkutsk a great many soldiers tried to board our train but the train porters were expecting the effort and managed to close and lock the doors in time to prevent many soldiers from entering the cars. The car steps are crowded with them and why they do not freeze and fall off I cannot imagine. I can see that some of them are asleep and the train is certainly not steady. I am obliged to pity them but the lack of organization, discipline, law and order is very apparent. "Free Russia" as translated for us from the many posters is not entirely free for us; we are practically prisoners in our car and there is ample evidence that "freedom" means more to these people than we understand the word to mean; it also means more for them than they intend it shall mean for us, which is annoying!

Walter did not wear his uniform to-day and he will keep it out of sight for the present. It is evident that the uniform of an officer is regarded with—suspicion, shall I say, by "free Russian soldiers," another frequent quotation from the posters that are growing more frequent.

Something certainly *is* the matter with the Russian Army!

Thursday, May first.

The wonderful weather we have been having has failed us, and changed for the worse; so has the Russian political situation as viewed from a "Wagon Lit" window. Soldiers have now forced their way into the train in spite of the verbal protest of the Russian Army officers and the train officials, sometimes breaking down car fittings to accomplish their purpose. During the night we were awakened each time the train stopped by soldiers attempting to force an entrance into our car. It seems they do not break doors and windows in this car because they have been taught that the "Wagon Lits" are foreign property and there is still left a small amount of respect for foreigners and foreign property; our American friends tell us that the Russian officers use as an argument with the soldiers who are trying to influence them to let the train alone "What will the foreigners think of free Russia?"

Soldiers have practically filled all cars but ours on the train and it is only a question of time when to desire to ride free will overcome the respect for foreign property. It is now very difficult to get to the dining car because one must climb over soldiers in all vestibules and corridors. Poor food, foul air, dirt, discomfort and cold are beginning to affect me unpleasantly and I am not well. Fortunately I have some simple remedies in my hand bag, but I am assured that the Russian Grippe germ will not yield to simple remedies! I must not become really ill, for I am obliged to go on; there is no place to stop. Today we saw evidence on the part of some soldiers to observe law and order and to prevent "joy riding" on this train by those without railroad tickets. The effort was a mild one and did not have an appreciable effect.

May fifth.

This has been an exciting day. I am feeling much better but have an annoying sore throat.

We arrived at Vologda at one o'clock in the afternoon; it is a junction for Moscow and Archangel; the station was "jammed" with soldiers, also with peasants of both sexes and all ages. Here we saw the first members of the "White Guard" of which we have been hearing rumors for several days.

Some fine looking Russians, armed and wearing a white band on one arm, boarded the train and removed, by persuasion and force, every soldier except one.

We are due in Petrograd at ten o'clock tonight but we will not arrive at that hour; no one in the train can tell us when we *will* arrive. The railroad service is sadly demoralized and even from the car window we can see that other industries are in a similar condition. It is now nine o'clock in the evening and I am writing by the daylight that enters the compartment window. We find the white nights a very great comfort when the dynamo furnished no light in the car.

When you receive this you will know we did reach Petrograd. We must not undress for we *might* arrive while asleep and I wish to escape as soon as possible. Oh! How I will welcome unlimited fresh water and a tub!

Please give our love to _____ and _____ and.

I will write to you again when I am temporarily settled and partly comfortable.

Affectionately yours,

Petrograd

Kirocynayan, Vosyem, Petrograd

May 29, 1917.

Well— My dear __

A very busy week has passed and it is fortunate for my promise to you that I have taken notes, as I could never remember all that takes place any more than I can remember all the Russian I hear. We are in our temporary apartment; moved in the rain just after I wrote you last week. The rain stopped after we had moved and we have had fine weather generally, though it snowed the day before yesterday. What would you think if it snowed nearly all day in Washington on May 20th?

We have had a luncheon at the handsome apartment of Consul Winship, a dinner with our American friends of the Siberian Railway trip who live in the most modern apartment in the city, which is situated across the Neva, a dinner with our Counselor, Mr. Butler Wright, and his wife, have been to the ballet with Ambassador Francis and to a luncheon given us at the Restaurant Donon, so you see we are having a few diversions.

The Russian Ballet! The Russian Ballet dancers! No, they are butterflies! Each representation is a pantomime of an interesting fairy or other story and I shall never tire of seeing them.

Our more critical friends say that even the stage suffers on account of the revolution and that mistakes are made for which a punishment would have been awarded "before the revolution," but it seems perfection to me.

To this ballet school also very small girls of excellent families are sent; many stars are developed to shine brilliantly; the training of the artists does not cease until they are retired for age. It will be a calamity indeed if this Russian art becomes a thing of the past, for nothing more beautiful and graceful can take its place.

I have taken up active work, sewing, here in the American Lazaret. The Americans of Petrograd started this hospital for Russian soldiers where they have all worked and spent money to a very great advantage indeed. By their efforts they have shown many a wounded Russian soldier what comfort really is, and have taught them trades wherewith they may, though crippled, earn a livelihood. When the soldiers go to their homes after being discharged from the American Lazaret each one carries with him a bag of clothes and other useful articles, the amount of which depends on the size of his family. Touching, appreciative letters have been received at the Lazaret, written by these men from their homes, and Miss Potter has translated many, having them printed in a pamphlet.

Certainly this group of American patriots deserves credit it will never receive for the "American Propaganda" it has spread, the good effect of which cannot be denied. I am glad to add my mite to the great work.

The soldiers and sailors in and near the Black Sea have remained in a state of discipline far in advance of any others of which I can learn, except the ever faithful Cossacks.

On Saturday last a large Committee from Sevastopol, made up of sailors from the Russian Black Sea Fleet and of soldiers from the Sevastopol Garrison arrived in Petrograd and held an open meeting to which all were invited, with patriotic intent.

Enthusiastic speeches were made by members of the Committee urging the necessity of remaining in the war. Evidently this group has also decided that "all is not well in Russia"! Our Ambassador made a fine speech which was most excellently interpreted by a Russian Naval Officer and which was received with much cheering by the audience, but from what I have seen I suspect that a Russian audience is always ready to cheer the latest speaker.

There has been an arrangement by which those attached to foreign Embassies and Legations could purchase flour, butter, eggs and a small amount of wood from the Russian Government. We have not been able to profit by that arrangement and it appears it may, like other conveniences, quite disappear. The struggle for food and fuel has begun in earnest. It is lucky, first, that Summer will soon be here and, second, that we brought considerable foodstuffs with us.

The general unrest has begun to crystallize in a menacing series of strikes. Managers of factories are being forced, at the muzzle of many pistols and rifles, to increase wages to a degree that can only result in closing the factories, and this at a time when the output of every factory is needed more than ever before, and the wages received absolutely essential to maintain life. Also, at a time when raw materials, in some cases, cost *one thousand times* what they formerly cost!

Imagine prohibitive wages under those conditions! Men in charge of large business offices in Petrograd and Moscow are being similarly forced to increase salaries beyond all possibility of remaining in business. Probably geese that lay golden eggs have never before been murdered on such a large scale, and the final result is inevitable; every industry so attacked must fail; the number attacked is increasing daily.

We are very cheerful for it would be useless to be otherwise, but one can't help seeing what is so evident as the ultimate ruin of Russia.

It is all so interesting to me as I get it day by day from those I meet who have helped to make the history and from those who saw it being made. I only wish I could give you all I receive but time and space will not permit.

As a matter of news, I can tell you that Finland is showing signs of "secession"; I am not in a position to advise you as to the right of the wrong of this, but I believe Russia will lose that interesting part of her former Empire. (There are other parts of Russia from which signs of a similar uneasiness come, and all is *less* well in Russia.)

We walk about the streets at night, sometimes with an interpreter, viewing the bread and other food lines. Even now, when it is cold after the sun sets low, long lines of men, women and children sleep all night on the pavements in front of provision shops waiting for them to open in the morning. Some of these lines extend for several blocks.

These "bread lines" and the riots they caused really started the revolution prematurely in March. Working people from the suburbs whose factories had closed swarmed into Petrograd, where police and Cossacks patrolled and threatened the mob. At the same time regiments of soldiers were kept ready to move from their barracks. Immediately before the final crush, shops were closed and cars stopped running.

This latter measure is a common one in Petrograd and is put into effect, apparently, for two purposes: to prevent the transportation of the mob and to preserve the cars!

There was a clash between the mob and the police (who were reinforced by Cossacks) on March 10th, but, though many shots were fired, probably few were killed or wounded and the mob began to believe that the soldiers would not handle it as severely as they had in former times.

The next day, Sunday, March 11th, more firing took place and it seems that more than a hundred people were killed in different parts of the city, but by late that night, when many more of the troops had been called out, all seemed quiet and the law-abiding began to hope that the end had come.

The Nevsky Prospect has always been a gathering place for disorderly crowds and a large part of it was closed to traffic that night to prevent mobs gathering. But during the night the disorderly mobs had organized and the next day they appeared as real revolutionists, with objectives in view and a determination to capture Petrograd, which they proceeded to do, for during this day practically all the garrison of the city, about 25,000 men, went over to the revolutionists, though there was considerable fighting among the soldiers and many were killed, a large percentage of the dead being officers.

It has always been difficult to learn the number of killed during the street fighting in Russia. The authorities have removed the dead to prevent facts from being known; the relatives of the dead remove and conceal them to avoid becoming implicated in the riots.

Prisons and jails were among the buildings taken and it was at this time the political, military and criminal prisoners were released in wholesale numbers. Many people were killed, officers who refused to give up their arms were murdered on the spot, the mob showing no mercy to anyone who failed to comply instantly with its demands. Red flags began to appear and all other flags to disappear, as well as all symbols representing the Empire.

At this time it was reported that loyal troops were on their way to Petrograd to suppress the revolution and preparations were made by the revolutionists to meet them, but it is reported that, while there was some doubt as to the attitude the advancing troops would take, the majority of the revolutionists were firm in the belief that they would join in the revolution.

Now I have written enough for this week. I intend to continue my notes and write you just a little bit more of this history with each letter I send you. We are expecting mail early next week and it will be most welcome.

Always Affectionately yours,

Kirochnaya, 8, Petrograd

June 5, 1917.

My other dear Son:

My last letter went to your brother but of course you will have seen that as well as my former letters before you receive this. Real correspondence is out of the question for we estimate that about three months will be required to receive an answer to a letter written from either end of the line. Even that period is uncertain, so do not be surprised if you fail to receive prompt answers to questions!

We are fully enjoying the warmer fine weather which reduces the fuel question to that necessary for cooking. Our need became so great we had to borrow wood from the Dvornik (a sort of janitor who carries wood from the basement to one's apartment). Your father, after continued effort, managed to procure about two cords of wood which, without decrease by theft, will last us a month.

There is a remarkable system of what is called in the Far East "cumshaw" and in the United States sometimes called "graft," we have discovered in connection with the wood proposition. One buys wood by the sahjen, about two-thirds of a cord; each sahjen contains ten visiyankas; one pays for a sahjen and *nine* visiyankas are delivered; of these nine the Dvornik gets one (plus a wage from the owner of the house plus a monthly money gift from the occupant of the apartment). The remainder eight visiynakas shrink some-what when other occupants of apartments find it necessary to borrow, as we did! There is a system of wood tickets supposed to protect the owner of the wood from such losses, but in this case protection does not protect.

We have again been to dinners and luncheons and teas, making new ac-quaintances and becoming better acquainted with those we have met before. It is perfectly legitimate to ask a hostess in Petrograd where she found any part of the dinner and what she had to pay for it!

Many Russian officers have called at your father's office with a request, in each case, that they be sent to the United States to join our Army or Navy.

The number of these callers increases and not a day passes without one or more coming for such a request. It is difficult to convince them that our laws prevent what they desire, and while they cannot have their wish gratified one must be sorry for them. There is very little in sight for them in Russia; many of them come in disguise; they are in hiding because they were more or less prominent under the old régime and they would be killed or imprisoned if recognized now. Your father invites some of them to luncheon or dinner with us and they are sources of valuable information as well as interesting narrative. They are so confiding; they trust us absolutely and do not hesitate to tell anything they know! In addition, they are charming guests and we like some of them very much indeed.

It may be, as stated, that only fifteen per cent of the population of Russia is educated, but even if that is true my short experience here shows that percentage to be very *well* educated. It is not wonderful that the Russians are linguists; the deeper I get in the study of their own language, the more reason I see for their ease in mastering and using others!

Your father is obliged to have his office in our apartment and, to my great satisfaction, he has obtained the services of a very attractive young lady as interpreter. Her father was a Colonel on the personal staff of the Czar and when the crash came he was arrested as a "suspect" and imprisoned for seven weeks in the Fortress of Peter and Paul. The young daughter decided she must utilize her excellent education to help the family and I am very glad she is to come here.

The food problem becomes more difficult though the Government seems at times stronger and we hope that reconstruction has really begun. Occasionally one sees soldiers drilling in the streets and drill grounds, though the number is very small as compared with the number of soldiers in Petrograd; some are leaving from time to time, with more or less flourish ostensibly for "the front," but the tales we hear from officers returning from the various fronts and wishing to go to America confirm our suspicions that not many of them reach a "front" and my belief that Russia, as a factor of the war against Germany, has ceased to exist! From now on her military force and activity will become less and less. How can one help believing that this collapse, so helpful to Germany, is largely inspired by that despicable country!

Just now we hear much of the "Kadets," a political party, and it will interest you to know where the name comes from. The initials of Konstitutional Democrat" are "K.D", plural, "K.D's"; from those the word "Kadets" is simple. (in Russian "C" is pronounced as our "S," therefore "K" for "Constitutional"; "D" is pronounced "day").

This party, which seems to include those most interested in what looks to us like a sane government, is in the lead, both in the Ministry and with the people. They are, just now, backed by the Cossacks, which materially strengthens their hands. The trouble with all these political affairs in Russia is that, while to-day all seems serene and the Ship of State on a course for a safe harbor, tomorrow the entire situation may be reversed! I have never heard of such a kaleidoscopic control, and again my belief in German influence is strengthened, for every marked change is for the worse, as I see it; we are not permitted to congratulate ourselves for long at a time!

The "white nights" become more white; at midnight one can read ordinary newspaper print in the streets. Now we know why the heavy double curtains are at the windows and why one pair is so dark in color.

We have learned that an American Commission, headed by Mr. Elihu Root, and composed of some of our noted men, will soon be in Petrograd. As a matter of fact we knew it a long time ago but were not supposed to mention it. Probably you knew all about it before we did. We are hoping great hope for if German and misguided Russian efforts are *properly* fought now it will mean much to the Allies. If only the enormity of the efforts required and the necessities to carry them out can be realized in the capitals of the Allies, all may not yet be lost in Russia, but that looks like an impossibility, for those of us actually here can hardly realize to-day that what we *know* happened yesterday really took place.

How much more difficult for those thousands of miles away and who have never seen Russia to realize the conditions!

I promised to give you an outline of the Temporary Government here, but that will not be easy since both personnel and policy change rapidly. On March 16th the new Government was formed, the Ministry being quite like the one under the Czar, though of course with different Ministers to replace those arrested by the revolutionists. Since then the Ministers have changed rather rapidly and it is useless to name all that have been in office; some of them are now in prison! Apparently it is unfortunate that the original Ministry could not have lasted longer, for I am assured that it contained "the best men in Russia."

The principles of the Provisional Government, as published and issued to the people, met with general approval and were adopted with the apparent intention of establishing a real government for and by the people. There were, of course, paragraphs intended to ensure the safety of those who had made the success of the revolution possible, and there were small "jokers" indicating that the horny-handed son of toil, whether or not he possessed ability intended to help run the show.

The personal safety of former political prisoners was also assured by the document which made no mention of any variety of offenses that might have made them prisoners.

Probably there was some distrust by the representatives of the soldiers and workmen toward the Ministers, who were educated, and therefore in that class we hear so much of now in a despised manner as the "Bourjewie," by which they mean "Bourgeois." The Ministers, some of whom are still in office, were comparatively young and vigorous men who could have done very well, no doubt, in spite of inevitable mistakes if they had been permitted by the "Soldiers and Workmen's Deputies" to really govern. It seems that the Ministers have never had any actual power and what they had is decreasing, the large body of men with the long name (above) permitting nothing of which they do not approve.

It is all very well to talk of a government by and for the people, but what exists here now is not that at all. It is a rule by a very few men who have *usurped* the power and, from all I can learn, is very much more "autocratic" than the Czar's government ever became, also mostly inspired by hatred, more deadly and lacking many of the comforts obtainable under the old régime! Almost any reasonable advocate of a democratic form of government would become converted to Monarchy if forced to believe that Democracy means what we see here.

The *real* power is vested in a secret committee elected by the "Soldiers and Workmen's Deputies" (I am beginning to dislike that term). That group with the long name is made up of nearly three thousand members presumably representing the classes named *in Russia*, but really representing those in and about Petrograd. A very large class, the Peasants, are only represented as some soldiers are peasants. The "S. & W. D." form a body too large to govern intelligently—too many personal interests are involved; it is too ignorant, selfish and brutal to really govern a country.

I can learn of no real reason for the brutal excesses that took place during, immediately after and in the name of the Revolution.

These were shown in their worst form and greatest extent at Kronstadt, but were general over the country; I suspect they resulted partly from hatred, individual and class, as well as from a condition that can be expressed as "drunk with power" or "intoxicated with freedom." Possibly the excesses show "the real nature of the beast."

It is evident that some officers, in times past, took advantage of the great power they had over their men; possibly this brought on a class hatred against the officers; evidence in this respect is conflicting, excellent observers stating that the feeling between the officers and men was all that could be desired, and other excellent observers stating that the officers were cruel and brutal; doubtless they were at times, but it is certain that many of the officers brutally tortured and murdered did not deserve their fate because they, individually, had mistreated their men.

"Election" of officers began after the success of the revolution was assured and it resulted in some ludicrous exhibitions; we see some of them daily. Committees in companies, regiments, armies, ships, divisions, fleets were formed to administer and direct them. The effect upon routine and efficiency need not be described.

Time presses and I must end this letter. Please pass it along as arranged. All of our love to you our dear boy.

Affectionately,

Mother

Kirochnaya 8, Petrograd

Sunday, August 19, 1917

My dear,

There is still a dearth of exciting news, though a great deal happens. Detail would bore you for they would sound so like in each I write you; therefore I will again generalize by saying that everything here grows steadily worse.

By that statement I mean that Russia is no longer in "our war" and cannot be brought back in it. And when I consider what that means to the United States and our Allies, the lack of food and other physical comforts fades into insignificance, and the Russian-Army-Rearward-Marathon is the most important thing in the whole world!

More details of the horrible crimes committed by the fleeing soldiers continue to be given me by the wives of Russian officers who have escaped with their lives from the fast melting fronts and they are too terrible to put into print. Use your imagination; try to remember everything unpleasant of which you have ever heard as happening to human beings; those, and more, are happening to Russians, but the saddest part of it all is that crimes are being committed by Russians! Yet we are told that these men can govern.

I have yet to hear of a court of justice punishing a criminal, though of course many punishments, including death, have been assigned without trial; think of it!

We have been again to the beautiful estate of Colonel Vsevolosky near Petrograd. There was a large party for the week-end, and where the terrible conditions in Russia were temporarily ignored, a very pleasant gathering.

Walter had some excellent ptarmigan shooting, and, in addition, some much-needed exercise, of which he gets too little. The visit further impressed me with the pitiful situation in which nice Russians now find themselves. The guard of officer friends remains at this beautiful place but their number is too small to keep off a large force. Such a force may arrive at any time, yet the bravery of these good people permits them to act as though nothing threatens; how I wish I could help them!

Heretofore the St. George Cross was a decoration given only for military service of the highest character, so you can imagine that the wearers of it would form a body of rather superior persons.

Some of our friends are members of the St. George Society and, through them, we have met many other members. I am told that the Cross had more recently been awarded for no service whatever, this furnishing another example of destruction.

Small social affairs continue and my days at home are becoming most interesting "functions." Friends bring their friends and my circle is enlarging rapidly. We brought a supply of sugar and tea with us so I shall not run short of them, but it is a problem to find something more substantial to serve.

The drinking water is also a problem! One cannot drink the city water in safety because it is taken from the Neva where it is an open sewer. Bottled water is becoming very difficult to obtain and is unreliable when found. To boil and filter the city water is beyond the comprehension of a Russian cook—so we are obliged to attend to that detail ourselves, as are many other housekeepers.

We hear that the Germans have decided to occupy Riga; the word "capture" hardly supplies, for when they want it seriously the "Red" Russians will run away! I fancy the Huns will be more comfortable in Riga next winter than in the trenches outside.

To-day we went to a solemn service at St. Isaac's Cathedral; I would like to describe that singing for you but words fail me. I would not have missed the music I have heard in Russia for a great deal; it appeals to me more than ever.

News from Ukrainia is bad; more secession, with a little government and army of their own; fights between Ukrainian "army" and Russian soldiers; ultimatum from Ukrainia to Petrograd to immediately remove all Russian soldiers from her boundaries; Huns waiting to march in and pickup spoils of provisions! It is all so sickening when one realizes the benefits the Germans are getting from the Russian turmoil!

One member of the Root commission stated in my hearing before he left for the United States "there is plenty of food in Russia"!

If you hear that statement, you may deny it in my name. There is plenty of food here for a *large* flock of Canary birds; there is even enough for the army; there is enough for the civilian population, but there is not enough for all three of those. I form a part of the civilian population, do marketing and I *know*.

So many of our friends here have lost weight since we arrived; our arrival is not the cause of the loss of weight but there is every other reason why one should lose weight here!

The ex-Czar and his unhappy family have been removed from Tsarskoe Selo and taken to—where? We cannot learn. There was considerable talk of an escape or a rescue, and it is generally believed that Mr. Kerensky, who seems to be the only "Ministry" Russia has now, decided to remove them all to a "safer" place in Russia for the ex-Royal family.

My friends are very complimentary about my success with this very difficult language, and I really surprise myself at times with my ability to make myself understood. Its study certainly furnishes one with a never-failing occupation, which, in itself, is a very good thing to have at this particular time!

Now we know that the Root Commission has reached Washington as do our Russian friends, and that knowledge on their part is a source of frequent embarrassment to us. They ask; "Why did your Root Commission come to Russia?" "The Root Commission did a great deal of talking here and made many promises; they are in Washington now, but where is the help they promised?" "Why does the rich United States help all her other Allies so wonderfully and do nothing for Russia?" As I cannot answer any of those questions to my own satisfaction, I am obliged to "beat around the bush" considerably when my Russian friends ask them!

Russia is a wonderful land and one which offers all kinds of opportunities to American business men. That is, if and when law and order are established, citizens of the United States could reap harvest of legitimate wealth here if armed with the good will of the people. That good will existed in a marked degree not long ago. It is being driven away by our enemies, who, with a different object, ask the Russian "proletariat" the same questions my friends ask me.

Of course I appreciate how difficult it is for any one so far away as you are to realize just what is needed here, but! I am sure you *can* realize those here charged with the duty of knowing certainly do know more than you do! That simple problem of "*Why*" is the hardest one for us to solve.

Since I began this letter I have had some callers and one related to me the report of a Russian officer who had been at Tornopol when the Russians beat such a disgraceful retreat from the German advance. This officer reports that the Germans took moving pictures of the Russians engaged in the most terrible excesses against their own people, and that the Russian soldiers committed much worse crimes against their fellow citizens than the Germans did in 1914 in Belgium! Isn't it a horrible mess?

I have read much Russian history since my arrival here and it is really remarkable how it is repeating what has happened from time to time since there began to be a Russia!

We hear of some excellent work done in Vladivostok by the men on liberty from the U.S.S. *Buffalo*. It is reported here that they refused to meet or to have anything to do with the Russian sailors there, on the grounds that the Russians were mutinous and approved of the actions of their fellows who murdered their officers! That is reported to have made a great impression on the Russian sailors in Vladivostok and it has even done some good here. Just think how that effort could be multiplied by a comparatively small force of *Armed* American troops! There are *so many efforts* that could be made! It is the total absence of effort that makes one wonder to a headache!

Our mail communication grows worse. I have just received replies to letters written nearly four months ago. I have no means of knowing how our plan to pass these letters around is working, but you will readily realize that I cannot write letters of this size to many people!

Please, all of you, send us newspaper clippings—it is easier than sending the papers and will give us a great variety of news, of which we need all we can get. I never before realized the value of "news from home"—I suppose because it was never so difficult to obtain!

The activities of the women soldiers increase, but their successes do not. Their original intention to shame the men soldiers has failed utterly. We hear remarkable stories of Cossacks being placed on guard to protect the women soldiers from the remainder of the Russian army!

The big question here is: "Will the Germans take Petrograd?"

They *can* take it at any time, but I still believe they will not make the effort. Everything here is going fine for the Germans, so there is no good reason for them to send an army here. They will take Riga and as much of the surrounding country as they need to make themselves snug for the winter, but I am not alone in being unable to decide what the German General Staff plans to do!

Now I must attend to important housekeeping; routine goes on in the home even if all outside in Russia is upset.

Much love to all of you from both of us.
Affectionately yours.

French Quay, 8, Petrograd

September 14, 1917.

My dear

Well, there has been plenty of excitement during the past week but little has happened except for a relatively small number of people! Petrograd is a busy little place, I assure you.

A great many people have left the city with all their personal effects, and all exits are crowded. Railroad transportation is more in demand than ever. I cannot understand why they leave Petrograd as they do for we hear of nothing but disorders all over Russia, and I can learn of no locality that is really *safe.*

In the meantime Walter has made plans for a means of escape for the American colony, in case an escape becomes necessary. Times are uncertain and threats are many; we *may* have to run some day; it is certainly better to have a plan than no plan.

The Red Cross Mission had a farewell dinner at the Hotel Europe and many members leave for home very soon, the remaining few staying here to carry on their work. The American Red Cross Mission to Roumania has been represented here by a few of its members, also, so you see we have had quite a number of fine Americans about.

The political events have been too numerous to list, but the most important item would be that all but four Ministers resigned after "Korniloff's Revolution" failed, and Kerensky is stronger than ever.

I am still strong for Korniloff, in spite of his failure, and I believe him to be a true patriot. I wish I could believe the same of Kerensky.

There are many *dark* rumors and a rather settled conviction that General Korniloff has been "double crossed" (I hate that term, but that's what they all say!) by Kerensky. Korniloff was certainly deserted by many he had a right to suppose would uphold him in his great effort to save Russia. I have read considerably about General Korniloff, his history and career, and no one will be able to convince me he is a traitor as he has been branded by Kerensky. Read again the speech of General Korniloff in my last letter; is that the language of a traitor? *Never!*

The net result of this last effort is that Russia is worse off than ever, and we have been shown that many who promised to assist General Korniloff in his supreme effort turned at the last moment and also turned traitors, for

General Korniloff was Russia's last hope. I have seen enough now to be firmly convinced that this country will go from bad to worse until foreign aid in sufficient force cleans it up.

Korniloff is said to be a prisoner, but I will only believe that when convinced that *all* the Cossacks have turned Bolsheviki! Some of those stationed in Petrograd have been contaminated, and I am not surprised at that, for some educated Americans have been that same, much to my surprise and disgust, but it *will* be a shock to me if the majority of the Cossacks give up all their traditions and become the brutes their fellows in the Army have become.

General Alexieff is Commander-in-Chief now, but what General Korniloff could not accomplish will not be done by the new Commander. He will only last a short time in his high office.

The women soldiers have been more than ever in evidence; they now sing as they march about the city, a custom among Russian troops. They claim to be strong for Kerensky; I trust them to remain honest in their convictions more than I trust any of the men soldiers!

There are the usual thousands of rumors, but one that seems true and difficult to explain is that General Krimoff, who was believed to be in active command of the forces proceeding to Petrograd in favor of General Korniloff was ordered to Petrograd, arrived, had a consultation with Kerensky, then committed suicide. *Why?*

I must give you one example to show you why I do not enthuse over Kerensky, why I doubt his ability and motives.

When the Leninites (Anarchists) took Petrograd in July, Kerensky ordered the Cossacks out against them; when the Cossacks were reported nearing Petrograd to establish a Military Government it was said, "Kerensky armed the Anarchists against the Cossacks." I have heard such an exhibition called "carrying water on both shoulders."

Some Russians (and others) now boldly denounce Kerensky.

By the way, the anarchists will not give up the arms and ammunition with which they have recently been furnished by the Kerensky Government; they will keep them, and we will hear from them when they are ready to make a noise.

The recent excitement gave the soldier-murderers another chance to slake their thirst for blood and there have been many more officers murdered. Shooting is common in the streets, but no one seems to know what it is all for. Probably it is being done by *armed criminals* taking advantage of the conditions to ply their trades of murder and robbery.

Our newspapers from the States annoy me very much! They have the most misleading articles about Russia in them. How I should like to reply to some of those articles and give real facts! Of course, by the time such replies could reach an editorial desk they would be ancient history, for no one not a stenographer can really keep Russian history up to date, although, by changing names and dates, much that has happened here since my arrival would be described by histories of events here one hundred, two hundred, three hundred years ago!

Our mail service grows worse and worse, in fact we have nothing that deserves the name of "service," but I have been fortunate in being able to send out some of my letters by friends, not all of them Americans, leaving for more healthy locations; I hope you will receive all of them, for I want some of you, at least, to know what is really going on here.

I am keeping copies of all the letters, for I will find them interesting proof hereafter, to convince myself that certain things really did happen! We even find ourselves to-day wondering if what we saw yesterday really did take place!

Recently a French aviation officer who had fought with the Russians for two years was murdered by Russian soldiers in a most brutal manner and no real reason for it. It looks as though none of the Allies will be safe here very long. However, we may be safe for weeks, months, even years; queer people, these Russians, they acknowledge it!

For several hours during the "last revolution" no "Russian Government" could be located; so many believed that Korniloff would succeed almost without effort that Ministers were not very prominent—in fact none could be found for a time! The Allied Ambassadors and Ministers have been meeting often lately; we live quite near three Embassies and I can see the diplomats when they arrive. I have heard the Diplomatic Corps offered to mediate between the opposing factions. Walter says this again reminds him of other revolutions he has seen.

The press in Petrograd is a joke; only what is permitted by the government is published; much of it we *know* to be false, so we suspect the remainder.

We have just received some very fine mail written in July; you see the question of real correspondence is quite impossible.

In spite of the revolution my first "day" in my new home was very well attended and many were made happy by the chocolate cake I am able to supply with my tea. It is really a pleasure to see some of the Russians at tea; they so enjoy sugar, jam, white bread, and the many other things they cannot get at all, and we would not have if we had not brought them with us.

I have been to the opera and the ballet again; they are still wonderful, but one takes chances in going out at night; to see the Russian opera and ballet is worth a chance or two! I shall never tire of them but, alas, their days are numbered—I am afraid they must go, with all else that is attractive here; all *is* going fast.

Very many thanks for the lovely letter I had from you in the last mail, and for the newspaper clippings. I will write more briefly and intimately to you in a letter not one of this series.

In the meantime,

Affectionately yours,

8 French Quay, Petrograd

November 7, 1917.

My dear

NOW, my dear, There is some excitement, and as I write the atmosphere is punctuated by all kinds of shots, rifle, pistol, machine guns, field pieces and large guns aboard ships!

Walter and Miss Gueradhy are at the telephone getting reports from various parts of the city and I am putting down my impressions while they are fresh in my mind. It is midnight, but I am not sleepy!

Yesterday Walter was at the Admiralty, making his routine visit, when his friend there advised him to get home quickly, saying; "They are going to try again, these people!" On his way home he heard much shooting and saw the bridges being opened to prevent the Anarchists from crossing them. He came to the Lazaret for me and advised the other ladies to get home as quickly as possible, further advising them to come to our house if unable to get home.

After we reached our apartment, we telephoned to all Americans we could reach, advising them of the trouble. There was street fighting, but not serious, and by midnight all seemed quiet, though there was an occasional shot. Mrs. Volkeapaa had been unable to reach her home so came to us for dinner. We telephoned to her husband who managed to get to our house and later took her home.

This morning we heard that the Anarchists had repeated their effort of last July, only more successfully, and the entire city was in their possession, though fighting continued all day in the streets. Miss Gueradhy, the interpreter, very pluckily came in the morning but the fighting was too severe in the afternoon and she prepared to remain here to-night, after telephoning her mother.

There seemed to be no let up in the fighting. We all prepared for bed, when very heavy guns were heard, and we learned by telephone that the Russian Cruiser *Aurora* is in the river, bombarding the Winter Palace. We can see the Fortress of Peter and Paul from our front windows and the flashes of field guns there, apparently also firing at the Winter Palace.

Fortunately for the information we so desire, Walter has many friends in different parts of the city to whom it has been his custom to telephone in cases like this, and to-night the system is working so he is getting reports from all of them. They indicate that fighting is general all over the city, but hardest about the Winter Palace, where it seems that most of the Ministers of the Provisional Government have taken refuge. We have been promised this uprising for several days, in fact I wrote you last July that it would come, but, believing the Government knew as much as I did, it seemed they would be prepared for it, but the city has again fallen an easy prey to the better organized anarchists, who have had some German assistance this time in their organization.

We now have a considerable store of provisions in the house and will not suffer if forced to remain indoors, though it is another item of interest here that no one stays at home simply because there is street fighting! We even go to the ballet and opera, dodging those sections of the city where we hear shooting, both going and returning.

We are wondering to-night if all the various threats of the anarchists, made in their speeches during the past few months, will be carried out! The threats included making as much misery as possible for those they do not like, and I believe they have the desire and intention to do that very thing. I have not heard of any threat or plan to really better conditions, except that it has been threatened that those who lived in large handsome homes must give up some of their rooms to those less fortunate.

You should have seen us hiding our precious canned fruit, vegetables, condensed milk, cocoa, etc., we received from the States!

It will take a search party a long time to locate all of it; not even our domestics know where it is.

To-day one of the naval officers Walter knew at Oesel Island came here with the customary request that he be sent to the United States to serve in our Navy. There have been many rumors of what happened at Oesel Island when the Germans captured it, and this officer confirmed many of them. I will only give you one sad incident, which will convince you what horrible creatures are now in power here.

The officer who invited us to visit them at Oesel Island had his wife and two beautiful children with him there, a girl and boy. He was in command of the forces on the Island and had made plans to remove his family if the place fell. He remained with his men during the few minutes they resisted the Germans, and followed them in their mad retreat, going to his house to take his family on board ship. What he saw in his house caused him to shoot himself; his own men in retreating had outraged the wife and daughter and had murdered all three of his family. Could men be worse?

Yes, these are the people some Americans with brains are urging us to trust, bear with, uphold, and *acknowledge!*

Another robbery took place in our *immediate* neighborhood; a post and telegraph office was robbed, the young woman in charge at the time being brutally murdered. The number of such cases is increasing all the time, but I only give you the few as examples!

Nothing really worse than what has happened since we have been here can happen; the only way in which it will change is for a greater number of the same things to happen. Even their fiendish ingenuity can probably not devise worse tortures than have been and are being inflicted. Of course their successes during the past two days will inflame all their passions and make times worse in the respect that more will suffer. The "searching parties," which are really "looting parties," will now have a more free hand, and their activities will increase.

It is a source of great satisfaction to me that my husband, soon after his arrival here, announced the great need for foreign troops and for propaganda; he could get no one in authority to agree with him, but he has continued his efforts and now, as if it were quite a new idea, many are saying, "We must have foreign troops and active propaganda."

His ability to say "I told you so" does not help the situation a bit, so he does not say it. What he does say is, "You'd better hurry, or it will be too late!"

Troops *could* have been brought here and successful propaganda, or rather counter-propaganda, for there was much of the German variety already, *could* have been carried on, but no one seemed to be able to see the necessity for them.

In some of our mail I read of the servant troubles in the States; I rather suspect that you are infinitely better off than we are in that respect! Probably none of your servants believe they have the *right* to murder you if they so desire!

One more of the best generals Russia had, Dukhonin, has been murdered, and so they go, always the best, though Alexieff managed to be relieved by Dukhonin without being killed. The new Commander-in Chief is a second lieu-tenant, who will do just as well as any, for there are no armies left to command.

The latest official robbery came out a few days ago. Everyone living in an apartment the rent for which is one hundred and fifty roubles per month or more is required to furnish the robber rulers of Russia with two warm articles of clothing. As I have not seen any apartments that cheap, the order is a very general one.

At last we have a courier mail service, but that is a comfort that will not last long for already the British Embassy has had to discontinue its couriers. Just now the Bolsheviki are particularly cross with the British because two Russians with criminal records are being held in custody in England. This simply shows that they are no respecters of persons or governments, and our turn is likely to come at any time. It is a great pleasure to see our couriers, though; fine, big, real men.

Just now we have no electric light from midnight to five in the morning, and it will soon be reduced very materially. We are ready for all reductions, except that our electric door bell is on the lighting circuit! Walter could install a bell easily enough but one cannot be found.

Germans are thick in Petrograd now. They have offices and are "advising" the Bolsheviki, who, by the way, have taken the most famous girls' school in the country, Smolney Institute, for their Headquarters. I suppose it is no secret that the Germans are here for I met one quite openly at a tea recently.

Just now I hear no shooting, and I am sleepy, so I will stop. There will certainly be many people leaving here now, so I will have this ready to send by the first one of whom I learn.

You need not worry about us for we will be safe as long as anyone is, and there will be foreigners in Petrograd for a long time yet.

Until next time,

Yours faithfully,

French Quay 8, Petrograd

February 20, 1918.

My dear

This has been no time for writing letters! All of our previous surcharged atmosphere has been a mere nothing as compared with the last ten days. To be sure, the betrayal of Russia into the hands of Germany has continued successfully, and really nothing very *new* has turned up, but all that has gone before has now begun to pyramid, probably as per plank and the air is heavy.

The anarchists have again threatened the American Ambassador and his staff, but I cannot see that any of them are awed!

The thing that is properly causing uneasiness now is the rapid advance of a German Army in this direction. Possibly it advances for the sole purpose of driving the Allied Representatives from Petrograd.

Now it is too late to interfere with the success of the plans for destruction whoever made them; destruction is an accomplished fact.

I report that the Bolsheviks have changed the Russian calendar to make it coincide with ours! That will be a comfort to foreigners living in Russia and to business men with associations here.

The number of Russian officers who wish to join our Navy has increased with the decrease of Russia. One who had command of a destroyer when the Germans captured Riga Gulf told us that after the "fight" (!) was over and he was in retreat he overtook a Russian Battleship underway, but going very slowly; he went near, but saw no one and his hail was not answered. He finally put his destroyer alongside the battleship and some of his officers went on board. The battleship was *entirely deserted* but one of her engines was running as were her dynamos! Battle flags were flying and the ship was normal in all respects except there was not a soul on board! He could only find one place where she had been hit by a German shell, and no damage had been done there.

He sunk the ship with one of his own torpedoes to prevent the Germans from getting her. And *that* is the way the "brave Red Russian sailors" (!!!) won the battle of Riga Gulf!

Four days ago Walter and I received orders to shovel snow in the streets. The order reads: (Translation.)

"Mr. Walter and Pauline Crosby are detailed for forced labor (to shovel snow) on 18/5 February. The first named from 9:00 to 12:00 noon; the second named from 12:00 to 3:00 p.m."

Walter declined to consider the order and announced that neither of us would do the work concerned; threats were made which have not yet been carried out. I have just learned for the first time that Walter has had a loaded carbine near the front door for some time, and he announces that there will be a very pretty fight when they try to make us shovel snow!

I did give another dinner party, and it will probably be the last one. The effort is simply too great for all concerned.

Yesterday we called at the Spanish Legation; the wife of the Chargé d'Affaires told me they had potatoes and tea for luncheon, only, and that, so far as she knew, there was nothing in the house for dinner!

The Embassy is trying to get a train ready to take all of us out by way of Siberia. Apparently it will soon be time to leave! I may *bring* this out of Russia! At any rate it will leave by the first reliable means and I hope you will receive it.

Always affectionately,

Yours.

CHAPTER FOURTEEN

~

Emma Goldman

An Anarchist in Russia

Emma Goldman was a Russian-born American anarchist, author, and lecturer. She was born on June 27, 1869, in Kovno, in the Jewish pale of settlement, then part of Russia, now in Lithuania. Most of the Jews there were poor, discriminated against, and subject to pogroms carried out by the government; they could not own land and lived in urban centers, where they found work in shops or factories. The Goldman family were lower middle class and were not prosperous, but they held fast to their Orthodox Jewish faith. They moved to Koningsburg, East Prussia, where her father, Abraham, found work and Emma went to school. There she was exposed to German culture and literature, which she favored throughout her life. She had a rebellious streak as a child and later as a teenager.

In 1881, the family moved to St. Petersburg, Russia, for employment opportunities. Emma went to school and wanted to continue her education in hopes of becoming a doctor, but the family could not afford it, and she found work in a glove factory. There were some bright sides in the move to St. Petersburg for her. The city offered culture, an exposure to radical politics and literature, and some personal independence. She was introduced to radical literature, reading Nikolai Chernyshevsky's *What Is to Be Done?* And she knew about the Nihilist martyrs.

Tsar Alexander III assumed power in 1881 after the assassination of his father, Alexander II. Once in power, Alexander III stifled political dissent and passed anti-Semitic laws and quotas for Jews. The political repression and restrictions against Jews made Emma hate the tsar and motivated her to join her two stepsisters, Lena and Helene, who had immigrated to America and settled in Rochester, New York. Emma joined them in 1886, and her parents the following year. There she worked in a textile factory and in 1887 married Jacob Kersner, a tailor who had boarded with the family. The marriage did not last, and she divorced him, but when he begged her to marry him again, she assented; however, they divorced again.

In 1889, once her marriage ended, Emma left Rochester and moved to the Lower East Side of New York City, which she called home until she was deported in 1919. The Chicago Haymarket Square riot in 1886 took place to protest the killing of two strikers of the McCormick Reaper Company, and the subsequent trial of the seven anarchists unjustly accused of throwing a bomb was a turning point in Emma's life. She followed the trials closely, and the outcome led her to take the first step toward anarchism and leftist politics. In New York, she met immigrants like herself who were socialists and anarchists.

Anarchism and radical politics attracted Jewish immigrants from Russia who prized personal freedom and were anti-government, anti-religion, and anti-private property. In New York cafes, Emma met fellow anarchists, including Alexander Berkman—who was a lifelong friend, her lover, whom she held as her ideal—and Johann Most, who developed her ability as a fiery speaker.

Emma went on a lecture tour and became involved in the labor movement, supporting strikes. In 1892, the Homestead strike of workers of the Amalgamated Association of Iron and Steel Workers against the Carnegie Steel Corporation energized Emma and Alexander. A clash between the armed union workers and the Pinkerton Guards resulted in the death of nine workers. The two collaborated on planning their response. Emma obtained money for a pistol that Alexander used to shoot Henry Clay Frick, the president of the corporation. The attack failed, Frick was injured, and Alexander was arrested and sentenced to twenty-two years in prison, commuted to fourteen. Emma was not implicated in the assault. But then, in 1893, she was arrested for promoting a riot after a speech to striking workers in New York City and was sentenced to a year in jail. She made good use of her time in prison, reading and studying medicine.

To earn a living, Emma's interest in medicine led her to work as a practical nurse. Needing additional training, she decided to go to Vienna. Then, in 1896, she returned to the United States, where she worked as a nurse and midwife, as well as continuing her anarchist activities as a speaker. Her work with immigrant women with unwanted pregnancies led her, later on, to support and speak on birth control, although she never supported the suffragettes' call for voting rights for women.

On a speaking tour in Chicago, Emma met Leon Czolgosz, who was interested in anarchism. In 1901, Leon assassinated President William McKinley, who had been visiting the Pan American Exhibition in Buffalo, New York. After his arrest, Leon reported that Emma inspired him to assassinate the president. She was hunted down and surrendered to the police in Chicago but was later released, as she had not conspired with Leon in the crime. After this, Emma Goldman was well known—and anarchists faced hostility and attacks.

After a brief hiatus, Emma returned to political activity and speaking engagements. In 1902, the government passed a law that prohibited the entry into the United States of individuals who opposed organized government or were members of an organization that opposed government. The threat of deportation and an infringement of free speech was implicit in this legislation. Emma joined the Free Speech League and gave speeches to liberal organizations. She reached out to the American radicals and the Left and worked to build connections with them.

She founded *Mother Earth*, and the first edition was published in 1906. The magazine included articles on cultural topics and historical figures, but, more importantly, it introduced international anarchism to Americans. Both European and American writers contributed to it. The magazine remained in print until the federal government banned it in 1918. Goldman left the editorship of the magazine to Alexander Berkman and continued lecturing in cities and on university campuses, now arranged by a new lover and fellow anarchist, Benjamin Reitman. Given anarchist support for strikes from 1907 to 1908, her appearances were often canceled, and she was arrested.

By 1905, Emma supported a new union, the Industrial Workers of the World, that organized skilled and unskilled workers and was anti-government and pro-revolution. The union practiced direct action and orchestrated strikes to bring down the capitalist system. She supported their goals and their right to hold meetings; defended their leader, William Haywood; and gave the IWW publicity in *Mother Earth*.

With the advent of the United States' entry into World War I and the passage of the Selective Service Act in 1917 that required men to register for military service, Emma Goldman and Alexander Berkman organized the No-Conscription League, as they opposed war between capitalistic governments. She was against war between nations, though not war or revolution to overthrow governments and capitalism. They both gave speeches and wrote handbills opposing conscription, and on June 15 they were arrested and charged with attempting to prevent draft registration. The jury found them guilty and sentenced them to two years in prison and a $10,000 fine. Their lawyer appealed the case, and they were free for a brief period. Once out of jail, she wrote articles and spoke in support of the 1917 Russian Revolution, while their lawyer brought their case before the Supreme Court and lost. Hence, in 1918, they were both back in prison, she in Missouri and he in Atlanta.

In the summer of 1919, they were both released, having served their sentences. The country was in the midst of a "red scare" and labor strikes, while the federal government was in the process of deciding whether or not to deport Emma Goldman to Russia, her home country. Her citizenship had been revoked by the United States government previously, and she was deported on December 21, 1919, sailing aboard the *Buford* for Russia, along with 249 others, including Alexander Berkman.

They were taken to Petrograd first, where they received a warm reception. The city was not as she remembered it; it looked broken down, dirty, and deserted and had lost its sense of vitality. They soon met with Russian anarchists who reported that they were harassed, their meetings disrupted; some were executed, while others served jail terms. Even more unsettling was the masses who were suffering. They had little food or fuel; inflation was rampant; they were not in charge of the factories; they could not travel without a permit; the Tcheka was powerful and abusive, and the newspapers suppressed any opposition. Political freedom was unheard of. Any criticism of the regime was considered counter-revolutionary. The social inequities were obvious; the political elite had access to food and goods that the average citizen did not have. Emma was put up in a first-class hotel and could use American money to buy whatever she wanted. She found that distressing, but she maintained her faith in the revolution until the end of their visit.

Both Emma and Alexander wanted to obtain work that would benefit the people and the revolution, but they were turned down when they offered help. Finally, they joined the staff of the Museum of the Revolution, located in the Winter Palace, where they were to travel by railroad in Russia and gather manuscripts and memorabilia for the museum's archives. This gave them an opportunity to move about freely and see the country firsthand.

At first, they headed to the Ukraine to assess current conditions. During their travels, they were taken to schools and institutions that were model ones to show the progress the Communists had made, but not to those that were poorly equipped. The bureaucrats they met were inefficient and corrupt. Discrimination against the Jewish population still existed. While government pogroms ceased, the White Army had taken over, only to continue the pogroms. When Emma and Alexander returned from their travels, they decided to end their collaboration with the museum that had been taken over by the Communists.

For Emma, the Kronstadt Rebellion was the last straw. The sailors supported the demand of the masses for food and fuel in Petrograd, as they had supported the Revolution of 1905 and 1917. The government considered them counter-revolutionaries and attacked the fortress, killing a number of sailors and government troops. Before the government's response, Emma and Alexander had written a letter to the chairman of the Petrograd Soviet of Labor and Defense recommending that the Red Army not be used against the demonstrators, but it was to no avail.

Emma had wanted to believe in the justice of the Russian Revolution, with its promise of freedom, equality, and economic and political justice. She held fast to her ideals until the reality of the situation forced her to confront the truth. Disillusioned by the economic conditions, the loss of political liberty by the people, institutionalized terror, and the arrest of anarchists, the couple decided to leave Russia. They were under suspicion, spied on, and moved out of their quarters. Unknown to them, they had been under surveillance by the Bolsheviks and the United States government since their arrival nearly two years earlier. Now it was time to go. But where *could* they go?

They applied for passports and left Russia in December 1921, finally ending up in Germany, where she wrote a book about her experiences in Russia entitled *My Disillusionment in Russia*, which was published in 1923. A second volume entitled *My Further Disillusionment in Russia* followed in 1924. She wanted to let the public know what the real Bolshevik regime was like and that she had been wrong about her support for the Bolsheviks. At the same time, she made clear that she had not been wrong about the concept of revolution itself; revolution was necessary, but under the guidance of anarchists, who preached brotherhood, justice, and equality.

In 1924, Emma left Germany for England, but she did not find an outlet for her political activities there. The following year, she married James Colton, an English anarchist and coal miner. Their marriage gave her British citizenship and the right to travel. From there, she went to Canada, where she lectured, and in 1928 finally moved to Saint Tropez, France, where she settled down to write her autobiography, *Living My Life*. As the years went on, she still believed in anarchism, although she was less sure that it would be achieved.

In 1932, Emma continued her lecture tours in Europe and Canada, where she spoke against the dictatorships in Russia, Italy, and Germany. In 1934, she was allowed to return to the United States for ninety days but with the

Emma Goldman
Library of Congress

caveat that she could speak only about literature and drama, not politics. She longed to move back to the United States, where she had spent most of her personal and political life, but she was still considered too dangerous. She returned to Saint Tropez but sold her home to be in Nice with Alexander Berkman, who had cancer. He died on June 28, 1936, from a self-inflicted gunshot wound.

The Spanish Civil War from 1936 to 1939 drew Emma Goldman in as a last possible success for an anarchist victory. She directed the preparation of English language propaganda for the anarchists in London and raised money for the displaced. She also made three trips to Spain, visiting Barcelona, the center of anarchist politics, but soon the conflict became an international one, and the Left received the support of the Communists. The nationalist government took issue with rebellious anarchists and cracked down on them. With the takeover of Spain by the Fascists in 1939, the anarchist cause was lost. Despite her despair over the results, Emma went to Canada that year to raise funds for the Spanish.

In 1939, the Second World War began in Europe. Emma hated Communist Russia and Nazi Germany, and she opposed the world war, as she always had opposed war between nations, believing that nothing good would come of war.

She returned to Toronto and in February 1940 suffered a cerebral hemorrage; she died on May 14, 1940, at the age of seventy. She was buried at Waldheim Cemetery in Forest Park, Illinois, now at last back in the country that she was exiled from and longed to return to.

Emma Goldman wrote the following books: *Anarchism and Other Essays* (New York: Mother Earth Publishing Associaton, 1910); *The Social Significance of the Modern Drama* (Boston: Gorham Press, 1914); *My Disillusionment in Russia* (Garden City, NY: Doubleday, Page and Co., 1923); *My Further Disillusionment in Russia* (Garden City, NY: Doubleday, Page and Co., 1924); and *Living My Life* (New York: Knopf, 1931; Oriole Press, 1932).

The following selections are from *My Disillusionment in Russia* and *My Further Disillusionment in Russia*.

～

My Disillusionment in Russia

The Bolshevik Regime

I had come to Russia possessed by the hope that I should find a new-born country, with its people consecrated to the great, though very difficult task of revolutionary reconstruction. And I had fervently hoped that I might become an active part of the inspiring work.

I found reality in Russia grotesque, totally unlike the great ideal that had borne me upon the crest of high hope to the land of promise. It required fifteen long months before I could get my bearings. Each day, each month added new links to the fatal chain that pulled down my cherished edifice. I fought desperately against the disillusionment.

Then came Kronstadt. It was the final wrench. It completed the terrible realization that the Russian Revolution was no more.

I saw before me the Bolshevik State, formidable, crushing every constructive revolutionary effort, suppressing, debasing and disintegrating everything. Unable and unwilling to become a cog in that sinister machine, and aware that I could be of no practical use to Russia and her people, I decided to leave the country.

Two years of earnest study, investigation, and research convinced me that the great benefits brought to the Russian people by Bolshevism exist only on paper, painted in glowing colors to the masses of Europe and America by efficient Bolshevik propaganda. ... But in reality, the Russian people have gained nothing from the Bolshevik experiment. To be sure, the peasants have the land; not by the grace of the Bolsheviki, but through their own direct efforts, set in motion long before the October change.

The Russian workers, like the peasant, also employed direct action. They possessed themselves of the factories, organized their own shop committees, and were virtually in control of the economic life of Russia. But soon they were stripped of their power and placed under the yoke of the Bolshevik state. Chattel slavery became the lot of the Russian proletariat. ... Try as I might I could find nowhere any evidence of benefits received either by the workers or the peasants from the Bolshevik regime.

Petrograd

I found Petrograd of 1920 quite a different place. It was almost in ruins, as if a hurricane had swept over it. The houses looked like broken old tombs upon neglected and forgotten cemeteries. The streets were dirty and deserted; all life had gone from them. The population of Petrograd before the war was almost two million; in 1920 it had dwindled to five hundred thousand. The people walked about like living corpses; the shortage of food and fuel were slowly sapping the city; grim death was clutching at its heart. Emaciated and frostbitten men, women, and children were being whipped by the common lash, the search for a piece of bread or a stick of wood. It was a heart-rending sight by day, an oppressive weight at night.

Inequality

The feature that affected me the most was the inequality I witnessed in my immediate environment. I learned that the rations issued to the tenants of the First House of the Soviet (Astoria) were much superior to those received by the workers in the factories. To be sure, they were not sufficient to sustain life, but no one in the Astoria lived from these rations alone. The members of the Communist Party, quartered at the Astoria, worked in Smolny, and the rations in Smolny were the best in Petrograd. Moreover, trade was not entirely suppressed at that time. The markets were doing a lucrative business, though no one seemed able to explain to me where the purchasing capacity came from. The workers could not afford to buy butter which was 2,000 rubles a pound, sugar at 3,000 or meat at 1,000.

Moscow

Coming from Petrograd to Moscow is like being suddenly transferred from a desert to active life, so great was the contrast. On reaching the large open square of the main Moscow station I was amazed at the sight of busy crowds, cabbies, and porters. The same picture presented itself all the way from the station to the Kremlin. The streets were alive with men, women and children. Almost everyone carried a bundle, or dragged a loaded sleigh. There was life, motion, and movement, quite different from the stillness that oppressed me in Petrograd.

I noticed considerable display of the military in the city, and scores of men dressed in leather suits with guns in their belts. "Tcheka men, our Extraordinary Commission," explained Radek. ... Here in Moscow they seemed everywhere. ... What struck me forcibly besides the display of militarism, was the preoccupation of the people. There seemed to be no common interest between them. Everyone rushed about as a detached unit in quest of his own, pushing and knocking against everyone else.

The Russian People

The Russian people even after four years of war and three years of revolution remained unsophisticated. They were suspicious of strangers and reticent at first. But when they learned that one had come from America and did not belong to the governing political party, they gradually lost their reserve. Much information I gathered from them and some explanation of the things that perplexed me since my arrival. I talked frequently with the workers and peasants and the women in the markets.

The forces that led up to the Russian Revolution had remained *terra incognito* to these simple folk, but the Revolution itself had struck deep into their souls. They knew nothing of theories, but they believed that there was to be no more of the hated *barin* (master), and now the *barin* was again upon them. "The *barin* has everything," they would say, "white bread, clothing, even chocolate, while we have nothing." "Communism, equality, freedom," they jeered, "lies and deceptions."

The Anarchists and the Revolution

At a conference of the Moscow Anarchists in March I first learned of the part some Anarchists had played in the Russian Revolution. In the July uprising of 1917 the Kronstadt sailors were led by the Anarchist Yarchuck;

the Constituent Assembly was dispersed by Zhelezniakov; the Anarchists had participated on every front and helped to drive back the Allied attacks. It was the consensus of opinion that the Anarchists were always among the first to face fire, as they were also the most active in the reconstructive work. ... I learned that the Anarchists had virtually helped the Bolsheviki into power. Five months later, in April 1918, machine guns were used to destroy the Moscow Anarchist Club and to suppress their press. The field had to be cleared of "disturbing elements" and the Anarchists were the first to suffer. Since then the persecution of the Anarchists has never ceased.

Industrial Militarization

The Ninth Congress of the All Russian Communist Party, held in March 1920, was characterized by a number of measures which meant a complete turn to the right. Foremost among them was the militarization of labour and the establishment of one-man management of industry, as against the collegiate shop system. Obligatory labour had long been a law upon the statutes of the Socialist Republic, but it was carried out, as Trotsky said, "only in a small private way." Now the law was to be made effective in earnest.

The first works to be visited were the Putilov, the largest and most important engine and car manufacturing establishment. Forty thousand workers had been employed there before the war. Now I was informed that only 7,000 were at work.

At the Putilov office we were cordially received, shown about the various departments, and then turned over to a guide. There were four of us in the party, of whom only two could speak Russian. I lagged behind to question a group working at a bench. At first I was met with the usual suspicion, which I overcame by telling the men that I was bringing the greetings of their brothers in America. I inquired about their work, their lives, and their attitude toward the new decrees." As if we had not been driven enough before," complained one of the men. "Now we are to work under the military *nagaika* (whip). Of course, we will have to be in the shop or they will punish us as industrial deserters. But how can they get more work out of us? We are suffering hunger and cold. We have no strength to give more." The men were bitter and resentful.

The great flour mill of Petrograd, visited next, looked as if it were in a state of siege, with armed soldiers everywhere, even inside the workrooms. The explanation given was that large quantities of precious flour had been vanishing. The soldiers watched the millmen as if they were galley slaves, and the workers naturally resented such humiliating treatment. They hardly dared to speak. One young chap, a fine-looking fellow, complained to me of the conditions. "We are here virtual prisoners," he said. "We cannot make a step without permission."

The Bolsheviki

During the several months I had heard and seen enough to become somewhat conversant with the Communist psychology, as well as with the theories and methods of the Bolsheviki. I had come to realize that the Communists believed implicitly in the Jesuitic formula that the end justifies all means. In fact, they glorified in that formula. Any suggestion of the value of human life, quality of character, the importance of revolutionary integrity as the basis of a new social order, was repudiated as "bourgeois sentimentality," which had no place in the revolutionary scheme of things. For the Bolsheviki the end to be achieved was the Dictatorship of the Proletariat. Everything that advanced that end was justifiable and revolutionary. In short, I had come to see that the Bolsheviki were social puritans who sincerely believed that they alone were ordained to save mankind.

Schools

One thing grew quite clear to me: I could not affiliate myself with the Soviet Government: I could not accept any work which would place me under the control of the Communist machine. The Commissariat of Education was so thoroughly dominated by that machine that it was hopeless to expect anything but routine work.

I had also learned a great deal about the system of favoritism and graft that prevailed in the management of the schools and the treatment of children. Some schools were in splendid condition, the children well fed and well clad, enjoying concerts, theatricals, dances, and other amusements. But the majority of the schools and childrens' homes were squalid, dirty, and neglected. Those in charge of the "preferred" schools had little difficulty procuring everything needed for their charges, often having an over-supply. But the caretakers of the "common" schools would waste their time and energies by the week going about from one department to another, discouraged and faint with waiting before they could obtain the merest necessities. The well-kept schools were for show, for the foreign missions and delegates who were visiting Russia. Everything was lavished on these show schools at the cost of the others.

Working with the Museum of the Revolution

The Museum of the Revolution is housed in the Winter Palace, in the suite once used as the Nursery of the Tsar's children. The secretary of the Museum, M. B. Kaplan, received me very cordially and expressed "the hope that I would join in the work of the Museum." He and another member of the staff spent considerable time with me on several occasions, explaining the plans and purposes of the Museum. They asked me to join the expedition which the Museum was organizing, and which was to go south to Ukraina and the Caucasus. Valuable material of the revolutionary period was to be gathered there, they explained. The idea attracted me. Aside from my general interest in the Museum and its efforts, it meant non-partisan work, free from Commissars, and an exceptional opportunity to see and study Russia.

The Trade Unions

The Printer's Union had been suppressed and its entire managing board sent to prison. The Union had called a public meeting to which members of the British Labour Mission were invited. There the famous Socialist Revolutionist Tchernov had unexpectedly made his appearance. He severely criticized the Bolshevik regime, received an ovation from the huge audience of workers, and then vanished as mysteriously as he had come.

The Bakers Union, a very militant organization, had also been suppressed, and its management replaced by Communists. Later I met some of the bakers and found them much embittered against the Communist Party and the Government. I inquired about the condition of their union, telling them that I had been informed that the Russian unions were very powerful and had practical control of the industrial life of the country. The bakers laughed. "The trade union are the lackeys of the Government," they said. "They have no independent function, and the workers have no say in them. The trade unions are doing mere police duty for the Communist State."

At Kursk

Our first stop was Kursk. Nothing of importance was collected there except a pair of *kandali* (iron handcuffs) which had been worn by a revolutionist in Schlusselburg. It was donated by a chance passer-by who noticing the inscription on our car, "Extraordinary commission of the Museum of the Revolution," became interested and called to pay us a visit.

Kursk is a large industrial centre and I was interested in the fate of the workers there. We learned from our visitor that there had been repeated skirmishes between the workers and the Soviet Authorities. A short time before our arrival a strike had broken out and soldiers were sent to quell it. The usual arrests followed, and many workers were still in the Tcheka. This state of affairs, the Tolystan thought, was due to general Communist incompetence rather than to any other cause. People were placed in responsible positions not because of their fitness but owing to their party membership. Political usefulness was the first consideration and it naturally resulted in general abuse of power and confusion. The Communist dogma that the end justifies all means was also doing much harm. It had thrown the door wide open to the worst human passions and discredited the ideals of the Revolution.

American Anarchists in Kharkov

In the evening our American friends visited us. Each of them had a rich experience of struggle, suffering, and persecution and I was surprised to learn that most of them had also been imprisoned by the Bolsheviki. They had endured much for the sake of the ideas and had been hounded by every government of Ukraina. ... The communists were no different; they also persecuted the Anarchists as well as other revolutionists of the Left. Still, the anarchists continued their work. Their faith in the Revolution, in spite of all they endured, and even in the face of the worst reaction, was truly sublime.

Militarization of Labour

During our stay in Kharkov I also visited the Department of Labour Distribution, which had come into existence since the militarization of Labour. According to the Bolsheviki it became necessary then to return the workers from the villages to which they had streamed from the starving cities. They had to be registered and classified according to trades and distributed to points where their services were most needed. In the carrying out of this plan many people were daily rounded up on the streets and in the marketplace. Together with the large numbers arrested as speculators or for possession of Tsarist money, they were put on the list of the Labour Distribution Department. Some went to the Donetz Basin, while the weaker ones went on to concentration camps. The communists justified this system and method as necessary during a revolutionary period in order to build up the industries. Everybody must work in Russia, they said, or be forced to work.

The Kharkov Concentration Camp

We found a number of prisoners working in the yard, digging a new sewer. It was certainly needed, for the whole place was filled with nauseating smells. The prison building was divided into a number of rooms, all of them overcrowded. One of the compartments was called the "speculators apartment," though almost all its inmates protested against being thus classified. They looked poor and starved, every one of them anxious to tell his tale of woe, apparently under the impression that we were official investigators.

There were in the camp White officers taken prisoner at the Polish front, and scores of peasant men and women held on various charges. They presented a pitiful sight, sitting on the floor for lack of benches, a pathetic lot, bewildered and unable to grasp the combination of events which had caught them in the net.

More than one thousand able-bodied men were locked up in the concentration camp, of no service to the community and requiring numerous officials to guard and attend them. And yet Russia was badly in need of labour energy. It seemed to me an impractical waste.

Traveling by Rail in the Ukraine

In the general dislocation of life in Russia and the breaking down of her economic machinery the railroad system had suffered most. The subject was discussed in almost every meeting, and every Soviet paper often wrote about it. Between Petrograd and Moscow, however, the real state of affairs was not so noticeable, though the main stations were overcrowded, and the people waited for days trying to secure places. If one was fortunate enough to procure the necessary permission to travel, and a ticket, one could manage to make the journey without particular danger to life or limb. But the farther south one went the more apparent became the disorganization. Broken cars dotted the landscape, disabled engines lay along the route, and frequently the tracks were torn up. Everywhere in the Ukraina the stations were filled to suffocation, the people making a wild rush whenever a train was sighted. Most of them remained for weeks on the platforms before succeeding in getting into a train. The steps and even the roofs of the car were crowded with men and women loaded with bundles and bags. At every station there was a savage scramble for a bit of space. Soldiers drove the passengers off the steps and the roofs, and often they had to resort to arms. Yet so desperate were the people and so determined to get to some place where there was hope of securing a little food, that they seemed indifferent to arrest and risked their lives continuously in this mode of travel. As a result of this situation there were numberless accidents, scores of travelers being often swept to their death by low bridges.

Day and night the terrible scenes kept repeating themselves at every station. It was becoming a torture to travel in our well-equipped car. It contained only six persons, leaving considerable room for more; yet we were forbidden to share it with others. It was not only because of the danger of infection or insects but because the Museum effects and the material collected would have surely vanished had we allowed strangers on board. We sought to salve our conscience by permitting women and children or cripples to travel on the rear platform of our car, though even that was contrary to orders.

Anti-Semitism in the Ukraine

I had learned in Moscow, in connection with the arrest of the Zionists there, that the Bolsheviki were inclined to consider them counter-revolutionary. But I found the Poltava Zionists very simple Orthodox Jews who certainly could not impress one as conspirators or active enemies. They were passive, though bitter against the Bolshevik regime. It was claimed that the Bolsheviki made no pogroms and that they do not persecute the Jews, they said: but that was true only in a certain sense. There were two kinds of pogroms: the loud, violent ones and the silent ones. Of the two, the Zionists considered the former preferable. The violent pogrom might last a day or a week; the Jews are attacked and robbed, sometimes even murdered; and then it is over. But the silent pogroms continued all the time. They consisted of constant discriminations, persecution, and hounding. The Bolsheviki had closed the Jewish hospitals and now sick Jews were forced to eat *treife* in the Gentile hospitals. The same applied to the Jewish children in the Bolshevik feeding houses. ... They were all the time exposed to insult and indignities, not to mention that they were doomed to slow starvation, since all trade had been suppressed. Anti-semitism throughout the Ukraina was more virulent than even in pre-revolutionary days.

Kiev

In Kiev antagonism to Communism was intense, even the local Bolsheviki being bitter against Moscow. It was out of the question for anyone coming from the "centre" to secure their cooperation unless armed with State powers. The Government employees in Soviet institutions took no interest in anything save their rations. Bureaucratic indifference and incompetence in

Ukraina were even worse than in Moscow and were augmented by nationalistic resentment against the "Russians." Here the atmosphere was charged with distrust and hatred of everything Muscovite.

Odessa

I have seen a great deal of sabotage in various Soviet institutions in every city I had visited. Everywhere the numerous employees deliberately wasted their time while thousands of applicants spent days and weeks in the corridors and offices without receiving the least attention. The greater part of Russia did nothing but stand in line, waiting for the bureaucrats, big and little, to admit them to their sanctums. But bad as conditions were in other cities, nowhere did I find such systematic sabotage as in Odessa. From the lowest to the highest Soviet worker, everyone was busy with something other than the work entrusted to them.

The Tcheka and Corruption

Not a day passed but that people were arrested for trading in tsarist or Kerensky money; yet it was an open secret that the Chairman of the Tcheka himself speculated in valuta. The depravity of the Tcheka was a matter of common knowledge. People were shot for slight offenses, while those who could afford to give bribes were freed even after they had been sentenced to death. It repeatedly happened that the rich relatives of an arrested man would be notified by the Tcheka of his execution. A few weeks later after they somewhat recovered from their shock and grief, they would be informed that the report of the man's death was erroneous, that he was alive and could be liberated by paying a fine, usually a very high one. Of course, the relatives would strain every effort to raise the money. Then they would suddenly be arrested for attempted bribery, their money confiscated and the prisoner shot.

It was not possible that Moscow did not know about these things, the Zionists asserted. The fear of the central power was too great to permit of the local Tcheka doing anything not approved by Moscow. But it was no wonder that the Bolsheviki had to resort to such methods. A small political party trying to control a population of 150,000,000, which bitterly hated the Communists, could not hope to maintain itself without such an institution as the Tcheka. The latter was characteristic of the basic principles of Bolshevik conception: the country must be *forced* to be *saved* by the Communist Party. The pretext that the Bolsheviki were defending the Revolution was a hollow mockery.

The Press

In a country where speech and press are so completely suppressed as in Russia it is not surprising that the human mind should feed on fancy and out of it weave the most incredible stories. Already, during my first months in Petrograd, I was amazed at the wild rumors that circulated in the city and were believed even by intelligent people. The Soviet press was inaccessible to the population at large and there was no other news medium. Every morning Bolshevik bulletins and papers were pasted on the street corners, but in the bitter cold few people cared to pause to read them. Besides there was little faith in the Communist press. Petrograd was therefore completely cut off, not only from the Western world but even from the rest of Russia. An old revolutionist once said to me: "We not only don't know what is going on in the world or in Moscow: we are not even aware of what is happening in the next street."

Death of John Reed

From a copy of the *Izvestia* that fell into our hands en route, we learned the sad news of the death of John Reed. It was a great blow to those of us who had known Jack. The last time I saw him was at the guest house, the Hotel International, in Petrograd. He had just returned from Finland, after his imprisonment there, and was ill in bed. I was informed that Jack was alone and without proper care, and I went up to nurse him. He was in a bad state, all swollen and with a nasty rash on his arms, the result of malnutrition. In Finland he had been fed almost exclusively on dried fish and had been otherwise wretchedly treated. He was a very sick man, but his spirit remained the same. No matter how radically one disagreed with Jack, one could not help loving his big, generous spirit, and now he was dead, his life laid down in the service of the Revolution, as he believed.

Disillusioned Communists

Several other Communists I knew in Petrograd were even more embittered. Whenever they called on me, they would repeat their determination to get out of the Party. They were suffocating—they said—in the atmosphere of intrigue, blind hatred, and senseless persecution. But it requires considerable will power to leave the party which absolutely controls the destiny of more than a hundred million people, and my Communist visitors lacked the strength. But that did not lessen their misery, which affected even their physical condition, although they received the best rations and they had their meals at the exclusive Smolny dining room.

The Third Anniversary of the Revolution

The third anniversary of the October Revolution was celebrated November 7th (October 25th old style), on the Uritsky Square. I had seen so many official demonstrations that they had lost interest for me. Still I went to the Square hoping that a new note might be sounded. It proved a rehash of the thing I had heard over and over again. The pageant especially was a demonstration of Communist poverty of ideas. Kerensky and his cabinet, Tchernov and the Constituent Assembly, and the storming of the Winter Palace again served as puppets to bring out in strong relief the role of the Bolsheviki as "saviours of the Revolution."

Kronstadt

In February 1921, the workers of several Petrograd factories went on strike. The winter was an exceptionally hard one, and the people of the capital suffered intensely from cold, hunger, and exhaustion. They asked an increase of their food rations, some fuel and clothing. The complaints of the strikers, ignored by the authorities, presently assumed a political character. Here and there was also voiced a demand for the Constituent Assembly and free trade. The attempted street demonstration of the strikers was suppressed, the Government having ordered out the military *Kursanti*.

When the Kronstadt sailors learned what was happening in Petrograd, they expressed their solidarity with the strikers in their economic and revolutionary demands, but refused to support any call for the Constituent Assembly. On March 1st, the sailors organized a mass meeting in Kronstadt ... the resolution became the basis of the conflict between the Kronstadt and the Government. It voiced the popular demand for Soviets elected by the free choice of the people ... the Kronstadt sailors, far from being counter-revolutionists, were devoted to the revolution. The Petro-Soviet, its passions aroused by Bolsevik demagoguery, passed the Zinoviev resolution ordering Kronstadt to surrender on pain of extermination.

On March 7th Trotsky began the bombardment of Kronstadt, and on the 17th the fortress and city were taken, after numerous assaults involving terrific human sacrifice. Thus Kronstadt was "liquidated and the counter-revolutionary plot" quenched in blood. The "conquest" of the city was characterized by ruthless savagery, although not a single one of the Communists arrested by the Kronstadt sailors had been injured or killed by them. Even before the storming of the fortress, the Bolsheviki summarily executed numerous soldiers of the Red Army whose revolutionary spirit and solidarity caused them to refuse to participate in the bloodbath.

Kronstadt broke the last thread that held me to the Bolsheviki. The wanton slaughter they had initiated spoke more eloquently against them than aught else. Whatever the pretenses in the past, the Bolsheviki now proved themselves the most pernicious enemies of the Revolution. I could have nothing further to do with them.

Persecution of Anarchists

In connection with Kronstadt, a general raid on Anarchists took place in Petrograd and Moscow. The prisons were filled with these victims. Almost every known Anarchist had been arrested, and the "Golos Truda" in both cities were sealed by the Tcheka.

It had become the established policy of the Bolshevik Government to mask its barbaric procedure against Anarchists with the uniform charge of banditism. This accusation was made practically against all arrested Anarchists and frequently even against sympathizers with the movement. A very convenient method of getting rid of an undesirable person: by it anyone could be secretly executed and buried.

While the Communists were passing eloquent resolutions of protest against the imprisonment of revolutionaries in foreign countries, the Anarchists in the Bolshevik prisons of Russia were being driven to desperation by their long imprisonment without opportunity for a hearing or trial. To force the hand of the Government, the Anarchists incarcerated in the Taganka (Moscow) decided on a hunger strike to the death. The French, Spanish, and Italian Anarcho-Syndacalists, when informed of the situation, promised to raise the question at an early session of the Labour Congress. Some, however, suggested that the Government be first approached on the matter. Thereupon a Delegate Committee was chosen, including the well-known English labour leader, Tom Mann, to call upon the Little Father in the Kremlin. The latter refused to have the Anarchists released on the grounds that "they were too dangerous," but the final result was that they would be permitted to leave Russia; should they, however, return without permission, they would be shot.

The hunger strikers in the Taganka accepted the conditions of deportation. They had for years fought and bled for the Revolution, and now they were compelled to become Ahasueruses in foreign lands or suffer slow mental and physical death in Bolshevik dungeons.

Education and Culture

State monopoly of thought is everywhere interpreting education to suit its own purpose. Similarly the Bolsheviki, to whom the state is supreme, use education to further their own ends. ... The proletarian dictatorship has completely paralyzed every attempt at independent investigation. The Communist criterion is dominant. The least divergence from official dogma and opinion on the part of the teachers, educators, or pupils exposes them to the general charge of counter-revolution, resulting in discharge and expulsion, if nothing more drastic.

The mechanistic approach to art and culture and the *idée fixe* that nothing must express itself outside of the channels of the State have stultified the cultural and artistic expression of the Russian people. In poetry and literature, in drama, painting, and music not a single epic of the Revolution has been produced during five years.

The political dictatorship of the Bolsheviki with one stroke suppressed the social phase of life in Russia. There was no forum for even the inoffensive social intercourse, no clubs, no meeting places, no restaurants, not even a dance hall. I remember the shocked expression of Zorin when I asked him if the young people could not occasionally meet for a dance free from Communist supervision. "Dance-halls are gathering places for counter-revolutionists; we closed them," he informed me. The emotional and human needs of the people were considered dangerous to the regime.

Deportation

The first to be deported by the "revolutionary" Government were ten Anarchists, most of them known in the international revolutionary movement as tried idealists and martyrs for their cause.

To remain longer in Bolshevik Russia had become unbearable. I was compelled to speak out and decided to leave the country. Berlin Anarchists had made a demand upon the Soviet Government that passports be issued for Alexander Berkman, A. Shapiro, and myself to enable us to attend the International Anarchist Congress which was to convene in Berlin in December, 1921. It was just one year and eleven months since I had set foot on what I believed to be the promised land. My heart was heavy with the tragedy of Russia. One thought stood out in bold relief: I must raise my voice against the crimes committed in the name of the Revolution. I would be heard regardless of friend or foe.

Failure of the Russian Revolution

It is now clear why the Russian Revolution, as conducted by the Communist Party, was a failure. The political power of the Party, organized and centralized in the State, sought to maintain itself by all means at hand. The central authorities attempted to force the activities of the people into forms corresponding with the purposes of the Party. The sole aim of the latter was to strengthen the State and monopolize all economical, political, and social activities—even all cultural manifestations. The Revolution had an entirely different object, and in its very character it was the negation of authority and centralization. The Russian Revolution reflects on a small scale the century-old struggle of the libertarian principle against the authoritarian.

CHAPTER FIFTEEN

~

Marguerite Baker Harrison

A Spy in Russia

Marguerite Baker, born in 1878 in Baltimore, Maryland, to a life of privilege and wealth, never imagined that one day she would be a spy for the United States and spend most of a year in a Soviet prison. Growing up, she attended a private girls' school and spent a semester at Radcliffe College, before her mother pulled her out over a romantic attachment to an unsuitable young man and took her to Europe in hopes that she would meet and marry a titled Englishman. Instead, Marguerite married Thomas Harrison of Baltimore in 1901; had a son, Thomas, in 1902; and settled down to life as a young matron involved in social and charitable works. Her life was changed when her husband died at age forty-two in 1915. Marguerite needed to find work to supplement her income and found employment as a reporter for *The Baltimore Sun*, reporting on social news, musical events, and wartime news. She also informed the United States government of suspected German spies living in Baltimore.

Restless for adventure, Marguerite was sent abroad in 1918, armed with credentials from her newspaper, ostensibly, to show a film to American troops and to report on economic and social conditions in Berlin; in addition, she was to identify potential enemies. In Paris, she met Army Colonel Ralph Van Deman, who gave her instructions for her first espionage mission in Germany. When she returned to Baltimore, she met with General Marlborough Churchill, head of the Military Intelligence Division, and offered her services as a spy. She was forty years old and fluent in three languages, but not Russian. Even so, she was hired without any training and sent as a journalist, with code name B, to Russia in 1919. Her stated mission was to gather intelligence and find out the fate of Americans imprisoned in Russia.

She arrived in Moscow in 1920 with a passport but no visa. The Cheka knew she was a spy and allowed her to meet with Soviet officials and file her reports on social and economic conditions—only after they passed the censors. She was arrested on charges of espionage and, as prisoner #2961, was put in isolation in the notorious Lubyanka Prison, then moved to a cell she shared with seven other women prisoners. The women developed a spirit of camaraderie, and Marguerite was helpful to her fellow inmates. To survive, she kept to a daily routine of exercise, played games with the prisoners, sang songs, and mended the inmates' clothing. She was not only the first female foreign intelligence agent; she was also a double agent. The Cheka demanded, on condition of her release, that she provide them with information, and, feeling she had no choice, she assented.

Given the harsh conditions and the lack of nutritious food, she became ill and was moved to the Novinsky Women's Prison. Conditions were better there, and she received medical help. Meanwhile, officials of the Associated Press, Lord Beaverbrook, and United States Senator Joseph I. Francis of Maryland worked for her release. Senator Francis went to Moscow, visited her in prison, and convinced officials to free her with the promise that the United States would provide food aid to Russia during the famine. Marguerite was released from prison, ill with tuberculosis, and returned home. Back in the United States, she wrote and gave talks about her time in prison and urged the United States to recognize the Soviet government. She felt that isolating Russia would lead only to war and anarchy and that it was better to pursue a policy of peace and food. She believed that the moral imperative of the people would lead to the government they wanted.

In June 1922, Marguerite left for the Far East to write a series of articles for *Cosmopolitan* magazine. She visited Japan, then went to the Far Eastern Republic that had fallen into Soviet hands, where she was again arrested by the GPU on charges of espionage, taken to Moscow, imprisoned in the Lubyanka, and released after two months. Ever the restless wanderer, she went to the Middle East in 1923 to collect information on the oil fields for the U.S. Army, using her involvement in a film documenting the migration of the Persian Bakhtiari tribe to their summer pasture as a cover for the mission.

In 1926, Marguerite gave up her work as a spy and married Arthur Blake, an aspiring English actor. The couple honeymooned in Morocco, bought a chateau in France, and settled in Hollywood, where Arthur hoped to have an acting career. Marguerite wrote articles and gave speeches in the 1930s and

'40s to supplement their income. When World War II began, she offered the FBI her services as a spy, but they declined.

After her second husband's death in 1947, Marguerite rented an apartment in Baltimore to be near her son. She continued to travel abroad until she suffered a stroke in 1966. She died a year later at age eighty-eight.

Marguerite felt that her most important accomplishments were the establishment of the Children's Hospital School in Baltimore in 1905 and her being a founding member of the Society of Women Geographers in 1925, not her service to her country as the first female foreign intelligence agent.

Her published work include her autobiography, *There's Always Tomorrow: The Story of a Checkered Life* (New York: Farrar & Rhinehart, 1935), *Marooned in Moscow: The Story of an American Woman Imprisoned in Russia* (New York: George H. Doran, 1921), *Red Bear or Yellow Dragon* (New York: George H. Doran, 1924), and *Asia Reborn* (New York: Harper & Brothers, 1928).

The following selections are from *Marooned in Moscow*.

⌒

Marooned in Moscow

Taken to Lubianka Prison

I asked permission to pack the necessary articles to take to prison with me, and this was immediately granted. Although warned that there was not room for much luggage in the automobile, I managed to take a bag containing toilet articles, a change of underwear, some chocolate and cigarettes, an army bedding roll with a pillow and a steamer rug and my big fur coat.

When the search was over I was asked to sign a document witnessed by the Commandant, certifying that the search had been conducted in a proper manner, my room was closed, locked and sealed with a large red seal. I was then taken to the waiting motor, a fine English car, and driven through the silent moonlit streets to the prison of the secret section of the Cheka, which is in a building on the Lubianka, in the heart of Moscow's business district, formerly the property of the "Rossia" Life Insurance Company. From the outside it looks like anything but a prison. On the ground floor, a row of unoccupied shops, divided by temporary unpainted wooden partitions, serve as offices for the Cheka. The car stopped outside of one of these, and I was taken into a small dingy room, with a railed space at the end, behind which

Lubyanka Prison
Internet Public Domain

were sitting two Checkists in front of a large deal table covered with documents and papers. Lined up along the railing were a number of other people who had evidently been arrested, all men except myself. I was the last in the line, and it was more than an hour before my turn came to fill out the questionnaire presented to me by the men behind the table. It was a most elaborate affair, evidently invented only for Russians, for among the questions to be answered were whether I had any relatives in the Red or White Armies. When this was over my money was again counted, my valuables were all taken, including my wedding ring, and I was given a receipt for them, as well as for my typewriter and Kodak.

This done, the Commissars behind the table yawned, locked up their gooks and disappeared and I was left alone with half a dozen soldiers. Then I was subjected to the only personal indignity I experienced during my ten months' imprisonment.

One of the soldiers, who was what we would call a fresh guy at home, proceeded to search me on his own account, accompanying the proceedings with a number of witticisms which, fortunately, I did not know enough Russian to understand, but sent his companions into roars of laughter. They seemed to think it especially funny when I protested on the ground that I was an American.

"Much good being an American will do you here, citizenness," returned my tormentor scornfully.

Finally they had enough, and I was taken through a labyrinth of ground floor passages and up three flights of stairs to the office of the Commandant, where I surrendered my receipts and was searched again, this time in a perfectly correct manner. The commandant, whom I afterwards got to know quite well from his daily visits, was the living image of "Kaiser Bill," and my Russian companions always called him "Vilgelm" behind his back. Officially we addressed him as Citizen Commandant. He was a rigid disciplinarian, but absolutely just, and was always willing to listen to any reasonable complaints or requests.

By this time it was nearly six o'clock. I was desperately tired, and very thankful when I was taken to my room on the floor below. Here again the first impression was not that of a prison, though as a matter of fact the "Lubianka 2" is the strictest prison in Moscow. Except for the armed sentinel at the door, the winding corridor into which I was taken might have been the hall of any second-class hotel anywhere in Europe. On both sides were numbered rooms. We stopped opposite number 39, the door was unlocked, the light turned on "for five minutes so that you can undress if you want to," my guard informed me, the door was banged and locked, and I found myself in a small single room already occupied by three women.

Two were lying on the floor, and one on a bed of three boards laid across wooden horses and covered by a thin straw pallet. The only other articles of furniture were a deal table, and the *parashka*, a large iron garbage can, which is unpleasant but indispensable considering the fact that prisoners are permitted to go to the toilet but twice a day.

On hearing the key turn in the lock, all three of my companions, who had evidently been "playing possum," sat bolt upright and began deluging me with questions as is always custom in prison. Where was I from, why had I been arrested? I retaliated with a cross-fire in French and Russian, which resulted in the discovery that I was already acquainted with one of the prisoners, a pretty Jewish woman whom I had last seen at "The Bat," one of Moscow's best known vaudeville theaters. The second was a young girl employed in the Foreign Office. Both had been arrested a few hours before I was and professed to be ignorant of the charges against them. ... The third woman, a young Russian girl, had been for six weeks in solitary confinement. ... She had fallen in love with a Hungarian prisoner of war ... and was accused of being implicated in a plot for his escape, together with a number of Hungarian officers.

When our herring soup was served at noon, she assured me that it was fine for the digestion, and she told me that the six weeks in solitary confinement had been wonderfully soothing to her nerves.

The morning passed without any incident except our matutinal trip to the bathroom, where we all performed our ablutions together in a big tin trough with cold water. In the afternoon, I was taken to be photographed, full face, left and right profile, against a white screen on which my serial number was printed—as nearly as I can remember it was 3041.

That night, curled up in my bedding roll on the floor, for there had been so many arrests recently that there were not enough beds to go around, I slept well. Strange to say I was not in the least nervous. After many weeks of suspense, the worst had happened, and my first feeling was one of relief, for it must be remembered that my status in Russia had always been illegal. I had been arrested once before, and I knew that I was subject to rearrest at any time.

The next day, shortly after dinner, a soldier appeared. "Harrison," he demanded. "Here," I answered.

I followed my guard out into the hall, up and down a maze of stairways and passages, until I reached a familiar room, the office of Moghilévski, a member of the praesidium of the Checka, who had questioned me in the spring when I was detained for forty-eight hours on account of the fact that I had come to Russia from Poland, an enemy country, without the permission of the authorities.

Moghilévski is a tall, slender, dark man, tremendously earnest and intensely fanatical in his Communistic beliefs, utterly unsparing of himself and others in his work, but he has his human side, as I discovered when I noticed a beautifully bound copy of *Rabelais* lying on his desk. I remarked about this and he told me he had a weakness for old French literature.

I was put through a rigid cross-examination, lasting nearly three hours about my acquaintances in Moscow, my relations with foreigners, my relations with the prisoners to whom I had been sending food packages, and other matters, during which, while perfectly courteous, he made it quite plain to me that my position was exceedingly serious. My answers were not altogether satisfactory, and the examination ended with my being returned to my companions in room 39, with the admonition to think things over and refresh my memory.

I had not been back more than a few minutes, however, when one of the prison guards appeared again.

"Pack your clothes," he ordered. "Where am I going?" I asked. "You'll see when we get there," he answered.

I started to put on my fur coat. "You won't need that," he said, and then I realized that I was probably going to be transferred to solitary confinement, the thing I dreaded most, and I said good-bye to my new-found friends with a sinking heart and followed the escort down the passage. It was just as I expected. I was shown into an empty room, the key turned in the lock and I was left alone.

Odinochka

The autumn days are very short in Moscow, and it was already beginning to grow dark, so I could see little except that I was in a small box-like room about nine feet square, with a large window, the panes of which were whitened, so that I could not see out. There was a plank bed, a small table and the *parashka*, nothing more. It was very cold in the room, and for a while I walked up and down trying to keep warm and hoping that the light would soon be turned on. At that time I did not know enough of prison ways to realize that the guard had forgotten to turn on the light, and that I could knock, and ask him to do so. Later I learned to knock and ask for all sorts of things, from a needle and thread to darn my stockings to a light for a cigarette. When we were short of matches, we always knocked on the door, and when the eye of one of the prison guards appeared at the peephole, or *glazok*, which is covered on the outside by the swinging metal number plate, one of us would stick a cigarette through and get a light.

Ordinarily the peephole, though inconvenient if you happen to be doing anything against the rules, is not an unmixed evil, but in the *odinochka*, as solitary confinement is called, it is nothing more or less at first than an instrument of torture. The guards are instructed to keep a close watch on prisoners in the *odinochka*, so at least, every half-hour, day and night, the number plate is stealthily pushed aside and an eye appears in the peephole, gazes steadily for a minute, and disappears. For some time I was perpetually watching for the eye, but after a while I grew quite indifferent to it, and it did not even disturb my serenity when I was dressing, undressing, or engaged in any of the intimate mysteries of the toilet.

But to return to my first evening in the *odinochka*. In about an hour a boy appeared with a big copper kettle of the infusion of apple parings or dried carrots, which passes for tea in Russia these days, at the same time presenting me with a tin cup and a big wooden spoon and turning on the light. While I ate the remaining portion of my day's ration of three quarters of a pound of black bread, sipped my tea and nibbled a cake of chocolate, I looked around at my new quarters.

The room was very dingy, but fairly clean. The walls were covered with a faded flowered paper that suggested the old rooming-house days, and scribbled all over, as high as a man's head, with inscriptions in various languages. Some were funny, some defiant, others despairing.

I sat on the radiator to get warm, meanwhile taking stock of the situation. I had good cause to know that my position was very serious, but at the same time I figured it out that unless the United States actually went to war with Russia, it was unlikely that I would be shot. Knowing the policy of our administration, I decided that it would probably be a waiting game on both sides, and that the only thing for me to do was keep my nerve and my health as well, if possible, and wait to see what could happen. I had no reason either to complain of my arrest or to expect early liberation. It was simply the fortune of war.

When I judged it was about bed time, I lay down and tried to sleep, but sleep was impossible. My room was directly opposite the entrance door, where there was a constant stream of traffic. ... Finally I dozed off in sheer exhaustion. When I woke up it was light, and in a few minutes the door was opened and a woman's hand and arm appeared with a broom ... this was the signal for me to clean my room.

First, I made my bed, which process consisted in conducting a hunt for the bed bugs who had invaded the sanctity of my bedding roll during the night; then I knocked and asked to be taken to the toilet, where I took a sponge bath in cold water. Soon came the day's bread ration, and a portion of sugar for two days, about two and a half teaspoons ... sat down to breakfast after which I took a walk—five hundred times the length of the room and back. I repeated this every evening. At about eleven o'clock the Commandant appeared, took a quick appraising look around the room, and inquired if I had any request to make. I asked for paper, pencil and a few books. He told me that I must first have the permission of my *sledovatl*, the examining judge, but he did not explain that I might ask for permission; so I resigned myself to waiting until I was next called for cross-examination, as I thought I probably would be in a few days.

Dinner, consisting of a bowl of herring soup, followed by a bowl of Kasha, the Russian national dish, a cereal made of various grains, most of which are new to Western palates, was served at noon. I had already learned to eat kasha, but I never could go to the herring soup. Later the herring soup was varied by a thin meat broth, and on Sundays, when we had no supper, it was thicker and sometimes contained a piece of meat. Supper was served at five, and consisted of soup only, followed by tea. This was my regular prison fare for eight months.

In spite of all efforts to keep myself busy and amused, the first day and the succeeding ones were terribly long. I resorted to all sorts of expedients to pass the time. In my bag I found some paper cigarette boxes and a cardboard toothpowder box. Out of these I made a pack of tiny cards, with a pencil I had managed to hide, through all the searches of my belongings. I was playing solitaire very peacefully when my enemy of the peephole looked in, saw me, unlocked the door and ordered me to give them up, for cards are not allowed in the Cheka. Then I played jackstraws with dead matches and a bent hairpin. Then I sang under my breath all the songs I had ever known, recited all the poems I remembered and gave myself oral examinations in languages and history.

Finally, when my first week was nearly up, the monotony and isolation had got on my nerves to such an extent that I decided I could not stand it much longer, and resolved on a bold stroke. I wrote to Moghilévski and told him I had a very important communication to make.

The end of it all was that I was informed that while I had failed to give a satisfactory account of myself, that charges against me would not be pushed at the moment, and that my request to be transferred to another room would be granted.

I was transferred to the general room where I spent the next six months, with plenty of company, for we were rarely less than seven, and often as many as eleven or twelve for days at a time.

Imprisoned with Company

The room to which I was transferred was much larger than any I had seen before, but my first impression of it was that it was exactly the shape of the coffins that are used all over Europe. It was rectangular, about eighteen feet long, possibly seven feet wide at one end, and ten at the other. There were two windows, whitened of course, at either end. During the six months I lived there, I never saw the sun, moon, or sky, except twice, once in December, and again in February, when we were taken out to one of the public baths with an armed escort, and I never left the room except for our morning and evening trips to the toilet, or when I was summoned to a *dopros*. It was well heated by steam, but the atmosphere was terrible owing to the utter inadequacy of the ventilation and the chronic aversion of most Russians to drafts.

When I entered, it was occupied by seven women, some sitting, some lying on their beds. ... The women were just as conglomerate as their belongings. They all stared at me curiously, appraisingly, and, as I thought, in a rather unfriendly manner, but I afterwards learned to understand this apparent hostility and insatiable curiosity with regard to newcomers. Living as we did, in such crowded quarters, an addition to our number meant more physical discomfort; then she might be a spy. As a matter of fact, the Slavs are the kindest, gentlest, most hospitable people in the world, wonderfully lovable and sweet-tempered. I was thrown almost entirely with them during my term of imprisonment, for I suspect that I was purposely isolated from persons from Western countries, and I never once had an unpleasant encounter with any of my fellow prisoners.

Besides Russians I had Poles, Finns, Letts, Lithuanians, Estonians, Ukrainians and Jews as companions. They were drawn from every class of society, from great ladies to illiterate peasants; they represented every political party from monarchists to anarchists. There were some disagreements in our room of course, but on the whole we pulled together remarkably well and no backward male can ever tell me again that women are incapable of team-work.

Strange as it may seem, I was really very busy in prison, and while each day seemed interminable, the time on the whole passed very quickly. Realizing the importance of getting some exercise I used to do Swedish gymnastics morning and night, to the constant wonder and amazement of my companions.

Then there was the daily hunt for vermin. All the beds were infested with bed bugs and they had to be gone over several times a week. At first I did not realize the importance of special care of the hair, and consequently acquired what are known to the learned as peticulosis and to school children at home as "nits." It took me some time to get rid of them, and then only thanks to a good friend who gave me a fine tooth comb which was one of my treasures for the rest of my term of imprisonment. When we had prisoners from the South we were pestered with fleas. ... I always inspected my underclothes twice a day, for we had many cooties, especially when prisoners arrived from a distance, and cooties are not only disagreeable but dangerous in Russia, for they are carriers of the dreaded typhus.

In spite of all our precautions we had three cases of typhus during the winter. There were several cases of syphilis in the acute state. We had many cases of acute hysteria, and I was often kept busy for several hours applying cold compresses and administering valerian.

We obtained all simple remedies from the prison dispensary. Medical service, while not adequate, was fairly satisfactory. There was a woman physician in charge of the prison, and she made periodical rounds of inspection, usually once a week.

The problem of keeping clean took much time. Occasionally I cajoled one of the guards into bringing me a kettle of hot water from the huge samovar machine in the court which supplied the prison, but usually there was no hot water to be had, so I used to save hot tea morning and evening in empty bottles that had been sent to the prisoners with milk. At night I took a tea bath in a small earthenware bowl that had been sent me by the Czech-Slovak Red Cross, and in the morning I washed my underclothes in the same manner, one or two pieces a day. I made coarse lace with a crooked hairpin from linen thread drawn from an old bag, took Russian lessons from my companions and helped to mend the prison linen.

All the prisoners were allowed to wear their own clothes and no uniforms are provided, but those who are arrested without any luggage may obtain shirts and drawers, furnished once a week. The shirts we mended were sometimes *kasionni*, the regulation blouses, such as furnished the Red Army.

The work was purely voluntary. We liked it because it gave us needles and thread to mend our own clothes and the privilege of having scissors, which as a rule are strictly forbidden. I never realized before to how many uses one pair of scissors could be put. We employed them to cut our bread, open tin cans, trim our hair and finger nails, mend our shoes, and even to carve meat and sausage.

I believe, as a whole, the women prisoners under exactly the same conditions were relatively far more comfortable than the men. We took a great interest in keeping our room as clean as possible and we often managed to make our prison fare more palatable by simple expedients. For instance when the potatoes were badly cooked or frozen, as they usually were, we used to fish them out of our soup at dinner time, put them in one large bowl and mash them with a wooden spoon until they were reduced to a paste which we flavored with a little salt. Then we made them into croquettes and dropped them into our hot soup in the evening. Although we had a great many lice, I rarely saw a woman with underclothes as filthy as the prison underwear worn by the men. Of course it had all been boiled and laundered when we received it to mend, but the seams were coated with deposits of eggs from all sorts of vermin.

Besides, we were all very ingenious at inventing games and amusements. We had several packs of cards made of the mouthpieces of the Russian cigarettes, chessmen and checkers made of hardened bread and paper dominoes, all these being kept carefully hidden, for games are not allowed. One of our favorite past-times was fortune-telling with cards, at which most Russian women are adept, and in which they believe implicitly. Once we had books, for two blissful weeks at New Years'; but they were afterwards taken away from us. We often sang Russian songs in the evening after the lights were out, in an undertone, of course, for we were not allowed to sing or to speak in tones that could be heard outside in the hall. Most of these songs were traditional melodies that had been sung in prisons in Russia and Siberia for many decades. I learned a great many of them at the time, writing down the words, but they were all taken away from me when I left the prison.

Release of Prisoner 2961

My first act after greeting the friends who came to meet me at Riga was to indulge in the luxury of a tub bath for the first time in nearly a year; my second was to buy a Rigan outfit to replace the costume I had worn during my entire term of imprisonment, an exceedingly dirty suit of khaki cloth, a man's pongee shirt, a hat made in prison from the tail of the same shirt, and a pair of men's shoes sent me by the Czech-Slovak Red Cross. Then I had a real dinner. I stayed in Riga for several days, after which the senator and I left for Berlin, where I met many friends, among them Captain Cooper who had come from Warsaw to meet me. Ever since his escape from Russia in April he had been working unceasingly for my release. The best news I had in Riga was the confirmation of what I had already heard from Moghilévski: that owing to the Soviet Government's acceptance of the terms of Mr. Hoover's offer all the American prisoners would probably be in Riga within a week or ten days. In Riga I also saw lists of the packages containing food, clothing and toilet articles, which had been sent me during my imprisonment, none of which ever reached me.

In the few quiet moments I was able to snatch between calls, writing newspaper articles, and trips to the shops to replenish my scanty wardrobe, I looked back on the events of the past eighteen months, during which I had lived on black bread and Kasha. From a material standpoint I had suffered, it was true, but I felt that I had gained immeasurably from another point of view. I knew the heart of Russia, and no one in these troublous times of transition can ever know it unless he lives with the Russian people, both in and out of prison. I had gained a just perspective, and I felt that I understood all that is good and all that is bad, and all that is historically inevitable in the great upheaval which is, in spite of everything, modernizing Russia.

CHAPTER SIXTEEN

Clare Consuelo Sheridan

A Sculptor in Moscow

Clare Consuelo Sheridan was a well-known English sculptor and the first cousin of Winston Churchill through her mother, Clara Jerome, the elder sister of Churchill's mother, Jennie Jerome. Born into the British upper classes in 1885, she was educated at home by tutors and at schools abroad. She married Wilfred Frederick Sheridan in 1910, and they had three children: two girls and a boy. Her husband served in World War I and was killed at the Battle of Loos in 1915, leaving her a widow with two children; her daughter Elizabeth died in infancy in 1914. Clare sculpted an angel to put on her daughter's grave, which is what led her to develop her artistic talents by studying in England and France. Later in her career, she sculpted a bust of Herbert H. Asquith and one of Winston Churchill.

In 1920, Clare was introduced to Lev Kamenev, Bolshevik revolutionary and Soviet politician, and Leonid Kassin, the People's Commissar for Foreign Trade, both with the Soviet Trade Delegation to London. Sympathetic to the goals of the Russian Revolution, her aim in life was to sculpt Vladimir Lenin and Leon Trotsky, both of whom would advance her career and bring her some notoriety. While Kamenev and Kassin were in London, she had them sit for her and finished their busts. She traveled to the Island of Wight with Kamenev; those who knew her thought they might have had a romantic relationship. Kamenev invited her to Russia, with the promise that he would have both Lenin and Trotsky sit for her, as well as Felix Dzerzhinsky, Chairman of the Cheka, and Grigory Zinoviev, Chief Commissar of the Communist International. In September 1920, Clare left England without

Clare Sheridan
Library of Congress

telling anyone, although she felt guilty about leaving her children. Kamenev arranged an Estonian visa for her when they arrived in Stockholm, and she arrived in Russia in late September.

Clare spent the next two months in Moscow. Vladimir Lenin was the first to sit for his bust. He sat at his desk in the Kremlin and was busy answering telephone calls and doing paperwork while she worked, although he was not reluctant to talk to her. She struggled to achieve the image of him that she wanted to convey because of the lack of light in the room and his posture. But finally, she was successful.

Leon Trotsky was her next candidate to sculpt, and they talked about politics, the economy, and the revolution while she worked. He even offered to take her to the front in the midst of the civil war, but she did not take him up on that. Clare worked assiduously to capture the strength and character of Trotsky and thought that she did. He agreed. Several writers hinted at a romantic relationship between Clare and Trotsky, but she did not confirm that in her writings. During her free time in Moscow, Clare went to the ballet, the opera, and theatrical productions and dined out.

Clare declared that she was not a communist, even though she was supportive of the Bolshevik revolutionary program, believing that it would improve life for the people. Once she returned to England in November, her pro-Russian views made her a *persona non-gratia*. Even MI.5 had a file on her, given her trip to Russia and her politics. Because she alienated many of the British upper class with her support for the Bolsheviks, she decided to visit the United States, where she thought she would find a more welcoming environment. Her book, *Mayfair to Moscow: Clare Sheridan's Diary*, was published in 1921 and caught the eye of the editor of *New York World*, who offered her a job as a foreign correspondent. She took the job and interviewed Benito Mussolini, Mustafa Kemal Ataturk, and the Smyrna residents during the Greco-Turkish War.

Still fascinated by Russia, Clare returned in 1923 but became disenchanted with the revolution and was not welcome in the country. In 1924, both she and her brother, Oswald, made a motorcycle trip through Europe to the south of Russia, ending in Odessa. Clare then moved to Constantinople with her two children and devoted herself to sculpture. In 1925, she moved to Algeria. When her son died in 1937, she carved a memorial to him in wood. Interested in this new medium, she went to an Indian Reservation in the Rocky Mountains for further training and had a showing of her work in London.

During her later years, she converted to Roman Catholicism, lived in a Franciscan Guesthouse, and sculpted religious objects.

She died at age eighty-four in 1970 and is buried in the churchyard at Saint George's, Brede, Sussex, England.

Clare never abandoned writing about her life and interests. She had sixteen books to her credit, including *My American Diary*, *In Many Places*, *West to East*, *Stella Defiant*, *Across Europe with Satanella*, *The Thirteenth*, *A Turkish Kaleidoscope*, *Naked Truth*, *Green Amber*, *The Substitute Bride*, *Arab Interlude*, *Redskin Interlude*, *Without End*, *My Crowded Sanctuary*, and *To the Four Winds*.

The following selections are from *Mayfair to Moscow: Clare Sheridan's Diary*.

⌒

Mayfair to Moscow: Clare Sheridan's Diary

Meeting Two Bolsheviks

August 14th, 1920. Saturday.

According to Mr. Fisher's instructions, I called on Mr. M—— at his office at 10:30 and introduced myself.

He took me in a taxi to Bond Street to the office of Messrs. Kamenev and Krassin. We waited for about twenty minutes in an *antechambre*, and I felt a certain melodramatic thrill. Here was I, at all events in the outer den of these wild beasts who have been represented as ready to spring upon us and devour us! This movement that has caused consternation to the world, and these people, so utterly removed from my environment, these myths of what seemed almost a great legend, I was now quite close to.

While we waited Mr. M—— put me straight on a few points and pointed out many of the inaccuracies about Bolshevism that people like myself have gleaned, so I was in part prepared and protected against appearing too ignorant and foolish.

At last the word came and we were ushered into the office of Mr. Kamenev who received me amiably and smilingly. We started off immediately in French and discussed the subject of his being willing to sit for me. I then asked if a Soviet Government had obliterated Art in Russia. He looked at me for a moment in astonishment, and then said: "*Mais non!* Artists are the most privileged class."

He gave me fully to understand that Russia is most appreciative of Art and Talent and is anxious to surround itself with culture. He thought the bust had better be started soon, as one never knew what might happen from one moment to the next, "What caprice of Monsieur Lloyd George" might elect to send him out of the country at a moment's notice. So we decided on Tuesday next at 10 A.M. Mr. Kamenev then took us downstairs to Krassin's office. Mr. Krassin seemed very busy and preoccupied, and didn't quite know what I had come about, but he agreed to see me Wednesday at 10 A.M.

Sculpting Kamenev

August 17, 1920. Tuesday.

Kamenev arrived nearly punctually at 10 A.M. for an hour, but he stayed till 1 o'clock, and we talked the whole three hours, almost without stopping. I don't know how I managed to work and talk so much. My mind was really more focused on the discussion and the work was done subconsciously. At all events when the three hours were ended, I had produced a likeness.

My "Victory" was unveiled when he arrived, and he noticed it at once. I told him it represented the Victory of the Allies, and he exclaimed: "But, no! It is the Victory of all the ages. ... What pain! What suffering! What exhaustion!" He then added it was the best bit of peace propaganda he'd seen.

After a while Kamenev let drop a suggestion which did not fall on barren ground—he threw it out apparently casually, but I believe to see how I reacted to it. I had just been telling him that I had all my life a love of Russian literature, Russian music, Russian dancing, Russian art, and he said, "You should come to Russia."

I said I had always dreamed it—and that perhaps—who knows—some day . . .

He said: "You can come with me and I will get you sittings from Lenin and Trotsky."

I thought he was joking, and hesitated a moment, then I said: "Let me know when you are going to start and I will be ready in half an hour."

He offered to telegraph immediately to Moscow for permission!

Sculpting Krassin

August 18th, 1920. Wednesday.

Krassin arrived at 10 A.M. and found me reading the papers, sitting on the seat outside the door. Like Kamenev he stayed until 1 o'clock. He has a beautiful head and he sat almost sphinx-like, severe and expressionless most of the time. We talked, of course, but his French is less good than Kamenev's, and we broke into occasional German—it was a bad mix-up, but we said all we wanted to say!

Kamenev had talked to him about me and told him of the project of my going to Moscow. I said nothing about it till he first broached it!

Krassin is a Siberian. He explained to me that his father was a Government local official and that his mother was a peasant and one of twenty-two children. He himself was the eldest of seven and was brought up in Siberia.

At one o'clock I thanked him profusely for sitting so long and so well, and he seemed quite surprised at my stopping, and said: "You have done with me?"

August 26th, 1920. Thursday

Krassin offered me a third sitting and came again at 5 and stayed till after 7. War is averted, and he assures me that Kamenev under no excuse can possibly leave for Russia before a fortnight.

I worked hard, and Krassin's head is finished. I think it's good.

Near Moscow

September 20th, 1920. Monday

Zinoviev had just told him that the telegram announcing his arrival with me came in the middle of a Soviet Conference. It caused a good deal of amusement, but Lenin said that whatever one felt about it there was nothing to do but to give me some sittings as I had come so far for the purpose. "So Lenin has consented and I thought it was worth while to wake you up to tell you that—" Kamenev was in great spirits.

Sculpting Dsirjinsky

Moscow

September 27th, 1920. Monday.

Things began to move more rapidly now, and my patience is being rewarded. To-day Dsirjinsky sat for me. He is the President of the Extraordinary Commission, or as we would call it in English, the organizer of the Red Terror. He is the man Kamenev told me so much about. He sat for an hour and a half, quite still and very silent.

As I worked and watched him during that hour and a half, he made a curious impression on me. Finally overwhelmed by his quietude, I exclaimed: "How wonderful of you to sit so still." Our medium was German, which made fluent conversation between us impossible, but he answered: "One learns patience and calm in prison."

I asked him how long he was in prison. "A quarter of my life, 11 years," he answered. It was the revolution that liberated him. Obviously it is not the abstract desire for power or for a political career that has made revolutionaries of such men, but fanatical conviction of the wrongs to be righted for the cause of humanity and national progress. For this cause men of sensitive intellectuality have endured years of imprisonment.

Sculpting Lenin

Moscow

October 7, 1920. Thursday.

Michael Borodin accompanied me to the Kremlin. On the way he said to me: "Just remember that you are going to do the best bit of work today that you have ever done." I was rather anxious about the conditions of the room and the light.

We went in by a special door, guarded by a sentry, and on the third floor we went through several doors and passages, each guarded. The last room contained about five women at five tables, and they all looked at me curiously, but they knew my errand. Here Michael handed me over to a little hunchback, Lenin's private secretary, and left me. She pointed to a white baize door and I went through.

Lenin was sitting at his desk. He rose and came across the room to greet me. He has a genial manner and a kindly smile which puts one instantly at ease. He said he had heard of me from Kamenev. I apologized for having to bother him. He laughed and explained that the last sculptor had occupied his room for weeks, and that he got so bored with it that he had sworn it never should happen again. He asked how long I needed, and offered me to-day and to-morrow from 11 till 4, and three to four evenings, if I could work by electric light. When I told him I worked quickly and should probably not require so much, he said laughingly that he was pleased.

My stand and things were then brought into the room by three soldiers, and I established myself on his left. It was hard work for he was lower than the clay and did not revolve nor did he keep still. But the room was so peaceful and he on the whole took so little notice of me that I worked with great calm till 3:45 without stopping for rest or food.

During that time he had but one interview, but the telephone was of great assistance to me. When the low buzz accompanied by the lighting up of a small electric bulb signified a telephone call, his face lost the dullness of repose and became animated and interesting. He gesticulated to the telephone as though it understood.

Secretaries came in at intervals with letters. I asked him why he had women secretaries. He said because all the men were at the war, and that caused us to talk of Poland. I understood that peace with Poland had been signed yesterday, but he says, "No, that forces are at work trying to upset the negotiations, and that the position is very grave."

We talked about H. G. (Wells) and he said the only book of his he had read was "Joan and Peter," but that he had not read it to the end. I am told that Lenin manages to get through a good deal of reading.

During these four hours he never smoked, and never even drank a cup of tea. I have never worked so long on end before, and at 3:45 I could hold out no longer. I was blind with weariness, and hunger, and said good-by. He promised to sit on the revolving stand to-morrow. If all goes well, I think I ought to finish him. I do hope it is good, I think it looks more like him than any of the busts I have seen yet. He has a curious Slav face, and how ill he looks.

Moscow

October 8th, Friday.

Started work again in Lenin's room. I went by myself this time, and got past all the sentries with the pass that I had been given. I took my Kodak with me, although I had not the necessary Kodak permission. I put a coat over my arm which hid it.

I don't know how I got through my day. I had to work on him from afar. My real chance came when a Comrad arrived for an interview, and then for the first time Lenin sat and talked facing the window, so I was able to see his full face and in a good light.

The Comrad remained a long time, and conversation was very animated. Never did I see any one make so many faces. Lenin laughed and frowned, and looked thoughtful, sad, and humorous all in turn. His eyebrows twitched, sometimes they went right up and then again they puckered together maliciously.

I watched these expression, waited, hesitated, and then made my selection with a frantic rush—it was his screwed up look. Wonderful! No one else had such a look; it is his alone. Every now and then he seemed to be conscious of my presence, and give a piercing enigmatical look in my direction. The Comrad, when he left the room, stopped and looked at my work, and said the only word that I understand which is "carascho" (it means good), and then said something about my having the character of the man, so I was glad.

After that Lenin consented to sit on the revolving stand. It seemed to amuse him very much. He said he never had sat so high.

When the secretary had gone, he became serious and asked me a few questions. Did I work hard in London? I said it was my life. How many hours a day? An average of seven. He made no comment on this, but it seemed to satisfy him. Until then I had the feeling that although he was charming to me, he looked upon me a little resentfully as a bourgeoise. I believe he always asks people, if he does not know them, about their work and origin, and makes up his mind about them accordingly. I showed him photographs of some of my busts and also of "Victory." He was emphatic in not liking the "Victory," his point being that I had made it too beautiful.

Presently he said to me: "What does your husband think of your coming to Russia?" I replied that my husband was killed in the war. "In the capitalist Imperialist war?" I said: "In France, 1915; what other war?" "Ah, that is true," he said. "We have had so many, the Imperialist, the civil war, and the war for self-defense."

We then discussed the wonderful spirit of self-sacrifice and patriotism with which England entered upon the war in 1914, and he wanted me to read "Le feu" and "Clarte" of Barbusse, in which that spirit and its development is so wonderfully described.

Then the telephone gave its damnable low buzzing. He looked at his watch. He had promised me fifteen minutes on the revolving stand and had given me half an hour. He got down and went to the telephone. It did not matter; I had done all I could. I had verified my measurements, and they were correct which was a relief, and so, it being 4 o'clock and I mighty hungry, I said good-by.

He was very pleased, said I had worked very quickly, called in his secretary and discussed it with her, said it was "carascho." I asked him to give orders to have it removed to my studio, Room 31. Two soldiers arrived and carried it out. I asked Lenin for his photograph, which he sent for and signed for me.

Sculpting Trotsky

Moscow

October 18, 1920. Monday.

Trotsky's car came for me punctually at 11:30 A.M. I made Litvinoff come and tell the chauffeur that he was first to go to the Kremlin with me to fetch my things. ...

Trotsky's chauffeur, myself, and the plaster moulder who was there working, carried the things down to the car, and I was driven to a place some way off, the War Ministry, I think. Getting in was not easy, as I had no pass, and there was an altercation with the sentry. I had to wait until a secretary came to fetch me. He took me upstairs, through two rooms of soldier secretaries. In the end room there was a door guarded by a sentry, and next to the door a big writing table from which some one telephoned through into the next room to know if I could come in. It was not without some trepidation, having heard how very intractable he is (and knowing his sister) that I was ushered in, I and my modeling stand and my clay together.

From behind an enormous writing table in one corner near the window came forth Trotsky. He shook hands with me, welcomingly, though without a smile, and asked if I talked French.

He offered courteously to assist me in moving my stand into the right place, and even to have his mammoth table moved into some position if the light was not right.

The light from the two windows was certainly very bad, but although he said: "Move anything and do just whatever you like"—there was nothing one could do that would help. The room loomed large and dark. There were huge white columns which got in my way and hampered the light. My heart sank at the difficulties of the situation. I looked at my man, who was bending down at his writing desk. It was impossible to see his face. Then I went and knelt in front of the writing table opposite him, with my chin on his papers. He looked up from his writing and stared back, a perfectly steady unabashed stare. After a few seconds, realizing the absurdity of our attitudes, I had to laugh, and said, "I hope you don't mind being looked at." "I don't mind," he said, "I have my *revanche* in looking at you, and it is I who gain."

He then ordered a fire to be lit because he thought it was cold for me. It was not cold, it was overheated, but the sight and sound of the fire were nice.

Seeing that he was prepared to be amiable I asked him if I could bother him with measurements. "*Tout ce que voudrez*" [do whatever you want], he said, and pointed out to me how unsymmetrical his face is. He opened his mouth and snapped his teeth to show me that his underjaw is crooked. As he did so, he reminded me of a snarling wolf. When he talks his face lights up and his eyes flash. Trotsky's eyes are much talked of in Russia, and he is called "the wolf." His nose is also crooked and looks as though it had been broken. If it were straight, he would have a very fine line from the forehead. Full face he is Mephisto. His eyebrows go up, at an angle, and the lower part of his face tapers into a pointed and defiant beard. I dragged my modeling stand across the room to try for a better light on the other side. ... He explained to me that he is not as desperately busy as usual because there is Peace with Poland, and good news from the South. I told him that I had nearly gone to the Southern Front with Kalinin who wanted to take me. But that Kamenev wouldn't let me go because it was a troop train. Without hesitating a moment, he answered: "Do you want to go to the front? You can come with me."

Litvinoff later told me that Trotsky had asked him if I was all right and if it would be indiscreet or not to show me the Front. Litvinoff gave me a good character.

At 4 o'clock he ordered tea, and had some with me. He talked to me about himself, and of his wanderings in exile during the war, and how, finally, at the outbreak of the revolution he sailed on a neutral ship from the United States to return to Russia, how the British arrested him and took him to a Canadian concentration camp. He was detained a few months, until the Russian Government succeeded in obtaining his release.

He was particularly incensed at the British interfering with the movements of a man who was not going to Britain, nor from a British colony, nor by a British ship: "But I had a good time in that camp," he said. "There were a lot of German sailors there, and I did some propaganda work. By the time I left they were all good revolutionaries, and I still get letters from some of them."

At 5 I prepared to leave. He said I looked tired. I said I was tired from battling with my work in such bad light. He suggested trying electric light, and we agreed for 7 o'clock in the next evening. He sent me home in his car.

Moscow

October 19th, 1920.

"We will have an agreement, quite businesslike; I shall come and stand by the side of your work for five minutes every half hour." Of course the five minutes got very enlarged, and we talked and worked and lost all track of time. When the telephone rang, he asked, "Have I your permission?" His manners are charming. I said to him: "I cannot get over it, how amiable and courteous you are. I understood you were a very disagreeable man! What am I to say to people in England when they ask me, 'What sort of a monster is Trotsky?'" With a mischievous look he said: "Tell them in England." (But I cannot tell them!)

Toward the end of the evening, as Trotsky said nothing more about the project of my going to the Front, I asked him if he had decided to take me or not. He said: "It is for you to decide if you wish to come, but I shall not start for three or four days." I asked him to order the motor having realized that unless he sent for it I have to wait outside in the cold or look for it in the garage.

Moscow

October 20th, 1920.

This evening when I arrived Trotsky stood by the fire while I was warming and I asked him for news. He says that the German workers have voted in favor of joining the Moscow International which is very important. "England is our only real and dangerous enemy," he said. "Not France?" I asked. "No, France is just a noisy hysterical woman, making scenes: but England—that is different altogether."

He talked about the persistence of the Foreign press in decrying the stability of the Soviet Government. All the Governments of Europe, he said, had undergone changes in the last three years. He pointed to France, Italy, the Central Powers, Turkey, and finally Poland. The British Government was holding out longer than any other, but that was pretty rocky, and its ministers were constantly changing their posts. The Soviet Government was the oldest Government in Europe and the only one in which the Ministers retained their posts and displayed any unity, and this in spite of every effort on the part of the world to dislodge them!

He then busied himself at his table with papers. I worked for an hour and we never spoke. But he never disregarded me as Lenin did. I could walk round Lenin and look at him from all sides, while he remained absorbed in his reading and apparently oblivious of my presence. Whenever I go near Trotsky, he looks up sharply from his work, with piercing eyes, and I forget which part of his face I was intent upon. Towards the end of the evening, when my tiptoe stalking had aroused him, he asked me, "*Avec vous besoin de moi?*" [Have you need of me?] I replied yes, as always. He came and stood by the clay, but he is very critical, and watches it and me all the time, and makes me nervous. I undid and did it over again a good deal. The room was hot, and the clay got dry; it was uphill work. Never have I done any one so difficult. He is subtle and irregular. At one moment the bust looked like Scipio Africanus, and I could see he was dissatisfied, then when I had altered it and asked him what he thought, he stood for some time in silence with a suppressed smile before he let himself go: "It looks like a French Bon Bourgeois, who admires the woman who is doing him, but he has no connection with Communism!"

When at the end of the evening I was dissatisfied with my work and feeling suicidal I asked him, "May I come back and work to-morrow night?" "And the night after," he answered, and added laughing, that he would rig the place up as a studio for me, and that I could do General Kamenev. General Kamenev (who is no relation to Leo Kamenev) is the Commander-in-Chief and was a very distinguished Tsariste officer.

Moscow

October 21st, 1920.

I went to see my friend the plastermoulder who is working for so many thousand roubles a day in his studio. He is making piecemolds of the busts, so that I can have duplicates when I go. ... At 8 o'clock I went back again to the War Commissariat in Trotsky's car. On arrival I told him that I had got to get this work right to-night, and that he was not to be critical and look at it all the time and make me nervous.

He was surprised and said that he had no idea he had that effect on me, that all he wanted was to help. "*Je veux travailler cela avec vous.*" [I want to work with you on this.] His criticism he said was from intense interest, and that for nothing in the world would he be discouraging. He promised, however, to be good, and offer no opinion until asked. It was a better night for work. I felt calmer and it went pretty well.

The worst difficulties were surmounted. Trotsky stood for me in a good light and dictated to his stenographer. That was excellent. His face was animated and his attention occupied. I got all one side of his face down. He laughed, suggested another dictation, offered to stand in another position, and called back his stenographer. When we were alone again he came and stood close beside the clay and we talked while I went on working. We talked a little about me. He said I should remain in Russia a while longer, and do some big work, like my "Victory." "An emaciated and exhausted figure and still fighting and that is the allegory of the Soviet."

I answered him that I could get no news of my children and therefore must go back.

"I must return to my own world, to my own conventional people whose first thought is always for what the world will think. Russia with its absence of hypocrisy and pose, Russia with its big ideas, has spoilt me for my own world."

"Ah! That is what you say now, but when you are away—" and he hesitated.

Then suddenly turning on me, with clenched teeth and fire in his eyes, he shook a threatening finger in my face: "If when you get back to England *vous nous calomniez* [you will slander us] as the rest have, I tell you I will come to England *et je vous*." He did not say what he would do, but there was murder in his face.

I smiled: "That is all right. Now I know how to get you to England." (Then to fall in with his mood): "How can I go back and abuse the hospitality and the chivalrous treatment I have received?"

He said: "It is not abusing but there are ways of criticizing even without abuse. It is easy enough here to be blinded *par les saletes et les souffrances* [by the dirt and sufferings] and to see no further than that and people are apt to forget that there is no birth without suffering and horror, and Russia is in the throes of great *accouchement*."

To-night he sent me home alone in his car. He excused himself, saying it was the only time it was possible for him to walk. He kissed my dirty hand and said that he would always preserve a memory of "*Une femme, avec une aureole de cheveux et des mains très sals*." [A woman with a halo of hair and very dirty hands.]

Moscow

October 22nd, 1920.

Finished!

I worked until half after midnight. I think it is a success. He said so, but it has been such a struggle.

At midnight he was standing by the side of the work, rather tired and very still and patient, when suddenly I had the thought of asking him to undo his collar for me. He unbuttoned his tunic and the shirt underneath, and laid bare his neck and chest. I work like a fury for half an hour which was all too short. I tried to convey into my clay some of his energy and vitality. I worked with the concentration that always accompanies last moments. When I left he said to me, "*Eh bien, on ira ensemble au front?*" [Well, are we going to the front?] But something tells me that we will never meet again.

There is a French saying: *"On n'est pas toujours née dans son pays."* [One is not always born in one's country.] It equally follows that all are not born in their rightful sphere. Trotsky is one of these. At one time in his youth, what was he? A Russian exile in a journalist office. ... Now he has come into his own and has unconsciously developed a new individuality. He has the manner and ease of a man born to a great position. He has become a statesman, a ruler, a leader. The reason I have found him so much more difficult to do than I expected, is on account of his triple personality. He is the cultured well read man, he is the vituperative fiery politician, he can be the mischievous laughing school-boy with a dimple in his cheek. All these three I have seen in turn, and had to converge them into one clay interpretation.

Moscow

October 23rd, 1920.

I went in the morning to fetch away the bust and take it to my room in the Kremlin. I went at 11 before Trotsky had got there. These are the moments that take years off my life! It arrived, however, undamaged, which was little short of a triumph. When my plaster moulder saw it he exclaimed with pleasure. Apparently it is very like, and every one is pleased. As Trotsky is adored, I take it as a great compliment to my work that the Bolsheviks consider it good enough.

The relief of having accomplished him as well as Lenin is indescribable. I wake up in the night and wonder if it is true or a dream. Now I am completely happy; I have achieved my purpose. I have proved myself to these people, and they in return have proved their belief in me by their trouble and courteousness.

Thoughts on Leaving Russia

November 2, 1920.

My work here is ended, but I am loath to go. I love this place. I love the people who pass by me in the street. I love the atmosphere laden with melancholy, with sacrifice, with tragedy. I am inspired by this Nation purified by Fire. I admire the dignity of their suffering and the courage of their belief.

I would like to live among them forever, or else work for them outside; work and fight for the Peace that will heal their wounds.

~

Acknowledgments

Librarians have been especially helpful in obtaining books through inter-library loan for this volume. I extend my thanks to Willa Anderson of the Redwood Library, Newport, Rhode Island, and Michael Poisson of the Middletown Rhode Island Public Library. My cousin, Nadine Redding, led me to Elisabeth Vigée Le Brun, for which I am grateful.

~

Bibliography

Atwood, Elizabeth. *The Liberation of Marguerite Harrison: America's First Foreign In-telllligence Agent*. Annapolis, Md.: Naval Institute Press, 2020.

Babey, Anna M. *Americans in Russia, 1776–1917: A Study of the American Travelers in Russia from the American Revolution to the Russian Revolution*. New York: Coronet Press, 1938.

Beatty, Bessie. *The Red Heart of Russia*. New York: Century Co., 1918.

Cantacuzene, Julia. *My Life Here and There*. New York: C. Scribner's and Sons, 1923.

Cantacuzene, Julia. *Revolutionary Days: Recollections of Romanoffs and Bolsheviki, 1914–1917*. Boston: Small, Maynard & Co., 1919.

Craven, Elizabeth. *A Journey through the Crimea to Constantinople in a Series of Letters to His Serene Highness the Margrave of Brandenburg, Ansbach, and Bareith*. London: G.G. J & J. Robinson, 1789.

Crosley, Pauline. *Intimate Letters from Petrograd*. New York: E.P. Dutton, 1920.

Daschkaw, Ekaterina Romanova. *Memoirs of the Princess Daschkaw, Lady of Honour to Catherine II, Empress of All the Russias*. London: H. Colburn, 1840.

Eastlake, Elizabeth. *Letters from the Shores of the Baltic*. London: John Murray, 1842.

Gasper, Julia. *Elizabeth Craven, Writer, Feminist, and European*. Wilmington: Vernon Press, 2017.

Goldman, Emma. *My Disillusionment in Russia*. New York: Doubleday, Page and Co., 1923.

Goldman, Emma. *My Further Disillusionment in Russia*. New York: Doubleday, Page and Co., 1924.

Hapgood, Isabel. *Russian Rambles*. Boston: Houghton Mifflin and Co., 1895.

Harrison, Marguerite E. *Marooned in Moscow: The Story of an American Woman Im-prisoned in Russia*. New York: George H. Doran Company, 1921.

Holderness, Mary. *New Russia: Journey from Riga to the Crimea, by way of Kiev: With Some Account of the Colonization and the Manners and Customs of the Colonists of New Russia. To which are added notes relating to the Crim tartars.* London: Printed for Sherwood, Jones and Co. 1823.

Marsden, Kate. *On Sledge and Horseback to Outcast Siberian Lepers.* New York: Cassell Publishing Co., 1892.

Meakin, Annette. *A Ribbon of Iron.* New York: E.P. Dutton, 1901.

Morton, Marian J. *Emma Goldman and the American Left, "Nowhere at Home."* New York: Twayne Press, 1992.

Nerhood, Harry W., comp. *To Russia and Return: An Annotated Bibliography of Travelers' English Language Accounts from the Ninth Century to the Present.* Columbus: Ohio State University Press, 1968.

Sheridan, Clare. *Mayfair to Moscow: Clare Sheridan's Diary.* New York: Boni & Liverite, 1921.

Smith, Harold F., comp. *American Travelers Abroad: A Bibliography of Accounts. Published before 1900.* Carbondale: Southern Illinois University, 1968.

Vigée, Le Brun, Elizabeth. *Souvenirs of Madame Vigée Le Brun.* New York: Worthington, ca. 1879.

Waddington, Mary. *Letters of a Diplomat's Wife, 1883–1900.* New York: C. Scribner's and Sons, 1903.

Wilmot, Catherine. *The Russian Journals of Martha and Catherine Wilmot being an Account of Two Irish Ladies of Their Adventures in Russia as a Guest of the Celebrated Princess Daschkaw.* London: Macmillan and Co., 1934.

Wilmot, Martha. *The Russian Journals of Martha and Catherine Wilmot being an Account of Two Irish Ladies of Their Adventures in Russia as a Guest of the Celebrated Princess Daschkaw.* London: Macmillan and Co., 1934.

Index

Astoria, 244
Aurora, 232

Bakers Union, 248
balls, 38, 100
Baltic Fleet, 203–4
baptism, 68
barin (master), 245
battleship, deserted, 236
Beatty, Bessie, xiii; on Baltic Fleet, 203–
4; Bolshevik Revolution witnessed
by, 192; on Constituent Assembly,
210–11; on Korniloff affair, 202–3;
on Lenin, 210; on 1917, 202; on
peasants, 208–9; on Peter and
Paul Fortress, 205–6; on Petrograd
conditions, 210–11; on Proletariat
take over, 204–5; on Provisional
Government overthrow, 205; *The
Red Heart of Russia* by, 193–211;
on revolutionary justice, 207; on
Russian Church, 209–10; on Russian
Revolution, 191, 193–95, 207–8, 209;
on Soviet policy, 206–7; on trenches,
197–99, 201; on Women's Battalion,
200–202; WWI reporting of, 191–92,
195–202
beggars: in Moscow, 113–14; among
Tartar peoples, 62
Beggars' Hospital, 40–41
Berkman, Alexander: attempted
assassination by, 238; Museum of the
Revolution work of, 240–41; No-
Conscription League organized by,
239–40; in prison, 240
Blagoslavenny, 165
Blagovestchensk, 163–64
Bochkarevska, Marie, 199
Bolshevik regime: culture under, 274;
Goldman on, 241, 243–44, 247. *See
also* Communist Party
Bolshevik Revolution (1917), xiii;
anarchists in, 232, 233; anniversary

of, 254; Beatty witnessing, 192;
Cantacuzene, Julia, on, 186; Crosley,
Pauline, impacted by, 232–33, 234;
Crosley, Walter Selwyn, impacted
by, 232, 233, 234; death during, 234;
food during, 233; shooting during,
232–33; Winter Palace overthrown
during, 205, 232–33
Bonaparte, Napoleon, 42–43, 53
books, censorship regarding, 106–7
borders, unguarded, 182
Borodin, Michael, 276
Borovsky, Ivan, 194
Bouromka estate, 172, 185–86
Boxer Rebellion, xii, 143, 164, 167
bread lines, riots caused by, 220
Breshkovskaya, Katherine, 202–3
Brest-Litovsk, Treaty of, 191
Bronstein, Leo. *See* Trotsky
Buffalo, U.S.S., 228
Buford, 240
bureaucracy, 175

cabinet: crises of, 183, 194; in Peter and
Paul Fortress, 206
cab men, 108, 138
Canadian concentration camp, 280
Cantacuzene, Julia, xii, 169; on
Alexandra, 173–74, 177, 180, 182;
on Bolshevik Revolution, 186;
Bouromka estate of, 172, 185–86; on
Crimea train, 186–87; on Duma, 179,
180–81; jewel smuggling of, 188; on
Julia (Princess) salon, 174–75; on
Kyiv, 183, 184–85; Marie (Grand
Duchess) meeting, 173–74; *My Life
Here and There* by, xiii; on Nicholas
II, 180–81; on 1903, 174; on 1905,
176; on 1915, 178–79; on peasant
village, 173; on Petrograd, 183–84,
187–88; on Provisional Government,
181–82; on Rasputin, 177, 179–80;
as refugee, 186–89; *Revolutionary*

About the Editor

Evelyn M. Cherpak holds a PhD in history from the University of North Carolina, Chapel Hill. She has written over fifty historical and bibliographic articles. This is her fifth book. She lives in Portsmouth, Rhode Island.